Distributed by

Motorbooks International
Publishers & Wholesalers Inc.

Osceola, Wisconsin 54020, USA

The MGA, B and C

CHRIS HARVEY

The Oxford Illustrated Press

Printed in Great Britain

ISBN 0 902280 69 4
The Oxford Illustrated Press Ltd,
Shelley Close, Headington, Oxford

Distributed in the United States by
Motorbooks International,
729 Prospect Avenue, Box 2,
Osceola, Wisconsin 54020, USA

Contents

Acknowledgements

It is with a feeling of great sadness and gratitude that I write these acknowledgements to this book on some of the greatest sports cars ever made, the MGA, MGB and MGC: sadness that no sooner had I finished work on this book than British Leyland had to announce the end of the MGB and Abingdon, and gratitude that I have had the chance to drive so many great MGs over the years; gratitude also that I have had the privilege to laugh, eat and drink with hundreds of MG enthusiasts who helped me in so many ways. None more so than John Thornley, who has been up to his ears in MGs almost since their inception and has been the guiding light and inspiration behind the MG Car Club since it was founded in 1930. John retired from Abingdon long before this book was written, following illness: executives of his calibre fought many a successful battle to keep the dedicated workforce of this backwater of a big empire in business, and we feel sure that they would have managed it again.

Now the fight has been left to the MG Car Club (and John Thornley who still does a lot of work for them), the MG Owners' Club (with live-wire leader Roche Bentley) and the unions who represent what must be the most loyal and trouble-free workforce within British Leyland. They deserve to succeed and deserve the support of everyone who ever loved an MG, and they must run into millions all over the world.

Roche Bentley and everyone at the MG Owners' Club were tremendously helpful in compiling this book; so was Mike Ellman-Brown (who survived late-night phone calls), Gerry Brown and Ron Gammons, Barry Sidery-Smith, Vic Smith, Vic Young and Lorraine Nicholson of the MG Car Club in Britain; Norman Ewing in South Africa; James Stout, Len Renkenberger, Mike Hughes and Steve Glochowsky in America; Thomas Studer in Switzerland; Richard Ide in Belgium; and Bram Hoogendijk in Holland. Between them they also produced a mass of pictures which, with the never-ending efforts of Paul Skilleter, who was also responsible for the superb cover photography. I am also very grateful to Warren Allport of *Autocar*, Jim Lee of *Motor*, John Dunbar, Kathy Ager, Martyn Elford and Maurice Selden of London Art Technical, Owen Barnes and Colin Taylor Productions for their outstanding pictures.

I must also thank sincerely John Chatham, John Horne, Graham Mitchell,

Ian Shapcott, Nick Ferentinos, Steve Bicknell, Matthew Bracey and Anne Davis in Bristol, and Steve Brazier and Robin Ottaway in London, for telling me so much practical information about running an MG and helping me keep my own car on the road. I must also thank them, with Jane Marshall of Oxford Illustrated Press, Paul and June Skilleter and Tim Holder for helping keep me on the road in very difficult times, and last, but not least, Gloria Callaway for taking a deep breath and diving into yet another index. Without their help and encouragement this book would never have seen the light of day.

In memory of my wife, Margaret, who talked to her MG every day.

Colour Plates

I

The A, B and C of Sports Cars

YOU CAN drive anywhere in the world and you'll always find somebody who has heard of the MG sports car. In America and Britain in particular, the name is synonymous with everything that spells sports car. Enthusiastic motorists have argued about the definition of a sports car since they were first introduced, but most agree that it ought to be open, possess really competitive performance, and have roadholding that enables it to be driven far faster than normal cars and in complete safety. Ideally it should be a dual-purpose machine that can be driven to work during the week and used in all manner of events at weekends. It should need a minimum of maintenance and be economic. Above all it must be symbolic of a fun-loving image that extends even to everyday driving.

From the time that Morris Garages made special-bodied Bullnoses in 1922, MGs have been sports cars, and their most popular have been the MGA and MGB. Indeed, the MGB is readily acknowledged as the most popular sports car made by any manufacturer in the world. Manufacturers, such as Ford with the Mustang and General Motors with the Chevrolet Corvette, have produced more, and their cars have a sporty image. But they haven't been sports cars in the mould made famous by MG, Triumph, Jaguar, Healey and Porsche.

The MGA of 1955 was an instant best-seller and at once became the most successful machine to have been built at Abingdon, the world's biggest sports car factory. The MGB that followed was even more successful and passed the half million mark. It was in production for so many years (since 1962, in fact) that it acquired the enviable reputation of being a ready-made antique, a status previously achieved only by the Model T Ford, the Volkswagen Beetle and all Morgans.

The MGC of 1967 was Abingdon's white elephant; its designers were forced to compromise with an unsuitable engine that was so heavy that it ruined the roadholding that had been the hallmark of every MG before it, especially the MGA and MGB. Such was the lack of demand that only 9000 were made before they ceased production in 1969. Today the MGC has become a cult car, such is its relative rarity, and because of its good qualities. If you could live with the bad qualities, the good ones, such as a high top speed and seemingly effortless cruising, were great. The other variation on the MGA, B and C theme is the MGB V8, of which even fewer were made. It was a much better car than the MGC, a road burner

Facing page: 'Hurrah, hurrah, we bring the jubilee! Give the good old Berkshire boys yet another song. Sing it as we used to sing it fifty thousand strong, as we were marching through Abingdon . . .'
TRADITIONAL LAMENT ARRANGED BY
BRITISH LEYLAND

in the best traditions of Abingdon, but it was crippled by economic recession and already the few examples made between 1973 and 1976 are being keenly sought out by enthusiastic collectors.

What made the MGA, B and C sports cars so appealing to men and women of three generations? It was because they fulfilled a need for a cheap sporting vehicle that was also solid and reliable, and was available in open, hard top and fixed-head form, with two seats or a vestigial four. They are cheap to run and thoroughly dependable, yet they were not produced in such large quantities as to be too common. Seldom has so much loving care been lavished on such cars by their owners; positively ancient MGs are to be seen.

These universal sports cars were the product of two brilliant minds: those of their designer, Syd Enever and their inspiration, John Thornley. Both men were steeped in the tradition of Abingdon, having worked there since its earliest days and British Leyland must rue the day that they retired. No one has been able to produce such a popular sports car since, despite the dedication of corporate minds and massive expenditure on development. Enever and Thornley designed and developed their car on a budget that wouldn't have bought a doorskin today. They could do it because they were dedicated to their work and they were involved with and learned from the racing and record breaking which had fostered generations of MGs. Enever was the engineer behind MG's greatest record breakers, the special cars that took land speed records before and after the Second World War. The MGA's shape was based on EX135, the pre-war star, utilising saloon car components made by the company that was their parent at the time, the British Motor Corporation. In turn, the MGB was based on EX181, the post-war record breaker, using the same kind of mechanical components as the MGA.

Facing page, top: The MGA and its immediate ancestor, the MG TF, both owned in the 1950s by one of the marque's greatest supporters, Mike Ellman-Brown.

Facing page, bottom: Later, Mike Ellman-Brown's MGA was converted to wire wheels and his distinctive registration number, JJ88, was transferred to a brand-new Twin Cam, the last made.

Left: The pretty MGA fixed-head coupé, inspired by Jaguar's classic XK120 coupé, was introduced in the autumn of 1956.

The MGB that followed the MGA in 1962 became a classic in its lifetime. This is one of the rare automatic roadsters, a 1970 model.

Phenomenal reserves of strength are built into these cars with the result that they last well beyond the accepted six-to-ten year lifespan of many sports cars. The MGC should have been the best-selling sports car the world has ever known, because, in concept, it offered a much-improved performance over the MGB on which it was based, at a similar low price. But by the time it was introduced, Abingdon had lost control of engine design to other sectors of the vast empire which was to become British Leyland. 'The engine turned out to be half a hundredweight too heavy,' said Thornley, and Enever's precious balance—the foundation of every MG's fine roadholding—was destroyed. The car had lost the Abingdon touch but its other qualities, notably a maximum speed in the region of 120 mph, and, if anything, even more strength than the MGB from which it was developed, have ensured that it is still much sought after today.

The MGB V8 was a much more successful attempt at producing a really high-speed MG, but its Rover engine was in such demand for other vehicles that it died of starvation. It was also the last MG made by Enever and Thornley.

The fixed-head versions of the MGA, B and C were Thornley's way of producing first, a poor man's Jaguar XK120 (note the similarity between the MGA and XK120 body styles), and second, an Aston Martin for the man in the street. That was the MGB GT with its hatchback rear door. Enever's skill made these inspirations come true and these distinctive cars have justly remained popular despite the essentially open-car philosophy that had secured the success of the original MGA and MGB.

The sheer strength, and consequent weight, of the MGA, MGB and MGC has proved a handicap in top-flight competition. Nevertheless, works-prepared examples were quite successful in long-distance racing and in events on courses such as the Nurburgring, where roadholding was of prime importance. In club events, however, whether they be circuit racing or treasure hunts, MGs remain among the most

Above: The MGB GT introduced in 1966 had lines that were an incredibly good blend of the angular and round-ed. Again, like the MGA fixed-head coupé, it was inspired by an expensive grand touring car, in this case the hatchback Aston Martin DB 2/4.

Left: The MGC was launched in 1967 as the first really high-speed mass-produced MG. However compromises in design proved to be a handicap during its short production life. Later its good points, such as great strength and fast relaxed cruising, endeared it to so many people that the relatively few examples remaining are in great demand.

popular cars, again because of their excellent handling and also because they can take so much punishment.

It is no secret that girls like MGs. My wife used to talk to her MGB roadster as she patiently turned the engine over, waiting for it to fire. The MGB's engine might not be the easiest to start unless it is kept in immaculate tune, and it has been renowned for years as one of the most difficult to stop, for the same reason. Its hood might have been a horror to erect and its heating only marginal, but it always had a fascination for the young at heart, who want a car to be fun. They call it character, the sort of character that endeared me to my own MG, a unique combination of MGC roadster and Rover V8 engine built by John Chatham. It has all the strength, stability and durability of the MGC with a wonderful performance imparted by one of the best Anglo-American engines of recent years. And because

This is the MG that was killed by politics and economics, the MGB GT V8, the fastest, and to many, the most desirable MG of all. Sadly only 2591 were produced by the factory, although there is such a demand that brand-new ones are still being made from spare parts by specialist garages.

this engine weighs so little, the car is balanced like an MGB, which puts it among the top flight of sports cars.

Even maintenance can be fun on an MG, it is such a simple, old-fashioned car, and so rewarding to those who give it the attention it deserves. Spare parts are abundant—by classic car standards—and there's all sorts of ways of making it go quicker. Then there's the clubs. Between them, the MG clubs are among the strongest in the world, with membership spanning all age and income groups. No wonder: to have owned an MG is to have been one of a special breed. To run one today is to show that you aren't finished yet, you are still an individual, and you won't knuckle down to a boring tin-top existence. To use Abingdon's memorable words: 'You can do it in an MG'.

That makes it all the more of a pity that the MGB and Abingdon were under the sentence of death as this book was written. British Leyland could not have picked a worse time to announce this decision, at the end of a week in September 1979 in which the whole town had been given over to celebrating the 50th anniversary of MG production there. The resultant public outcry was fantastic, the biggest for any car since another peculiarly English institution, Aston Martin, was threatened with extinction in 1975.

British Leyland's chairman, Sir Michael Edwardes, explained why he had to axe Abingdon and the MGB. There just wasn't enough money to develop a new model and a rise in the value of the pound against the US dollar was making it unprofitable to market MGBs at their current price in the biggest export market, America. What he didn't emphasise was that British Leyland had just launched their open version of the Triumph TR7 in the United States. To quote the influential *Motor* magazine: 'The bitter tragedy for MG is that a previous Triumph-oriented management poured what resources were available into the development of the TR7 and the tooling-up of Speke for its production, instead of spending the money on the much more highly-regarded MG name and re-tooling Abingdon to build the new MG.'

What a way to repay the dedicated workforce at one of British Leyland's happiest, most loyal and most efficient factories. And then to suggest that the all-hallowed MG octagon badge might appear on a British version of a Japanese saloon. No wonder the MG enthusiasts howled with rage...

II

The MGA

PRACTICALLY everything about the MGA was new when it was launched in September 1955. The chassis, although developed from the preceding MG TF, bore little resemblance to that of the earlier car. The engine, gearbox and rear axle were new units designed for the entire BMC range, and the body was completely different to that of the MG TF. Even the interior was different: it was much simpler and more practical. Only the well-tried suspension and steering was like that of the T series.

The chassis was good because it was exactly as the designer, Syd Enever, had planned it; there were no compromises to save time or money which would have handicapped the car. This new frame was box sectioned as before, narrow enough at the front to allow a small, 28 ft, turning circle. Immediately behind the front wheels it swept out as wide as possible, allowing an internal cockpit width of 3 ft 9 ins. The frame held this width until just in front of the rear wheels, where it curved in again to clear the tyres and pass over the rear axle. The rival Triumph and Healey designers made the mistake of running their chassis members the easy way under the axle, which limited axle movement and resulted in the Austin-Healey and Triumph TR cars suffering from inferior roadholding for ten years until they were able to redesign the rear end.

Increasing the width of the chassis in the middle to the extent that Enever did would have made it very floppy and weak if he hadn't reinforced it by having a box-section structure built up to support the front bulkhead. This followed the body lines and provided much-needed rigidity. The amount of metal that went into the chassis to make sure it was absolutely rigid, proved to be the MG's strength in terms of safety and roadholding, but its weakness in terms of speed, for it made it a rather heavy car.

Widening the chassis meant that the seats could be mounted very low so that the occupants sat between the chassis rails rather than on top of them as in the T series. The mandatory six inches of ground clearance was retained but the overall height of the car was reduced to 4 ft 2 ins with the hood up (3 ft 7.5 ins to the top of the narrow, 11.5-inch deep, screen with the hood down). Sitting the passengers so low not only reduced the frontal area to 13.77 sq ft and lowered the car's centre of gravity, but meant that they had to sit with their legs outstretched almost in a

Left: The shape of things to come: four prototype MGAs were built in the spring of 1955 and registered LBL 301, 302, 303 and 304. The first three were raced at Le Mans in June with LBL 304, pictured here, as the spare. LBL 304 then became a popular car with executives at Abingdon; this photograph was taken in the paddock at Silverstone in July 1955 three months before MGA production started.

Below: The massive chassis of the MGA was built up at Abingdon from components supplied by Thompsons of Wolverhampton. Here two welders attach the tubular cross members and 'goalpost' scuttle (right) to the chassis rails.

horizontal plane. Enever therefore considered that it was essential to provide as long a cockpit as possible with a maximum of seat adjustment. In the event, the seats were made adjustable over a range of six inches with provision for remounting the runners, giving a total of one foot for alternative positions. That was enough to accommodate anybody between five feet and seven feet tall! A telescopic steering column was offered as an extra for people wishing to go to the extremes of this adjustment.

These dimensions fitted neatly into a wheelbase of 7 ft 10 ins with a front track of 3 ft 11.5 ins and rear of 4 ft 0.75 ins. Taking the body of the EX175 prototype as a base, the length worked out at 13 ft and the width to 4 ft 10 ins. Luggage accommodation was rather meagre even with a ten-gallon petrol tank under the floor, because the spare wheel and a comprehensive tool roll had to be accommodated in the slim tail. There was a 12-inch wide shelf behind the seats and under the tonneau panel. T series owners had happily put up with no luggage boot at all—they carried their cases on a rack at the back—so Abingdon offered a rack for the back of the MGA as an optional extra.

The doors were hinged at the front for safety and because the front shut panel was deeper. This meant there would not be so much strain on the hinges, which had caused the T series doors to droop on their rear mountings. But the clean sweeping lines of the car presented one problem: where could you mount a door handle? To have mounted it on the vertical side of the door would have spoilt the lines and been potentially dangerous for passing pedestrians; to have mounted it on top of the door would have spoilt the clean lines of the cockpit edge and been dangerous for the occupants who could have accidentally opened the door when the car was moving and to have set the door handle into the metal panel would have been expensive. So Abingdon came up with a splendid solution: they dispensed with door handles altogether and used a catch operated by a cord inside the door. You reached the cord from outside the car through a flap in the sidescreens.

In this way Abingdon saved BMC a fortune—but sometimes at the expense of the owner for the car was far from thief-proof. In this respect they consoled themselves with the thought that the T series had been equally easy to enter despite its door handles and if a thief really wanted to get into a roadster the soft top was hardly likely to be much of a deterrent. Anyway, most people drove roadsters with the tops off in all except the most vile weather in those days, so lockable doors didn't matter that much. There was no excuse, however, for the lack of a lock on the luggage boot lid, which was opened by a handle behind the passenger's seat on the right-hand-drive car, and behind the driver's seat on the left-hand-drive car (seeing as the majority of MGAs were intended for export). The lack of a luggage boot lock was sheer penny-pinching and was irritating because there was no other safe place to leave anything in the car—not even a lockable cubby hole in the dashboard.

The dashboard itself was a model of simplicity; the rev counter and speedometer were placed in front of the driver, and there was an oil pressure/water temperature gauge and a rather vague fuel gauge on either side of the central radio grille. These instruments could be swopped around from side to side according to whether the car was a right-hand-drive or a left-hand-drive version. The horn button was

Facing page: The MGA bodies were completed on the first floor of the factory, then lowered on to chassis pushed along the production line. In this picture, a series of left-hand-drive roadsters are being made.

mounted in the middle, beneath the radio grille, so that either driver or passenger could operate it. The theory was that in some hectic rally, the driver might be too busy to use the horn so the passenger could operate it instead. The passenger also had a rally-style map reading light which doubled for an interior light.

The fly-off handbrake was mounted on the right-hand side of the transmission tunnel, and was ideal for competition use. It could also lead to some intimate moments with passengers in left-hand-drive cars. A large (14.5-inch) spring-spoked steering wheel positively invited replacement with a woodrim wheel from one of the numerous accessory manufacturers. An interior mirror sprouted from the top of the dashboard, and was infuriatingly in the line of many a driver's vision. It made you wonder what odd positions MG's test drivers must have adopted not to have got it moved. Presumably they also had peculiar feet. The position of the pendant pedals made it impossible to heel and toe this sporting car unless your feet were very large and MG refused to do anything about it; this was probably because they had opted for a cheaper cable-operated throttle which meant the accelerator pedal had to move too far to make this practical. A mechanical linkage would have cost more.

Floorboards, carpeting, leather seats, leathercloth trimming and a passenger's grab handle which also supported the laminated screen completed the interior in the best British tradition.

To keep the basic price down some items which might have seemed essential were listed as extras. The heater and demister were the most glaring omissions from the standard specifications but in practice, few cars left the factory without them, and so, in effect, the basic list price was higher than quoted.

The steering wheel that started it all (*facing page*) . . . from one of the record breakers. Note how the production MGA's steering wheel (*above*) follows the same basic design. The production car's cockpit shows also the standard radio installation.

Left: Luggage boot accommodation was very restricted in the MGA, with the spare wheel and toolkit in their normal places. Fortunately a great deal of luggage could be stored behind the seats in the cockpit. Many owners fitted luggage racks on the boot lid, however, and some even carried the spare wheel there or with special brackets on the rear bumper. The car pictured is the much-tested fixed-head coupé, NJB 381.

The engine was as straightforward as the rest of the car: it was a conventional three-bearing overhead-valve pushrod unit. It fitted in with the rest of BMC's range, being produced by the same machinery at Austin's works in Longbridge. A 73.025 mm bore and 88.9 mm stroke gave it 1489 cc. The camshaft, pushrods, ports and manifolds were on the right-hand side of the engine as you opened the rear-hinging bonnet, with electrical items such as the starter, dynamo and distributor on the other side. This meant that the valves had to be in a line down one side of the cylinder head with a heart-shaped combustion chamber and siamesed inlet ports, and a central siamesed exhaust port collecting from cylinders two and three. The chain-driven camshaft also ran in three bearings, driving the oil pump, distributor and rev counter through separate shafts. Solid-skirt pistons of aluminium alloy were fitted with three compression rings and a slotted oil control ring. The gudgeon pins were clamped in the connecting rods which had lead indium big end bearings. The full-flow oil filter was fitted between the starter motor and the dynamo, whose belt also drove the water pump from the crankshaft.

It was a good, strong engine (it was used for everything from the MG sports car to saloons and commercial vans). When the renowned gas-flow expert, Harry Weslake, 'breathed' on it, it produced 68 bhp in its first MG installation, and 72 bhp soon after, at 5500 rpm on an 8.3 : 1 compression ratio. Twin semi-downdraught 1.5-inch SU carburetters were used with a single exhaust pipe. Everything was quite accessible under the bonnet although the dipstick could have been a couple of inches longer.

An 8-inch single dry-plate Borg and Beck hydraulically-operated clutch was used with a BMC four-speed (three synchromesh, crash first) box fitted with closer-than-average gears which gave overall ratios of 4.3 : 1, 5.908, 9.52, and 15.652 (reverse 20.468) on a standard 4.3 : 1 hypoid bevel rear axle. A lower, 4.55 : 1, axle ratio was available as an option. This gearing gave 17 mph per 1000 rpm in top gear and plenty of flexibility with 77.4 lb/ft of torque at 3500 rpm, after which the engine tended to sound rather busy! It was also prone to run on in its MG form and was frequently hard to start at temperatures below freezing—although MG enthusiasts accepted this with good grace.

They grumbled about the awkward props that had to be used to keep open the bonnet and bootlid, but MG did nothing about such cheap antiquated fittings providing they were dependable. They did, however, strengthen a weak-looking manifold anchorage for the throttle cable.

The same sort of principles applied to the suspension. The TF's wishbone and coil independent front suspension, which used an Armstrong lever arm shock absorber as a top link, worked very well, so it was carried over to the MGA. No attempt was made to reduce the steering's 2.75 turns from lock to lock because it was not possible to use a smaller pinion with the rack and the distance the hands had to travel could not be reduced by using a smaller steering wheel if the weaker among us were not to protest at the weight of the steering while parking. The rear suspension was the same as that fitted to the MG Magnette saloon; half elliptical springs with a three-quarter floating axle and a banjo-style casing. The traditional lever arm shock absorbers were retained. Pressed steel wheels were used with

5.60–15 tyres and an option of wire wheels (which Thornley and Enever considered to be a passing fad) was offered with 10-inch brakes all round with 1.75-inch wide drums.

It was all very traditional, including the twin six-volt batteries, which were very inconvenient to service. You had to remove the spare wheel and unscrew the luggage boot floor to get at them *once a week* if they were to be kept in good condition (but at least you could check the SU electric fuel pump at the same time). There was no alternative position for a 12-volt battery that would not have used up passenger space or badly affected the weight distribution, which was nicely balanced at 51.5 per cent front/48.5 per cent rear. The dry weight was 18.25 cwt despite the use of alloy doors, bonnet and bootlid with the pressed steel body.

Although Abingdon produced cheap sports cars, Thornley and Enever closely watched the trends among the more expensive cars and noted the success of the Jaguar XK120 and XK140 fixed-head coupés. These saloon-like sports cars were selling well and they decided that they could make one too, at a reasonable price. As it turned out, the MGA fixed-head coupé cost only £699 when the roadster cost £640 and weighed only 100 lb more. This fixed-head coupé was introduced in October 1956, with an optional factory hard top for the roadster as there was already a steady demand for hard tops made by accessory firms. Abingdon's chief preoccupation after aerodynamics was to make the tops as light and airy as possible; if they were too claustrophobic, they would not sell well, and it would not be worthwhile marketing them. First they got the shape right (it had to be small so that it did not slow the car down and so that it fitted in with the dainty styling), then they used as much glass as possible. The result was outstandingly attractive and practical, with an enormous rear window made from toughened glass and two pencil-thin struts for strength and rigidity. The fixed-head coupé was given a new wrap-round windscreen and wind-up glass side windows together with quarter-lights for ventilation. The door handle problem was solved neatly with a slim vertical exterior catch on top of the wing line and it was shrouded by the window frame. The steel hard top on the fixed head was welded in place at the Morris Bodies Branch before it was transported, painted and trimmed, to Abingdon for assembly. The roadster's hard top, of similar design, (allowing for the flatter windscreen), was supplied with neater sliding sidescreens which could be specified as an optional extra with the soft top roadster.

Production of the two variants of MGA was well under way when *Motor Sport* visited the factory in May 1957. They told how the power units arrived in covered trailers from Austins at Longbridge and the bodies from Morris at Coventry. The chassis rails came from John Thompsons at Wolverhampton for the tubular cross members and 'goalpost' scuttle to be welded in at Abingdon. *Motor Sport* said:

'The completed chassis frame is conveyed automatically (on part of an old overhead conveyor commandeered from Cowley) to a paint bath in which it is immersed and then lifted straight out and taken through an infra-red gas-agitated drying oven . . .

'After the engine has been delivered, often on a transporter arriving at

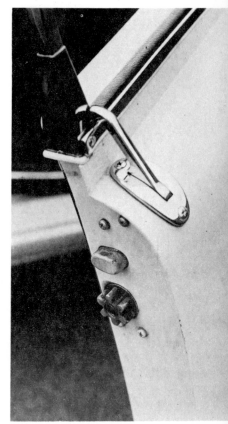

The neat exterior door handle fitted to the MGA fixed-head coupé. Abingdon got away without fitting any such handle on the roadster!

Right: Exposed view of the MGA
1600 chassis showing the engine and
disc brakes.

Facing page: The twin cam unit was a
tight squeeze into the MGA engine
compartment, although not so bad for
the factory operatives as they simply
lowered the body on top of it once it
had been installed in the chassis.

night to deposit its load "in the garden", manifolds, carburetters and mounting rubbers are fitted at Abingdon, as is the gearbox extension, although the casting for this is "bought out." The engine and other components are brought to the assembly lines on trolleys.

'The bodies are completed on the first floor of the factory and lowered by means of Feldo electric cranes to the assembly lines, along which the cars are moved by hand on steel runners or concrete runways. The MG floor trim is now part of the body and little remains to be done before the MGA body is ready to meet its chassis. The combination of the aforesaid "goalpost" scuttle member, wooden floor and the rigid "mantlepiece" or scuttle results in a satisfactorily stiff structure.

'A note in code on the windscreen advises the operatives as to whether bolt-on or centre-lock wire wheels are to be fitted, the type of lamps, speedometer required and whether left-hand or right-hand steering is specified. The brake master cylinder is bled *in situ*, after which it is slung on a "sky hook" to enable the body to be fitted on the chassis. After completion, MGA engines are lifted by means of Adegar hoists on travelling gantries, to be positioned for lowering into the chassis at the appropriate point on the assembly line.

'At the end of the assembly line steering is correctly tracked and the lamp beams adjusted, after which each car is taken, by one of a team of eleven test drivers, for a road test of about twelve miles over a standard test route.'

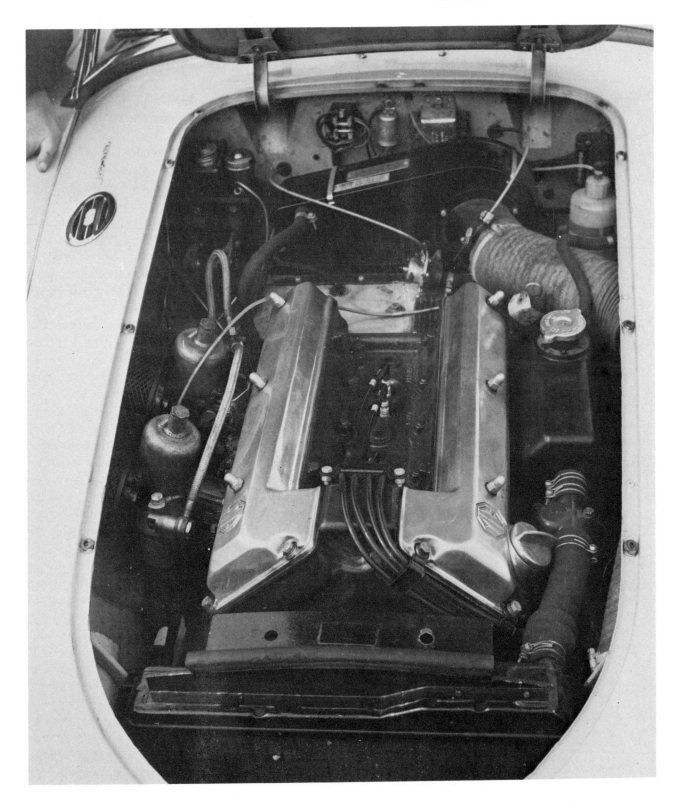

Thornley and Enever were not content to rest on their laurels with the MGA; John Thornley remembers with satisfaction the effect of tyre testing at Dunlop's track. A variety of production cars were put through their paces on all sorts of surfaces with the MGA finishing second only to the Aston Martin DB Mark III prototype. Resultant attention to the suspension settings in conjunction with improved tyres raised the MGA's speed round the trickiest test course by 3 mph and the changes were promptly made on production cars in 1957.

Meanwhile there was a good deal more happening on the four drawing boards in the tiny experimental department at Abingdon, and at Morris Engines in Courthouse Green, Coventry. They were planning ways of making the MGA go faster still for competition work, and this meant more power as not much could be done to improve the handling using basic BMC components.

A twin overhead camshaft engine like that in the Jaguar XK150, and used on various racing and record MGs since 1955, seemed the best avenue for development, although there was no immediate plan to substitute the twin cam engine in normal production cars. Thornley eventually secured permission to go ahead with development on a production racing unit 'provided it was B series from the gasket-face downwards. The intention seemed quite straightforward. All we had to do was put special camshafts on a new head, and fix up a drive [for them] from the front. Of course it entailed more than that and before we knew where we were we found that we could have done with a new block altogether! As so frequently happens in this sort of work, we could have saved ourselves a lot of trouble by starting from scratch—not that the result was much different in the eventual outcome. It just took us longer to design the production twin cam engine.'

Four years after work started on MG's new power plant, the Twin Cam MGA was introduced in 1958. Peak production was visualised at about twenty-five per week. To take full advantage of the 1600 cc international competition categories, the B series block was bored out to 75.4 mm to give it 1588 cc. This meant revising the water passages and extra machining at Courthouse Green after initial machining at Longbridge. 'About the only things which were the same were the bore centres,' said Thornley, although Abingdon had complied with the BMC dictate and saved costs on initial machining of the B series block. The twin cam engine had a complicated alloy casting at the front covering a primary drive from the crankshaft to a dummy shaft in the old camshaft housing, which now worked the rev counter from the back, the oil pump from the centre, and a duplex roller chain drive at the front with a repositioned distributor. The twin overhead camshafts worked the valves with bucket-style tappets like Jaguar's famous XK engine. The distributor had been moved to the right-hand side of the engine (viewed under-bonnet) because the twin 1.75-inch SU carburetters had been swopped to the opposite side of the engine. This was because the new alloy head, in which the valves were placed at 40 degrees to either side of the cylinder centre line, had its inlet moved to the left with the exhaust remaining on the right. With good breathing, the peak revolutions could exceed 7000 rpm and a revised crankshaft was used. Two-inch main bearings were retained with 1.875-inch crankpins, but narrower big ends were fitted to make room for thicker crank cheeks. This meant using

Head-on contemporary shot of the MGA Twin Cam that was tested by Roy Salvadori for *Sporting Motorist*. Standard MGA 1600s looked exactly the same from this angle.

heavier-duty big end bearings. The connecting rods were competition units using fully-floating gudgeon pins with heavily-domed, 9.9 : 1 compression ratio, pistons. As a result it was possible to extract 108 bhp at 6700 rpm with 104 lb/ft of torque at 4800 rpm, which meant that the car's gearing did not have to be changed. This new ensemble was completed with a large cast alloy sump so that oil pressure did not suffer at consistently high revs. An optional oil cooler was made available. The bulk of this new engine meant that the steering rack had to be moved forward an inch and the steering arms lengthened correspondingly. As a result the turning circle was increased by 4 ft 6 ins and the steering itself was not quite so responsive. However, the handling was unimpaired by new spring rates to support the heavier engine, so the chassis changes were deemed worthwhile.

Abingdon had done a good job of installing this much wider unit in the rather narrow engine compartment, but even after the head angle had been reduced from 90 degrees to 80, some of the ancilliaries were difficult to get at: the distributor was almost underneath one of the cam housings and the coil was buried beneath the heater trunking. All this made the engine difficult to work on and many suffered from poor maintenance. They also suffered from poor petrol, as five-star—virtually unobtainable in many countries—was vital to perfect timing for this engine's reliability. The use of chrome piston rings and chrome molybdenum treatment of the cylinder bores on the first 345 engines led to a high oil consumption and helped give the Twin Cam a bad name. The compression ratio was dropped to

8.3 : 1 from chassis number 2251 in 1959 and subsequently all twin cam engines rebuilt by BMC received these pistons. Power was reduced slightly, but reliability was much improved. The accessibility problem was helped by the fitting of detachable inner wheelarch panels from chassis number 592. The optional front anti-roll bar was fitted to all Twin Cams after chassis number 2275. Cars could be specified with either roadster or fixed-head body, although the lighter roadster was much more popular in Twin Cam form.

Once Abingdon had cured the Twin Cam's problems they concentrated on making the standard MGA more attractive. 'It had been in production for four years and there comes a time when you have to give the car a facelift, no matter how successful its basic shape has been,' said Thornley. 'Some people were on to their second and third MGA by then and were hanging on to the last one because they didn't wear out! They thought there was little point in buying a new one when a fresh model might appear any day.

'So we played about with different fronts and backs, but none of them were really satisfactory. Syd had done too good a job from the start! So we thought again: "What will persuade existing owners to carry on buying new cars?" The answer was simple: "Even better performance." Well, seeing as we didn't seem to be able to improve the shape we decided we must have more power, and better brakes to go with the extra performance. We already had a 1588 cc engine in the Twin Cam, so we decided to standardise on that capacity, and to use disc brakes at the front. We kept drums at the back to save money and to allow us to fit a decent handbrake.'

The result was the MGA 1600, introduced in May 1959. The engine was bored out like that of the Twin Cam and the moving parts were strengthened. Power went up to 79.5 bhp at 5600 rpm, with torque increasing to 87 lb/ft at 3800 rpm. Eleven-inch Lockheed discs were fitted at the front (with improved linings in the rear drums), instead of the 10.75-inch Dunlop disc brakes fitted all round on the Twin Cam; this was because it was intended to produce the MGA 1600 in far larger quantities than the Twin Cam. A ready identification point was the use of separate brake/tail lights and indicators on a plinth at the back with amber and white divided side lamps for parking lights and indicators at the front. The sliding sidescreens were standard. Badges bearing the legend '1600' were fitted on the bootlid and near the fume outlets on the front wings, although the separate number plate plinth remained unchanged. This was so that it could be easily and cheaply modified to accept the variety of number plate shapes used throughout the world. The lighting changes were dictated by changing British regulations.

The Twin Cam was withdrawn in 1960 after BMC competitions manager Marcus Chambers confirmed that its reputation for unreliability was giving MG a bad name in America. Only 2111 Twin Cam cars had been made in two years, leaving Abingdon committed to taking around four to five hundred sets of Dunlop disc brakes and wheels, it is estimated. These wheels could not easily be adapted for use on the standard car and the brakes were much different. Today British Leyland might have scrapped the surplus, or sold the parts at a 'knock-down' price, but Abingdon, long starved of good performance equipment and forced to

Rear view of the MGA 1600 with hood down (*facing page, top*) . . . and up *facing page, bottom*). The car, SMO 907, is the one tested by newspapers and magazines including *The Motor*, *Motor Sport*, and *Cars Illustrated*.

The MGA 1600 Mark II could be readily distinguished by its revised radiator grille featuring near-vertical bars. The standard bolt-on steel disc wheels, like many other parts of the car, were carried over from earlier models. This car had the 'luxury' sliding sidescreens.

make every penny count, simply kept on producing Twin Cam chassis with pushrod engines whenever anybody ordered a '1600 De Luxe'. Thornley had no intention of ordering any more of these components in bulk so the De Luxe was not officially listed as a separate model. No official records were kept of how many De Luxe models were made, but it seems reasonable to assume that there were no more than a few hundred.

The 1588 cc engine capacity caused disruptions at Longbridge however as no other car using the B series block used that capacity, so MG were brought into line in April 1961. As the MGA was no longer being considered for international competition (the Big Healey and Mini-Cooper were to the forefront of BMC planning), there was no need for it to stay within 1600 cc. So it was given a revised B series engine of a new capacity—1622 cc—that was to be used in other BMC products from October 1961. The reason for the choice of such an unusual capacity was that the new bore was 76.2 mm with the old stroke of 88.9 mm, better translated into the Imperial measures of 3 ins by $3\frac{1}{2}$ ins. Compression was raised to 8.9 : 1 to give 86 bhp at 5500 rpm with 97 lb/ft of torque at 4000 rpm and the rear axle ratio was raised to 4.1 : 1, giving overall ratios of 4.1, 5.633, 9.077 and 14.924 with a 19.516 reverse. This gearing was a more relaxed 17.9 mph per 1000 rpm in top gear. The engine was a good deal different in detail to that of the earlier B series units: it had a cylinder head with improved porting and breathing, bigger inlet valves and siamesed cylinders. The combustion chambers were reshaped and enlarged, which meant that new flat-top pistons had to be fitted to keep up the compression ratio. To emphasise these changes the radiator grille and rear lights were restyled and the new model was called the MGA 1600 Mark II and given new badges. But by 1962 sales had fallen well below the old peaks of more than 20,000 a year and a new model was long overdue, particularly as the much-improved Triumph TR4 was now on the market. The total production of MGAs was 101,081, made up of 58,750 1500s, 31,501 1600s, 8719 Mark IIs and 2111 Twin Cams including an unknown number of De Luxes.

By 1960, young British designers, such as D. N. Stephenson, were complaining that they were not getting opportunities to show their talent: they were having to spend years designing 'supersonic safety catches' or whatever before they were allowed near a complete car. So young Stephenson spent £2000 of his own money—a great deal in those days—building his own special-bodied MGA Twin Cam from aluminium sheets over a steel framework. This rather angular body was exceptionally interesting in that it had numerous features which were to appear on luxury cars in the future. The changes to the chassis, however, were minimal and economical. In fact, the only modifications were: The hydraulic operating cylinders for the clutch and brakes were altered to allow a more forward bonnet line and a more forward position of the windscreen; the steering column was shortened four inches to provide a more comfortable driving position and a new steering wheel was fitted; the hand brake was moved to a more accessible position on the right-hand side; two tanks of fifteen gallons total capacity were fitted either side of the body in place of the standard underfloor tank holding ten gallons; the spare wheel was housed vertically in the extreme rear of the vehicle. The changes to the tank position and that of the spare wheel tripled luggage space to 9 cu. ft. Access to the luggage boot was by the large, hinged rear window, which was made of Perspex. The individual seats were adjustable horizontally and vertically and the angles of the back rest and seat cushions could also be altered. These bucket seats also tilted forward to allow access to the luggage compartment and were instantly detachable for use during picnics outside or for cleaning the interior of the car. Lots of sound-deadening material made the Stephenson MGA Twin Cam considerably quieter than normal.

III

The MGB and MGC

I*T TOOK* Abingdon four years to design the MGB; four years to design a car that they expected to be in production for seven years at the most. Once the basic layout was evolved they spent countless hours either paring down the cost of seemingly minor items, or disregarding them either because they were not good enough, or because they were too expensive. They did their work so well that the car achieved well-nigh immortality as the most popular sports car the world has ever seen, the MGA notwithstanding. No manufacturer has been able to offer anything better at a lower price and so readily available since.

If Thornley and Enever were not allowed to go back to basics with their mechanical components, at least they were given a free rein with the body and chassis, although they had to be made at the right price. The only way in which they could improve the MGA body and chassis was to combine them. The result, they reasoned, would be lighter and more rigid, and if they could get the complete unit delivered to them in the manner of the MGA body then they could produce even more under the same roof, because they wouldn't have to finish off the welding and bolt the body and chassis together. The tooling for such a shell would be expensive but Thornley had his ways of getting round that. He decided that they would have to stick to the basic BMC mechanical components used on the MGA; they couldn't manage everything at once.

But despite reducing the wheelbase to 7 ft 7 ins and paring the body shape (based on the EX 181 record car), to a minimum, it became apparent that the finished car would be slightly heavier than the MGA if sufficient rigidity was to be built into the new monocoque. Enever always had trouble improving his designs!

It was decided, therefore, to use a B series engine bored out to 80.26 mm which gave 95 bhp at 5400 rpm and 110 lb/ft of torque at 3000 rpm for additional performance rather than marginally less. As Thornley would have said, it wasn't so simple as that. This amazing engine, dating back to an Austin design of 1947, really was on the limit of its production capacity. All the bores had to be siamesed except for a slim water passage in the middle of the block. This would have been considered most inadvisable ten years earlier, but casting techniques had improved so much that this 'stretching' operation proved most successful. New pistons with concave crowns, giving an 8.8 : 1 compression ratio, were fitted with main bearings increased

The definitive MGB roadster (*left*)
with the car that was its inspiration,
the EX181 record breaker of 1957
(*below*).

The unkindest cut of all: a left-hand-drive MGB GT split down the middle for a London Motor Show.

to a 2.125-inch diameter from 2 inches. As a result, the oil temperature was higher and an oil cooler was offered as an optional extra on the home market, and fitted as standard on export models. Abingdon was very anxious to keep down the price of the MGB on the home market as heavy purchase tax magnified any extra costs.

Other changes were confined to different carburetter needles, the air cleaner and exhaust system.

Besides stretching the engine, Abingdon managed to stretch the passenger compartment! The overall length was reduced to 12 ft 9.25 ins, but the front limits of the cockpit were moved forward six inches and the cockpit width was increased by an inch because there were no chassis members in the way. A massive built-in forward bulkhead, with deep box section sills, steel floor and transmission tunnel linked to a solid rear bulkhead, maintained rigidity without reducing the former extraordinary range of seat adjustment. As a corollary, the shelf behind the seats was increased to 16 inches in depth and the tonneau panel was cut away above it so that small children could perch on the platform. The stressed body skin helped strengthen the monocoque and the luggage boot lip was made deeper for this purpose. Very solid steel doors helped rigidity as well. The bootlid was also made of steel as the car tended to be rather nose-heavy on its reduced wheelbase and the bonnet was made from aluminium, as on the MGA. In this form, the weight—45 lb more than that of the MGA with wind-up windows, steel-panelled floor, doors and bootlid—was distributed at an acceptable 52.5 per cent in the front and 47.5 per cent in the rear. To achieve this the engine had been set back as far as possible, leaving a large amount of air between it and the radiator grille. An integral part of the structure was a massive detachable cross member for the front suspension, which, with the steering and rear suspension, remained substantially MGA. The bonnet opening had been made much wider for easier access, cheaper servicing, and the possible fitting of alternative engines, such as a V6 (which was under consideration and would have needed the extra width), or a straight six (which would have needed the air in front of the four-cylinder engine).

Front and rear spring rates were reduced by 25 per cent as the monocoque proved stiffer than the MGA's separate chassis arrangement, and one effect of fitting new 14-inch wheels was a reduction in unsprung weight. Front and rear tracks remained similar to those of the MGA at 4 ft 1 in and 4 ft 1.25 ins, but ground clearance was reduced to 5 inches to improve roadholding and reduce frontal area. In practice the MGB proved to be much easier to ground than the MGA, particularly when the springs settled. Overall height was 4 ft 1.5 ins with the hood raised, and 3 ft 9 ins to the top of the laminated screen with the hood down. The screen was actually bigger than that of the MGA at 13.25 inches deep but no deeper in effect because it sloped back at a more acute angle for better air penetration. Overall width was a little more than that of the MGA at 4 ft 11.5 ins.

The gearbox internals and rear axle remained almost exactly the same as those of the MGA except that the rear axle ratio was raised to 3.91 : 1, only a slight increase when the 14-inch wheels were taken into consideration. Overall ratios worked out at 3.91, 5.37, 8.66 and 14.21 with an 18.59 reverse. The gearbox did not need the 3-inch remote control extension that had been fitted to the MGA because of the revised cockpit.

The front brake discs were reduced in size to 10.75 ins to fit inside the new wheels while the rear drums remained at 10 inches. Optional wire wheels were available with 4.5-inch rims in place of the standard steel wheels, which have a 4-inch rim.

For the first time, the MGB roadster had locks on the doors and bootlid and a cubby hole in the dashboard, plus genuine door handles! 'I remember a time when Syd and I sat down for an hour-and-a-quarter with a 4s 1½d door lock in one hand and a 3s 11d one in the other, wondering which one we could afford.' Thornley said later. 'Over the years we had processions of people saying "Why don't you do this or that—it will only cost a couple of bob." By the time you have added up all those pennies you've put £20 on the price of the car, and—with purchase tax—you are halfway to the same price as your nearest rival.'

The rest of the interior was similar to that of the MGA except that it was modernised, with the radio location moved to the centre of the dashboard with the speaker in a console formed by the bulkhead reinforcement. This made room for the lockable cubbyhole on the passenger's side, with the horn button being moved to the centre of the steering wheel. Although the horn occupied a more modern position, the cubbyhole was thoroughly old-fashioned. It could be operated only by a key that it shared with the bootlid and as they were invariably kept on the same

Pint pot in a quart mug: the early B series engine (*facing page*) showing the radiator and its grille with masses of space in between. The later C series engine occupied this space fully (*left*).

ring as the ignition key, you couldn't open the cubbyhole when the engine was running. Abingdon still believed that people should prepare themselves for their journey and then concentrate on their driving, not fiddle about with bits and pieces in cubbyholes! Abingdon further justified it by saying that they could always use the spare set of keys. But at least the mirror mounting was changed—it was remounted on a central rod, out of the driver's lower line of vision—but like everything else on the MGB it had to work for its living. The rod helped increase the strength of the windscreen surround on the roadster, which was more subject to screen-shattering flexing than a steel-topped car. For some extraordinary reason, though, Abingdon insisted on retaining a number plate light (masquerading as a map reading light), on the passenger's side of the dashboard, when they still provided no room for pockets in the doors for maps, and no place for them anywhere else in the interior. If you had a map, and the hood was down, you had to hang on to it, or it would fly out of the back!

Soon after the MGB was released in September 1962, an optional glass fibre hard top became available with the two varieties of soft top. The soft tops were minimal rounded affairs so far as shape was concerned and came either as a standard build-it-yourself item or as a slightly more expensive foldback hood. The works hard top was smarter: its lines were based on those designed by Pininfarina for the back of the contemporary Austin A40 hatchback saloon. Numerous other

hard tops—with different, but no more attractive, lines—were offered by independent firms. The works hard top relied substantially on the roadster's inherent
stiffness for rigidity as it was of very light construction and floppy on its own. Its
overall weight, however, was similar to that of many of the hard tops made by
independent concerns because it had a glass rear window rather than the popular,
and lighter, Perspex. The advantage of the glass was that it improved rearward
vision. The optional tonneau cover was also given zipped slots so that seat belts
could be worn when it was in place for neat open car driving.

Overdrive was offered as a highly-desirable extra early in 1963. It was fitted
with an inhibitor switch worked by manifold vacuum, to prevent engagement
when the throttle was closed; in other words it only came in when the engine was
pulling, preventing jerky engagement. Its overall ratio was 3.14 : 1 on the standard
3.91 : 1 rear axle.

In August 1963, the removeable hood was abandoned in favour of the folding,
fixed-bottom, hood (at chassis number 19586). In February 1964, closed-circuit
crankcase breathing was introduced to meet new US regulations and the first major
mechanical change followed in September 1964, when the five-bearing version of
the B series engine was fitted. This was in common with the Austin 1800 saloon,
introduced at the same time. The idea behind using five main bearings rather than
three was to improve smooth running at high revs, but the MGB did not get the
Austin 1800's smooth new all-synchromesh gears. At this point (chassis number
48766) the oil cooler was made a standard fitting, a more modern electric rev counter
replaced the old mechanical device; and the vague fuel gauge was changed for a
steadier and more accurate hot-wire type. Engine numbers, which had been prefixed
18G with the three-bearing unit (or 18GA with closed-circuit breathing) now
became 18GB. The only other change of note before the introduction of the GT
model in October 1965 was the enlargement of the fuel tank to 12 gallons from 10
(at chassis number 56743), and the fitting of press button door handles.

Thornley was very keen to have the GT as he felt that it would increase
the MGB's sales scope dramatically, but, as usual, he didn't get it all his own way.
He would have liked to have lost a lot of weight off the bottom of the MGB to
compensate for the extra weight of the top. The stressed top would have made up
for the loss of rigidity overall. However, BMC opted for the cheapest alternative
in terms of development costs, fitting a Farina-style angular top to the rounded
roadster's bottom. It is to Enever's eternal credit that he managed to blend the
contrasting styles together so well, although he had no opportunity to lighten the
shell overall. That's why to this day the MGB GT is so much heavier—160 lb—than
the roadster. The rear end of the GT shell's underside was considerably redesigned,
to make way for the miniscule rear seats and a new Salisbury rear axle, but it was
still on the heavy side. There was one advantage in this: Enever was always keen on
even weight distribution and the GT was better in this respect than the roadster.
It had more weight at the back, which helped the handling. It needed stiffer rear
springs as a result (99 lb/in that had been produced for heavily-equipped police
versions of the MGB roadster, which normally had 93 lb/in rear springs), and
480 lb/in front coils in place of the 348 lb/in springs on the roadster because of the

Above: Cockpit view of the early MGB roadster with controls 'falling readily to hand' as they say.

Left: The automatic gearbox installation was especially neat and tidy in the MGB. Note the change of steering wheel in this 1970 model.

higher overall weight. Police GTs were fitted with 124 lb/in rear springs. All GTs were made with a front anti-roll bar from the start, and it was standardised on the roadster within a month (from chassis number 108039). Considering that it was developed with such economy, the GT was an extremely compact and efficient design. It had a roof 1.5 inches higher than that of the hard top roadster, with a screen 4 inches deeper and windows 1 inch deeper. The rear end had the A40 Farina-style hatchback door with a good-sized luggage platform above the spare wheel tray. Thankfully this door was fitted with concealed hinges and spring-loaded supports that made opening it a one-handed job; the roadster, however, kept its old bent wire prop.

The tiny rear seats on the GT were just about big enough to accommodate children up to about eight years old in reasonable comfort and could be used by an adult if the passenger's seat was slid right forward to give leg room. This was perfectly practical for the front passenger as he or she already had a vast amount of leg room.

Additional luggage-carrying space could be provided when the rear seats were folded down if their squab was removed.

In July 1967 the bigger and more robust Salisbury rear axle, with its attendant sheet metal changes, was adopted on the roadster (from chassis number 129187 with wire wheels and 132463 with disc wheels). Reversing lamps were standardised on all MG sports cars at about the same time.

The floorpan was modified next to accommodate the bulkier all-synchromesh gearbox introduced in October 1967. This MGB was designated Mark II by enthusiasts. At first glance it could be identified by its straight lever rather than the

bent one used before. Inwardly it was different also in that it had much in common
with the new six-cylinder MGC (described later in this chapter) and related Austin
three-litre saloon. The chief difference between the MGC and MGB versions of
this gearbox was in the casings, which were of individual design to match up with
their respective engines. The overall MGB ratios were 3.91 : 1, 5.40, 8.47 and 13.45
with a 12.1 reverse—an effective raising of the first and second gear ratios, bringing
them closer to the third gear, which was practically unchanged. At the same time an
automatic version was introduced with the popular Borg Warner Model 35 three-
speed gearbox. The overall ratios on this car were 3.7 : 1, 5.17 and 8.84 with a
7.73 reverse as a 3.7 : 1 rear axle ratio was normally used instead of the 3.91 on the
manual car.

Outwardly there was nothing to tell the difference between the manual and
automatic cars, and little to show for the change inside. 'The only evidence in the
cockpit is the lack of a clutch pedal and, instead of the normal short gearlever,
an even shorter sliding selector lever, with a lift-up tee handle to guard the reverse
and parking lock positions,' said *Autocar*. 'This moves very pleasantly, being
smooth and precise. Position D gives fully automatic changes up and down with
kickdown. L2 holds the intermediate gear from 54 mph to its maximum at 79 mph
(6000 rpm); below that speed it will kickdown. L1 holds low ratio from standstill
to a maximum of 48 mph.' It was an exceptionally-pleasant installation and a pity,
from the engineering point-of-view, that the idea of an automatic MGB was not
more popular with customers.

Other notable changes on the Mark II included the fitting of an alternator
with its attendent negative earth electrical system on all cars (in keeping with

improving trends in car electronics) and an energy-absorbing steering column on American specification models, with a special padded dashboard to meet US standards. This dashboard had a much better instrument binnacle in front of the driver with the oil pressure gauge in the middle, rather than tucked away behind the driver's left hand as on the British specification cars. The radio could be mounted in a central console, which was not altogether convenient as it made tuning difficult when the gearlever was forward in first or third gear—as it was frequently in traffic—just when the bored driver fancied a fiddle with the radio! This dashboard, which was distinctly Ford-like in appearance, surprisingly had no glove box or cubbyhole either. Dual circuit braking was also fitted to US-specification cars to meet new Federal standards, but it was left off cars where it did not have to be fitted, such as in Britain.

The penny-pinching over the brakes showed far more signs of corporate policy than that of Thornley or Enever: they were only too keen to standardise safety features.

Other changes necessitated by American regulations included the fitting of emission equipment to US-bound engines (18GF prefix). The performance did not

The MGB's luggage boot offered a good deal more space than that of the MGA.

suffer too much on these cars, however, as cylinder heads were improved in detail at the same time.

The next round of changes in October 1969 were purely cosmetic. All MGBs were fitted with a new black grille, Rostyle wheels in place of the old pressed steel wheels (wires remained an option) and Leyland badges on the wings. The steering wheel was also reduced from its antique 16.5-inch dimensions to 15.5 inches, with a more modern design. Reclining seats were also standardised (they had appeared on some 1968 cars) and the switches revised along the lines of American safety regulations. The horn push was transferred to the headlamp flasher stalk on the steering column, then returned to the steering wheel centre in August 1970 after the Americans disapproved. Two months later the bonnet and roadster bootlid were at last given self-supporting struts, a conventional interior light was fitted, the heater was improved (a long overdue revision) and the soft top was redesigned by Michelotti, who had been responsible for much Triumph work.

Road & Track didn't like the changes at all. They complained in one test: 'If the MG functions decently, it falls down on aesthetics and convenience. The styling has suffered rather than benefitted from the recent modifications, while the interior is decidedly unattractive. In most cases, needed improvements have been made as cheaply as possible (for instance the front of the hood—or bonnet in Britain—still has the raised form for the MG badge which has been moved to the centre of the grille, the rear bumper has been sliced apart to make room for a lower license plate mounting, the old dash structure has the new safety padding built on top of it, etc).' Somebody somewhere at Leylands noted all this and the Mark III MGB duly appeared in May 1971.

A new big-valve head was fitted for many markets, including Britain, and such engines were prefixed 18V. These were the best MGB engines ever produced. Later 18V engines reverted to smaller valves. All cars had a compromise grille somewhere between the old MGB style and the later black effort, which was generally approved; the interior was further redesigned with arm rests to give a more sumptuous look, and—more important—face-level ventilation was fitted. The US collapsible steering column was standardised and several items which had been extras such as radial-ply tyres, a tonneau cover for the roadster and heated rear window for the GT, became part of the standard specification in the face of mounting opposition from fully-equipped Japanese cars.

Various rubber or rubber-faced over-riders were fitted according to the market, the steering wheel was given slots to guard against idle fingers, and the windscreen wiper arms were painted black, rally-style, which also saved money.

Enormous overriders appeared on American models for the next year with hazard warning lights for the British market and radial-ply tyres everywhere. The optional brake servo also became standard and the steering wheel slots were filled in as they conflicted with some American regulations. Automatic transmission was withdrawn owing to a lack of demand.

Throughout this period, from 1971 to 1974, the engines on American cars had been progressively detuned to meet ever-changing emission regulations, but it was not until 1974 that the Americanisation of the MGB became really obvious. It

The distinctive GT badge on the rear quarter of an MGB GT.

sprouted its rubber bumpers and adopted a rather ungainly rise in ride height.

Considering the problems involved with the bumpers, the stylists did a remarkably good job, but it was only after five years that the writer actually heard anybody say that they liked them. These monstrous bumpers were fitted to meet California safety regulations which decreed that new cars should suffer no damage at all from a 5 mph impact. This entailed fitting massive steel beams at the front and back to support the dodgem-car style bumpers, adding 5 inches to the overall length and 70 lb in weight. Even worse, the ride height was raised 1.5 inches to save completely redesigning the shell with little done to combat the resultant strong roll oversteer. It was a classic case of legislation aimed at reducing accident injury causing the car to become more accident prone because its makers couldn't afford the money needed to redesign it completely, even had there been time. In addition, the engine had to be detuned so much with a reversion to the original small-valve cylinder head, a single Zenith-Stromberg carburetter and stangulating air cleaner, plus a catalytic unit in the exhaust manifold of California cars to reduce carbon monoxide, that it became 'too slow to get out of its own way', according to Thornley, speaking in retirement. In total, the American MGB had lost 25 bhp and gained a lot of weight.

Non-American MGBs retained the more powerful engine, but had to have the other changes made to save money in production. Instruments were standardised with the V8 model (described later in this chapter) and all models were fitted with twin stalk steering column controls. The optional Laycock D type overdrive with its 3.13 overall ratio was changed to the later Laycock LH unit with a 3.2 overall ratio, which was later made standard on all models from June 1975. The twin six-volt batteries were at last abandoned in favour of a single 12-volt one and sadly, the GT model was discontinued in the United States to give the new Triumph TR7 a clear run. An additional reason was that it was too heavy for the emission engine to give a reasonable performance.

During 1975, Abingdon produced 750 MGB GTs to celebrate what Leyland decided must be the company's fiftieth anniversary. These cars were all painted green with gold striping—the traditional colours of the legendary *Motor Sport* magazine which was also celebrating its golden anniversary that year—and were fitted with the cast alloy wheels and fatter tyres normally used with the V8, head restraints, overdrive and tinted glass. They didn't get much of a welcome from the enthusiasts, though. As historian Wilson McComb pointed out, MGs were in their fifty-second year of production. . . .

Attempts were made to improve the roadholding in the summer of 1976. From chassis number 41001, a rear anti-roll bar was fitted. This worked well to a certain extent, although fast drivers now found that it could cause the inside rear wheel to lift. The new anti-roll bar also meant that the fuel tank had to be redesigned to make room for it, cutting the tank's capacity by a gallon. The interior was redesigned yet again, and happily many of the features which had caused complaint during the model's fourteen years of production were eliminated. The pedals were remounted to make proper heeling and toeing possible, the cubbyhole lost its ignition key lock and the seats got a nice, but rather gaudy, nylon cloth trimming. The heater knobs were repositioned in a more conventional manner on a new console and the steering wheel was reduced in diameter (with the rack ratio being increased to 3.5 turns from lock to lock from 3.0, to compensate), besides being padded to meet new safety regulations. All cars were built in the V8 shell with its forward-mounted cross-flow radiator and twin electric fans, which were much quieter than the earlier belt-driven fan. This radiator needed an overflow tank, which was an advantage with emission-controlled engines, which tend to run hot. The GT also received tinted glass to heighten its upmarket image.

The MGC and V8

It had always been apparent that the basic MGB could take more power. Its handling was so good and its shell so strong that an engine transplant seemed to be the obvious way to improve its performance without adding much to the cost. Thornley and Enever tried a variety of different engines which could be obtained within the British Motor Corporation, but couldn't persuade the hierarchy to authorise production; they were told to see if the Austin-Healey's six-cylinder unit could be adapted first.

The main problem with this BMC C series engine was its great weight and height, which had been a handicap even in the hefty Austin-Healeys made alongside the MGB at Abingdon. This engine was demonstrably too big and heavy for the MGB, but there was room in the MG shell for a straight six like the C series if only it could be pared down a little. This didn't seem to be too formidable a task as casting techniques had improved by the mid-1960s, and Ford in America, for instance, were making a five-litre cast iron V8 that weighed only 480 lb against the three-litre C series engine's 611 lb. So when BMC decided to redesign the unit along the lines of their revision of the B series engine in 1964, they felt certain that they could reduce its weight to around 500 lb, at the same time as giving it

The spartan and cramped rear seat of the MGB GT (*above left*), proved to be more comfortable than it looked providing its occupants were small and preferably of not more than eight years of age. When folded down (*above right*), more luggage space was available, estate car style. The massive hatchback door of the MGB (or C) GT (*right*) gave good access to the luggage compartment.

seven main bearings instead of four, to make it smoother at high revs. It was also essential that the engine should be as compact as possible for use in a new Austin saloon in which passenger space was of paramount importance.

Therefore the C series block was redesigned with cylinder centres closer together to reduce its length by 1.75 inches while retaining its former vital statistics of 83.3 mm bore by 88.9 mm stroke (which gave a capacity of 2912 cc). Unfortunately the former Morris Engines works at Courthouse Green, Coventry, could get the weight down only to 567 lb—209 lb more than the B series engine it was to replace in the MGB shell to make the MGC and what was intended to be the Austin-Healey 3000 Mark IV. As it worked out, Donald Healey wouldn't put his name to it and Abingdon probably wished they hadn't either.

Enever was further handicapped in his task of fitting this heavy unit into the MGB shell by the decision to make the car available with optional automatic transmission. The Borg Warner Model 35 gearbox was a rather bulky affair, which posed special installation problems. Had the long six-cylinder engine been mounted further back for more equal weight distribution, the transmission tunnel would have had to move back, too. This would have restricted passenger space. There was an additional problem in that the main bulkhead would have had to have been redesigned and a new location found for the heater. This would have meant relocating the brake servo as well (probably in Jaguar saloon car style, in one front wing), with consequent redesign of parts such as flitch plates.

As the MGB stood there was a tempting amount of under-used space in front of the four-cylinder engine. It was calculated that the six-cylinder version of the MGB could be made to handle reasonably well if the new engine could be brought down to 500 lb. The new engine was similar in layout to the B series unit with pushrod-operated overhead valves and manifolds on the right-hand side (viewed underbonnet), with ancillaries on the left. Its cylinder head was modified for more easy acceptance of Federal anti-pollution devices but this, together with the friction of three extra bearings, reduced power and torque from 148 bhp at 5200 rpm and 175 lb/ft of torque at 3000 rpm, to 145 bhp at 5200 rpm and 170 lb/ft of torque at the noticeably higher figure of 3400 rpm. Nevertheless, this engine was still more than half as powerful again as the B series unit with a similar increase in pulling power. In manual form, it was fitted with a larger, 9-inch clutch and mated to a gearbox similar to the new all-synchromesh box fitted to the new Mark II MGB.

Enever did his best with this weighty problem. He had to redesign the front suspension to make room for the engine as the MGB's front cross-member got in the way. This meant using torsion bars, rather than coil springs, as the suspension medium, transferring the load back to a reinforced mounting under the seats. The shell was also substantially reinforced back to the floor pan, making it even stiffer than that of the MGB. Telescopic shock absorbers were also used at the front in place of the ancient lever arm devices because so much weight was concentrated over the front axle line. The small front bulkhead was scrapped and the radiator, with an oil cooler, was moved forward into the nose. The Girling front brakes were increased in size to 11.05 inches with rear drums by the same makers reduced to a 9-inch diameter (but increased in width to 2.5 inches), to cope with the extra

The 1974-model year MGB interior showing a cleaned-up dashboard and solid spoke steering wheel to prevent idle fingers becoming trapped in the slots of earlier spokes.

redistributed weight. Larger, 15-inch, wheels were fitted because of the car's additional performance potential. The steering rack was redesigned to run around the bottom of the far bigger engine and made lower geared (3.5 turns from lock to lock instead of 3.0) at the same time because of the extra weight and the increased skew angle of the pinion gear. A front anti-roll bar was fitted as standard and the spring rates were increased front and rear to near-MGA levels because of the extra power and weight.

The gearbox ratios were the same as those of the MGB on the early non-overdrive MGCs, giving overall ratios of 3.07 : 1, 4.24, 6.65 and 10.56 with a reverse of 9.5 : 1 and a higher geared (3.07 : 1) rear axle. Early MGCs fitted with a Laycock overdrive, which worked on third and fourth gear, had a closer-ratio gearbox and a 3.31 : 1 rear axle, giving overall ratios of 2.71, 3.31, 3.54, 4.33, 6.32 and 9.86 with a reverse of 8.87. Automatic cars shared the overdrive axle ratio, giving overall ratios of 3.31 : 1, 4.79 and 7.91 with a reverse of 6.92. This gearing gave 23.85 mph per 1000 rpm in direct top on the non-overdrive car; 27 mph per 1000 rpm in top in the automatic car.

Halfway through the production run from the car's introduction in October 1967 (from chassis number 4236 roadster, 4266 GT) an attempt was made to make

Facing page top and bottom: Front and rear views of the MGC roadster, showing its marked similarity in appearance to the MGB.

The massive C series engine (*right*), and the unit from which it was developed, the even bigger and heavier engine fitted to the Austin-Healey 3000 Mark III (*below*).

the MGC more responsive by fitting a 3.7 : 1 rear axle on overdrive cars and the 3.31 axle on non-overdrive machines and automatics. This meant that the closer-ratio gearbox could be standardised on manual cars and gave new sets of overall ratios: manual non-overdrive 3.31 : 1, 4.33, 6.32, and 9.86 with a reverse of 8.87; overdrive 3.03, 3.7, 3.96, 4.84, 7.61 and 11.03 with a 9.91 reverse. This gave 22.1 mph per 1000 rpm in top on the non-overdrive car and 24.1 in overdrive.

The rear axle was of tubular Salisbury type, but stronger than that of the MGB. The comparative overall weight to that of the MGB was 2460 lb against 2030 lb, the extra weight being fairly equally split between the engine and chassis modifications. Nearly all the changes were in the front end of the car, however, so the total weight distribution suffered to the extent of 55.7 per cent in the front and 44.3 per cent in the rear against the MGB's 52.5/47.5.

Outwardly, the MGC looked almost exactly like an MGB, except that it stood an inch higher off the ground because of its 15-inch wheels, and the bonnet sprouted bulges over the tall engine and its twin SU HS6 carburetters. The interior was the same and it 'could have been a world-beater,' said Thornley, 'had the engine not been half a hundredweight too heavy.'

Had Rover been within the BMC orbit in 1965 when the MGC was being developed, it might have been a different story. One of their executives had accidentally stumbled on a superb all-alloy V8 that had been produced by General Motors in America between 1960 and 1963. The Americans stopped production when their thin wall iron casting techniques improved sufficiently to make the alloy V8 an oddball in their range. Rovers started building it under licence just as the MGC was being introduced in 1967 and came within the same company umbrella when BMC was merged into British Leyland in 1968. This would have been the obvious engine to have fitted to the MGB shell for extra performance as it weighed only about the same as the existing B series engine and could be 'shoe-horned' into the engine bay with few modifications.

However, there were many other cars in the British Leyland range that needed this engine, especially saloons made by Rover, who had found the engine in the first place. Therefore, MG's designs on this engine took a back seat until Kentish garage proprietor Ken Costello started marketing the conversion in 1970. His Rover V8-engined MGBs received such acclaim that British Leyland had to follow suit with the MGB GT V8 in 1972. In essence, this factory car was a standard MGB GT with the V8 engine mated to an MGB gearbox.

A bigger, 9.5-inch, clutch and special ratios (which gave overall gearing of 2.52, 3.07, 3.87, 6.06, 9.63 and 8.65 reverse) were fitted with an overdrive as standard and a 3.07 : 1 rear axle. This arrangement took advantage of, and just about coped with, the engine's vastly-increased torque (193 lb/ft at 2900 rpm), in conjunction with stiffer rear springs, a larger-diameter propeller shaft, and fatter, 175-section, tyres. These were mounted on special wheels with cast alloy centres riveted to steel rims.

The Rover V8 pushrod engine used in the MGB GT V8 produced a comfortable 137 bhp at 5000 rpm in 8.25 : 1 compression ratio form with a bore and stroke of 88.9 mm by 71.1 mm, giving it 3528 cc. It was also used with a 10.5 : 1 compression

The MGB GT V8, looking very much like an ordinary MGB GT, except for its wheels and V8 badges. In an amusing manner, the V8 badges were carried only on the front, back and on the nearside of the car. There was none on the offside. Apparently, the idea was that people would wonder what was approaching them so fast and spot the V8 badge on the front; or alternatively the V8 badge on the nearside or back as the car overtook them. Should they overtake the car (and all production MGB GT V8's were right hand drive) they would seen no V8 badge. The car would look just like an ordinary MGB GT, which was fitting as nothing was supposed to overtake a V8 . . .

ratio in Rover saloons, giving up to 185 bhp. The lower figure was quite sufficient for the MGB as their gearbox (and rear springs) could not cope with the 226 lb/ft of torque produced by the higher compression engine. As it was, the gearbox proved to be on the limit of its capacity with 193 lb/ft of torque. Rover had a manual gearbox for the engine in 1973 but they needed them all for their own cars.

Three factors went against the MGB GT V8 being sold on the American market: it would have cost more than British Leyland could have afforded for the engine and body to have been adapted to meet US emission regulations; the fuel consumption looked like being too high with emission equipment; and General Motors had always seen the MGB as a competitor for their Corvette range. They tolerated the engine's use in the Morgan Plus 8 as that car had been outlawed from America by the safety regulations and only a handful were made per week. Abingdon's problems were made worse by the conviction that the MGB roadster's shell was not stiff enough to take the V8 engine, so all their development costs would have been concentrated on the GT, which Triumph wanted dropped to make way for the TR7. The stiffer MGC roadster shell could not be used as the tooling was long gone.

Leyland had been stung by criticism of the MGC's bulbous bonnet, so the Rover penthouse manifold was redesigned in order that twin SU HIF6 carburetters could be fitted at the back of the unit with a lobster claw air cleaner picking up heat from the exhaust manifolds. A special single exhaust system was used. These arrangements allowed the V8 engine to be accommodated under the MGB's bonnet

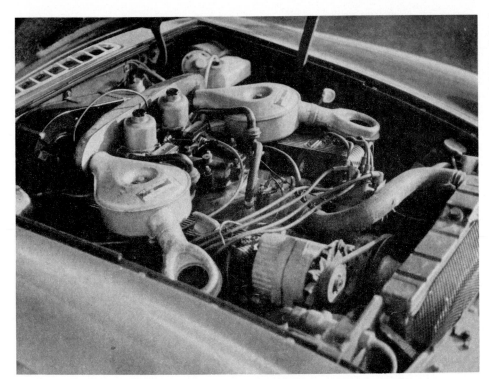

The Rover V8 engine was a neat, shoe-horn fit under the standard MGB bonnet because the complex lobster claw inlet manifold, pictured clearly here, kept the carburetters low, unlike those on the MGC which needed a bulge in the bonnet.

without any outward alteration. Inwardly, the main bulkhead was slightly modified, indentations were made in the flitch plates and the front bulkhead was removed to make way for the new engine. The steering rack was also moved down an inch, but the sump was still on the small side and the unit ran at a low pressure, so an oil cooler with remote filter was fitted as standard.

Tremendous interest had been shown in Ken Costello's conversions at a price of nearly £1000 more than the standard MGB GT. So Leyland pitched the V8's price only slightly below that but sales suffered as a result and only 2591 of these high-performance machines were made before production ceased. Early MGB V8s had a ride height of one inch more than the four-cylinder cars in anticipation of the changing American laws on bumper height, then they were standardised with the four-cylinder cars when the rubber bumpers were fitted. At this point all MGB shells were fitted with the V8's modified bulkhead. With a more sympathetic management, the MGB GT V8 could have been a great success.

IV

Road Testers' Reports

THE LARGER MG sports cars made since 1955 have been among the most popular tested by the specialist magazines: more than eighty tests have been published in Britain and America alone. Most testers liked the MGA and MGB, but the MGC came in for a lot of criticism. It is also significant that a quarter of the total British and American tests have been of modified MGs, mostly in the clubmen's magazine, *Cars and Car Conversions*. Obviously there has been no shortage of firms willing to spend time and money developing conversions to make the cars go faster.

Of the four most popular magazines that tested the **MGA** in its original guise in 1955, *The Autocar* extracted the highest maximum speed from a right-hand-drive pre-production car, LJB 370. They recorded 99 mph flat out with a 98 mph average from runs in opposite directions, and managed 0–60 mph in 15.6 seconds and the standing quarter mile in 20.2 seconds, with 27 mpg. John Bolster, of *Autosport*, who had been competing in sprints and hill climbs for years, recorded slightly better acceleration figures with the same car (0–60 mph 15 seconds, standing quarter mile 20 seconds) and fuel consumption (29 mpg) but could manage only 96.7 mph flat out. Of the car itself, he said:

> 'On driving off, one is at once impressed with the gearbox. It is as nearly crash-proof as anything I have driven outside the automatic class. The changes go through beautifully, and third gear is high enough for frequent use on the open road . . . the clutch is smooth in action, but can be made to slip if fast changes are attempted . . .
>
> 'The makers suggest 80 mph as a cruising speed, which seems to suit the car admirably. I had the speedometer on the 100 mark a score of times, under favourable conditions on the road. One tends to drive fast because the comfort is so good. The first impression is that the suspension is fairly hard, but this soon disappears, and at the higher speeds the comfort is most marked. There is none of that continuous up-and-down movement that mars so many modern cars. The stability is exceptional, and the MG corners fast under perfect control . . .
>
> 'Very powerful brakes are a valuable safety feature. They can be used hard and often without the slightest sign of fading . . . in fact they are more than

adequate for the speed and weight of the car.'

The Autocar agreed with Bolster in essence, although they couldn't make the clutch slip. In fact, they left black lines on the road surface with abrupt starts, but their test pre-dated Bolster's by a month, so perhaps the clutch was worn by the time he tried LJB 370. *The Autocar* were also quite happy with the exhaust note, describing it only as 'familiar' in contrast to *The Motor*, who tried another pre-production MGA, LJB 439, at the same time. They complained that the level of noise in the cockpit rose a good deal when the hood was up.

Their performance figures (with wheelspin) were slightly slower at 98.4 mph maximum (97.8 mph mean), a 16 second 0–60 mph time and 20.4 second standing quarter mile, with 26.7 mpg, but nevertheless they considered that the car needed higher gearing than its standard 4.3 : 1 rear axle ratio. They enjoyed the car, however:

'To drive the MGA on a winding road is sheer enthusiast's delight. Rack and pinion steering and small cars have always gone well together, and the lightness of the steering . . . is matched by a quickness and precision which might not be expected of the lock-to-lock figure of 2.75 turns. In this case the secret lies in an admirable example of useful and controllable oversteer. In point of fact, an improvement in the handling was found possible by inflating the tyres

Road test pictures fall into two categories: those with the cars spick and span before they went on test and those of the cars during some hectic trial. In this case, the fly-spattered front of *The Autocar's* MGA Twin Cam puts this picture in the latter category.

from the recommended fast-driving pressures of 18 psi front and 23 psi for the rear wheels to approximately 26 psi on all four. The effect of the oversteer then was merely that the driver, rather like a pilot in some types of aircraft, steered into a turn and then virtually centralised the wheel to keep the car on course. It was notable that to some tastes at least the extra sponginess of the tyres at lower pressure did not make for a more comfortable ride, and had the further disadvantage of causing tyre squeal on corners, otherwise entirely absent.

'Quite apart from steering characteristics, the cornering power of the car is extremely good, holding it down in a manner to give the driver complete confidence, and seeming almost indifferent to the type of road surface. As is often the case, a wet road gives an earlier indication of the car's behaviour when pressed to the limit on a corner, sliding of the rear wheels beginning quite gradually and being easily transformed into a controlled drift. Wheelspin is very easily provoked in starting from rest in the wet, due possibly to the combination of a small, high-revving, engine and a throttle control which on the left-hand-drive model under test was awkward in the extreme.'

Surprisingly, the Americans who tested a left-hand-drive MGA for *Road & Track* were quite happy about the accelerator pedal although critical of some other parts of the interior. 'Getting into the car, especially for the driver, is a little difficult, but once seated the new lower position is immediately noticeable. There is more pedal room, especially for the accelerator foot, but unfortunately the steering wheel interferes with the legs of a tall driver. The new centre armrest gives a feeling of security but the seat-backs are certainly very erect and the lack of support under the knees proved somewhat tiring toward the end of our 300-mile road test.'

Much of the rest of this test was devoted to a comparison with the MGA's predecessor, the MG TF. *Road & Track* were very enthusiastic about the new car, asking how MGs were going to meet the demand after recording performance figures as much as twenty per cent better than the TF 1500. They managed 97.5 mph on one run, with a 95.1 mph average and 0–60 time of 14.5 seconds, with a standing quarter mile in 19.3 seconds—the best acceleration figures recorded so far for the MGA. They noted that the TF 1500 was not much slower up to 50 mph, but really lost out after that as the MGA's streamlining became of greater advantage. The 0–60 mph time was nearly 2 seconds faster and the 0–70 mph no less than 4.8 seconds, with fuel consumption improved to 28–32 mpg from 20–23 mpg.

Five British magazines tested the MGA fixed-head coupé in 1957 and 1958 returning similar performance figures, all slightly faster than the roadster. The similarity between the figures—*Autosport*'s were best at 102 mph maximum, 0–60 mph in 14.2 seconds, standing quarter mile in 19.2 seconds and 26 mpg—was hardly surprising: the same test car, NJB 381, did the rounds of *Autosport*, *Motor Sport*, *The Motor*, *The Autocar* and *Sports Cars Illustrated*'s British edition! The reason it was slightly faster than the roadster was attributed to its more slippery shape and an extra 4 bhp for only an extra 32 lb in weight. Bolster, in *Autosport*, was happy to note that its clutch plate didn't slip, but thought that it rolled slightly more than the open car. He was of the opinion that it would sell like hot cakes in Britain because of 'our atrocious weather', although it was a pity that the spare wheel occupied so much of the luggage space. Without the wheel in place it would make a good long-distance tourer, said Bolster.

Bill Boddy on *Motor Sport* did not publish comprehensive performance figures—except for fuel consumption which was of critical importance at the time because of the Suez petrol crisis—but his report gave the impression that NJB 381 performed just as well for him as Bolster. Generally, he liked the styling, although he thought that even an octagonal hole in the front would have been preferable to the oblong grille. He appreciated the large expanse of glass but considered the best thing to do with the interior mirror—which obstructed his near-side line of vision—was to throw it over a hedge and fit the optional wing mirror.

Boddy was ten years ahead of his time in pointing out that sharp edges inside the car were potentially dangerous in an accident. However, he said: 'This body earns good marks, for chic appearance and well-thought-out detail work, and it is commendably free from rattles.' But he added: 'It scores a big black mark when all but the more agile first try to enter or leave it. The doors are large and quite properly trail, but they do not open more than about 45 degrees, which with the low floor and low roof line, renders dignified exit from an MGA virtually impossible for the elderly, who are in imminent danger of rupture or a slipped disc unless care and thought is applied to the manoeuvre.'

In common with *Autosport* and *Motor Sport*, *The Autocar* praised the MGA fixed-head coupé in general terms and found fault with the interior mirror. They also complained about the lack of ventilation with the windows closed and the draughts with them open. These points did not fail to escape the attention of *The Motor*'s road tester's either, although they were better able to express their appreciation of the body's qualities:

'We were particularly impressed by the robustness of the car and the entire absence of chassis wave or body shake even when speeds considerably greater than 80 mph were being sustained on Continental highways. This high stiffness factor not only ensures freedom from deterioration of door windows, window frames and other small items in the general structure but also gives the driver and passenger a psychological impression that high speeds can be maintained in safety, whereas some more flimsily built vehicles suffer not only from mechanical disabilities but also impose strain and anxiety upon the occupants. . . .

'Any resonant effects which may be introduced by the use of a closed body are more than offset by the reduced wind noise and buffeting which follow from the enclosure of the occupants and by reason of a well-designed and carefully positioned wrapround windscreen.'

The British edition of *Sports Cars Illustrated*, who carried out their test on NJB 381 some months after the other magazines and managed to extract 105 mph from it, praised the concept and said that, superficially, its styling was modern.

Customers can still collect their cars from Abingdon as they often used to. But before a completed car can be handed over, it must be road-tested, and most rigorously inspected by the gateman at the factory to make sure that nothing is amiss! Here the gateman of the day carries out his check on the last MGA Twin Cam made before it was tested and handed over to its one and only owner, Mike Ellman-Brown.

'Yet in some ways the car is old-fashioned. Although the tail is long, the bonnet is even longer, because, of course, much of the rearward part of the nose covers the occupants' leg room. The driver thus looks along an aristocratically long nose, which curves away to give good visibility close to the front of the car.'

They also summed up the British view of the MGA rather well: 'For pleasure motoring it is very hard to beat, so long as two seats are enough. It flatters the good driver, lets him enjoy himself and enters into the pleasure of the journey.'

This magazine's parent publication in America, also called *Sports Cars Illustrated*, or *SCI*, found the MGA's cornering ability 'quite awe-inspiring' but considered its ride 'naggingly choppy.' They liked the interior trim of the fixed-head coupé much better than that of the roadster (complaining particularly about the roadster's fibreboard inner door panels) and warned that it was possible to select reverse by mistake when changing hurriedly from third to second gear. They praised the economy—25 mpg—and performance (similar to the British figures), but found that 102-octane petrol was needed to combat running-on. They summed up by saying:

'Two anomalies result from the conversion of an originally laid-out right-hand-drive car to left-hand-drive. In the home-market model the very important combined oil pressure and water temperature gauge is located alongside the driver—as it should be—and the fuel gauge is in a corresponding position, in front of the passenger, where it need be referred to only occasionally. In the changeover to left-hand-drive the speedometer and tach migrate as they should to the new driver's position, but the vital oil-water instrument stays in its original spot, now out of the driver's field of vision. Similarly, the windshield wipers park to the left, out of the right-hand driver's way. In the left-hand version they still park to the left, just as the handbrake stays in foreign territory. Other objections: at its price the car could afford an ash tray; and, as reported of the roadster, the seat backs should be re-contoured to support the entire back instead of the shoulders.

'So much for negative comment, most of which is fairly trivial and can be corrected by the owner who cares. On the positive side there are many points in addition to those already mooted. The MGA's general and detail finish is excellent, actually rich in its appearance. So is its overall look, which wins admiring attention everywhere. It's a car in which the owner can take as much pride of possession as he might in other cars that cost much, much more. It belongs, perfectly, at the swankiest spa and has an urbane, cool distinction that the cherished T series, with its flavour of flaming youth, never could aspire to. The MGA coupe is the snuggest MG yet, the most comfortable in all kinds of weather and for all kinds of touring. Its necessarily limited luggage accommodation is no problem if you add the natty luggage rack option. It is the perfect car for rallying and it's ideally adapted to racing. It has the broadest appeal of any MG made.'

Road & Track were similarly impressed, adding that the 'fine fly-off handbrake, as before, is an aid in breaking the ice on a date!'

The next round of tests for the basic MGA concentrated on the 1600 roadster between 1959 and 1961, mostly with one machine, SMO 907. *The Motor* managed 100 mph flat out (96 mph mean) when it was hardly run in, returning a 0–60 mph time of 13.3 seconds and standing quarter mile in 19.8 seconds. These were better than the 1500's figures, but the real difference made by the extra torque of the new engine was seen in the 30–50 mph figures in top gear (10.6 seconds against 11.4) and 50–70 mph (13.3 against 14.9). In fact, *The Motor* were rather apologetic about the maximum speed, saying SMO 907's tubeless tyres were slower than the Road Speeds on their earlier car. They also commented on the outstandingly good balance of the new disc front brake/drum rear brake combination, saying that the squeal on gentle application was a small price to pay for such good retardation. *The Motor* appreciated the more relaxed manner in which the 1600 could be driven but said they thought the engine felt more harsh than that of the 1500. Fuel consumption with the tight new engine was up to between 23.5 and 25.5 mpg.

The Autocar tested an identical twin SMO 908, soon after and managed 101.4 mph (100.9 mph mean) although their 0–60 mph figure was slower at 14.2 seconds and standing quarter mile faster at 19.3 seconds! They agreed with *The Motor* over the harsh feel of the new engine but felt that it was unlikely to deter the enthusiast. Noise came in the same category: 'While not obtrusive at lower engine speeds, at 4000 rpm and above it is, perhaps, a little loud for town use, although the occupants of the car do not suffer from this so much as onlookers.

'One of the greatest advantages of the new MGA is that the increased power has improved the flexibility of the engine, and where previously one had to use first and second while crawling in heavy traffic, one can now employ second and third gears quite comfortably. In fact, it was found that the car would pull away from under 10 mph in top gear, though, of course, it is unlikely that any driver of this type of car would do so.'

At the same time as *The Autocar* were testing SMO 908, the redoubtable Bolster was trying to push SMO 907 past 100 mph for *Autosport*. He failed (97.8 mph maximum) but got the 0–60 time down to 12.8 seconds and standing quarter mile to 19.2 seconds, with 26 mpg overall. He blamed the lower-than-anticipated top speed on hood flap and also noted that the engine went through a rough period (which had also been reported by *The Motor*) at 5000 rpm. Bolster said:

'The car is definitely livelier than its predecessor, and perhaps the acceleration figures scarcely do justice to the increase in performance. This is because there is a rather marked tendency for one rear wheel to spin at the getaway, even on dry concrete. It is, in fact, necessary to be well on the move before full throttle can be applied on first gear. When the speed begins to rise, however, the very real benefit of the powerful engine can be felt . . .

'The engine is an instant starter and pulls well almost at once. The extra torque of the slightly bigger unit renders the car more flexible and one makes less use of the gear lever than formerly during normal touring. Considered as a fast touring car, the MG must be rated very high indeed. The occupants are well protected and the machine is comfortably sprung. It covers the ground in an effortless manner, and useful average speeds may be maintained without any undue feeling of strain.

'At low speeds the steering feels rather dead and is perhaps heavier than would be expected. At higher velocities, however, it comes into its own, being delightfully accurate and affording a fine sense of control. The gearbox is a splendid component, and it would be hard to better the easy and precise operation of that short and rigid lever. The clutch is well able to cope with the bigger engine; the brakes also are entirely free from vice and cannot be made to fade.'

Bill Boddy on *Motor Sport* considered the brakes to be impeccable in his left-hand-drive 1600 roadster, 899 CFC, tested in 1960 and he made a point of saying that his engine was astonishingly smooth 'and all too willing to take you well into the red.' Obviously the cars used by *The Motor* and *The Autocar* had suffered from their initial thrashing.

Boddy did not take performance figures, but Douglas Armstrong did when his turn came in SMO 907 in January 1961. By then this long-suffering car had done more than 20,000 miles and he commented in *Cars Illustrated*, the successor to the British edition of *SCI*, that 'the test car was old enough to be the model equipped with Lockheed disc brakes on the front wheels only. Later models are available with Dunlop disc brakes (and pressed steel, centre-lock, Dunlop wheels) on all four

Road test photography does not just cover the car being hammered all over the country and abroad; it means painstaking hours of picture-taking for photographers, of which this picture, of *The Autocar's* MGA fixed-head coupé, is typical. Without these numerous detail shots of the cars there would be a great scarcity of contemporary pictures of the cars, as factory files have a habit of going missing.

wheels'—an obvious reference to the mysterious 1600 De Luxe.

Armstrong tried hard but couldn't quite clear the magic ton, recording 99 mph flat out, with a 0–60 mph time of 14 seconds; but he did reduce the 30–50 mph time in top to 9.5 seconds.

SCI in New York and *Road & Track* in California both tested the MGA 1600 roadster in October 1960 and cleared 100 mph; 102 mph with the top down in the case of *SCI* and 103 top up for *Road & Track*. The Californian magazine praised the 1600 and finished by saying: 'We always go a little overboard on the subject of the MG, which is a first-love type of machine. We still say this is the best all-round sports car for use in America, especially for the new enthusiast.

'Having said that much, and having owned both a TC and an A, we think some criticism might be pertinent and excusable. The MG is primarily a street sports car, which is merely another way of saying that it isn't too well suited for competition. In the first place it's a little too big, too heavy, and too soft riding for serious competition. Perhaps it isn't intended to be raced, but, sentimentally perhaps, it would be nice to see the marque back in the fight.

'Minor criticism on the A concerns us too, because several annoyances have continued from year to year without correction. One of these is the totally inadequate ventilation. There is a fresh-air duct, but it lets in a mere whiff of air. The new sliding curtains help a little, but a real blast of air is needed near the driver's and passenger's feet, and the foot dimmer switch is impossible to find when you are in a hurry. The seats aren't too bad, but they're not too good either. A little more bucket shape and a quickly adjustable back would be worthwhile, even if available only as optional equipment. Something should be done about the spare tyre: there isn't any luggage space at all. And while we're about it, a simple external push-button release (with lock) on the lid would be handy when coming out of the store loaded with bundles (assuming you can get them in). As it is now, you fumble down around behind the seat and tonneau cover trying to find the elusive pull ring. The present battery location is quite impractical. To get at it, you must first remove the tonneau cover, then raise the side curtain storage case, then put up the top. After that we are getting close; merely remove six sheet metal screws and the rear floor comes out, exposing the battery (if it's still there after being ignored for six months). It would also be nice if something could be done to protect the grille from the current crop of lethal weapons protruding from the sterns of certain behemoths whose drivers insist on rather rough parking tactics. However, a standard guard would put several accessory firms out of business.

'All this may sound like grousing, but it isn't. It's carping. We could even go further and ask for a synchromesh first gear, a dual exhaust system, etc. The MG is an honest automobile, built to sell for under $2500, and we wouldn't want to see it become more costly. No car has done more to further enthusiasm for the sport. The MG has succeeded because it has the obvious value needed to sell—and, more important, the stamina and durability to keep enthusiasts enthusiastic.'

John Christy of *SCI* was absolutely captivated by the 1600 roadster. He packed 2000 miles of turnpike and tollway in New York, New Jersey, Pennsylvania, Ohio, Indiana and Illinois, and a quick trip to Detroit by secondary road into his test, then wrote, with the old T series in mind:

'It wasn't too many years ago that a long cross country haul in an MG could be looked upon as an adventure in frustration if much throughway or turnpike travel were on the itinerary. Secondary road travel was, and still is, another thing—the MG came into its own, sticking like glue and maintaining an average well above the capabilities of more staid machinery. But long straight turnpikes with their constant speeds and, from a sports car standpoint, 100 mph bends were not the MG's dish of tea. Then it became a case of constant hours-long buzzing at a sustained engine speed that seemed positively painful to the sensitive ear while domestic machinery went whooshing past.

'That day, gentlemen, is past—we guarantee it. It actually died with the TD and TF series, but not entirely. The MGA 1500 still retained some of the feeling that cruising speeds of 70 were somehow to be lumped under the various anti-cruelty acts. Not that the ubiquitous A wouldn't do 70—it would and much more . . . but it still didn't seem right. A steady speed of 65 or 70 in the 1500 is a matter of a bit more than half throttle. One knew one's foot was pushing the gasworks.

'No longer. With the 1600 things are different. So much so that only 100 cc are behind the difference. With a properly broken-in 1600 a steady speed of 70 mph is a matter of keeping one's foot out of it rather than pushing.'

At other times during his 2000 miles, Christy had cause to thank the power of the brakes and precision of the steering, 'dinging' a stray deer on the hoof with one front wing when 'in an ordinary car or one with inadequate brakes we would have wound up with a large amount of venison in the cockpit by way of the hood and windshield.' On one downgrade he saw 112 mph on an unusually accurate speedometer and he noted that the trunk lid no longer 'conducts rain water down into the trunk and onto the one thing you didn't want to get wet.' Beyond a shadow of doubt, it was the best touring MG yet, he said.

The Autocar tested a 1600 Mark II roadster, YJB 218, in July 1961, and although the engine and gearbox were still tight took half a second off acceleration times up to 70 mph and two seconds off the 0–80 mph figure (26.6 seconds down to 24.6) with a top speed of 102.3 mph (101.4 mph mean). Fuel consumption was up to 21 mpg driven hard, but it was noted that 35 mpg was attainable on the new 4.1 : 1 axle ratio if no more than 3–3500 rpm were used. High-speed cruising was even more relaxed and of the detail changes they gave special praise to the headlight flasher, and made a special complaint about the lack of locks.

Road & Track considered that their similar left-hand-drive car was too new for maximum performance testing, but agreed with *The Autocar*'s figures, adding that they considered 105 mph possible. They still liked the car very much but pointed out that although MGs were among the best-riding sports cars when they first used independent front suspension on the TD in 1950, they were now among the poorest. They were grateful for the new dimmer switch but still considered it inadequate for anybody not wearing ballet shoes and said: 'A pull-type starter switch is also an anachronism that can only lead to broken ignition keys when the car is left in a parking lot.'

SCI's successor, *Car and Driver*, really went to town on the MGA Mark II in 1961, devoting several pages to history and spending 3000 miles with their car. They carried out side-by-side tests with a 1600 owned by a gentleman from Abingdon, Pennsylvania, and found that the Mark II was 3.4 seconds faster up to 60 mph (12.4 seconds) and one second quicker over the standing quarter mile (18.5 seconds). During further tests giving the older 1600 a four-length start, the Mark II overtook it for a one-length lead over the quarter mile. 'The Mark II has, nevertheless, the characteristics of a distance runner rather than a sprinter,' said *Car and Driver*.

'While it's quick off the mark, it's at its top end that it really comes alive. Even in fourth cog, acceleration is forceful from about 3000 rpm up and from 4000 rpm it takes a second bite.

The much-used MGA 1600 roadster
SMO 907 pictured here during its test
by *The Autocar*.

'Fast cruising is enhanced by reduced wind noise with the top up. The second top bow is now attached to the fabric, eliminating the roar caused by wind buffeting in former models. It's not possible to talk in a whisper at that speed but at least you can hear yourself think.'

The test, which included all sorts of hints on how to improve your car in detail, went on to compare the Mark II with the recently-discontinued MGA Twin Cam; 'We were surprised to find when checking our research on MGAs that the performance of the Mark II is comparable to the Twin Cam in street form. Zero to 60 time for the off-the-dealer's-floor Twin Cam was about 13 secs and its time for the quarter mile was around 18.5 secs. Considering that the Twin Cam carried a considerably higher price than the Mark II and that its power was well over 100 bhp, the comparison puts the Mark II in a very favourable light indeed. . . .

'One of the new packages this year results from the death of the Twin Cam . . . for $250 over the basic price (of the Mark II) it's possible to get four-wheel disc brakes, knock-off disc wheels and Road Speed 5.90 × 15 tyres, all of which were standard on the Twin Cam'—another reference to the elusive 1600 De Luxe.

Considerably better performance figures were recorded by some of the magazines which tested the Twin Cam between 1958 and 1960. *The Motor*'s 1958 roadster, PMO 325, did 0–60 mph in only 9.1 seconds, although a standing quarter mile took 18.1 seconds. Top speed was 115 mph with 22 mpg overall, figures which *The Motor* found highly impressive:

'Perhaps the most revealing way to sum up this performance is to say that of all the cars so far tested by *The Motor* only machines built specifically for sports car racing would keep pace with this 1600 cc touring two-seater in a standing start match to speeds of 60, 70 and 80 mph (the 0–70 time recorded was 12.3 seconds and 0–80 16.2) . . .

'To what extent has racing performance been bought at the cost of inconvenience? There is, to begin with, a considerable increase in noise both mechanically from the engine and from the tailpipe when the throttle is opened at all wide. Neither is particularly objectionable at the speeds of normal traffic, but both can become tiring with the prolonged cruising at 90 mph or so which is a very practical possibility with this type of car.

'So long as 100 octane fuel can be obtained the engine is extremely docile at low revolutions and extremely smooth at high ones. On slightly lower grades it pinks only when pulling hard at low speeds, but has a very definite tendency to run-on . . . different styles of driving do not appear to affect an oil consumption of one pint for every 120 miles . . .'

The Motor praised the brakes, steering, handling and gear change, before concluding:

'Quarts into pint pots frequently take up a lot of the available space. The extra width of a twin overhead cam cylinder head has filled the bonnet to very near its capacity, and the engine is by no means as accessible as formerly. The dipstick, requiring as it does frequent attention, is almost completely hidden from view; a fault which could be most easily cured by fitting a long tube rising to the top of the engine. Similarly the distributor cannot be reached at all without first uncoupling the air duct to the interior heater.'

The Autocar were also enthusiastic about their Twin Cam roadster, PMO 326, recording the same top speed and a standing quarter mile of 18.6 seconds although their 0–60, 70 and 80 times were well down at 13.3, 17.3 and 22.5 seconds. The oil consumption was just as heavy and it had not improved by the time Bill Boddy tried PMO 326 ten months later in 1959. His performance figures were similar to those of *The Autocar* and later he said in *Motor Sport*:

'The keenly awaited Twin Cam MG came along to City Road in the merry month of May. The first one dropped a valve before I got near it but a subsequent model provided plenty of exhilarating performance and the noted "safety fast" by reason of disc brakes all round. With an engine willing to run up to 7000 rpm giving 88 mph in third gear, this MG really did get a move on, at the expense of considerable noise, rather heavy petrol thirst and a quite alarming consumption of oil. Since then the new 1600 cc MGA has been introduced, which could be a better car for all-round road motoring.'

The oil consumption problem certainly seemed to have been cured by the time Roy Salvadori tested a Twin Cam roadster, PMO 946, for *Sporting Motorist* in February 1960 as he made no mention of it although he noted the same points as other testers (and discovered that the wider engine meant a sacrifice of four feet on the turning circle) and recorded similar performance figures.

Road & Track and *SCI* in America carried out far more conclusive tests on the Twin Cam, giving rise to speculation about the state of tune and specification of PMO 325 and 326. *Road & Track* tried two cars, one in standard form and one with a 4.55 : 1 axle ratio and close ratio gearbox. The modified car equalled the best acceleration figures recorded by *The Motor* and *The Autocar* and reached 117 mph; the standard car's potential when properly tuned was put at a 10 second 0–60 and an 18.1 second standing quarter mile—which made you wonder whether the stock Twin Cam figures quoted by *Car and Driver* from *SCI* tests were ever in the right state of tune. *Road & Track* concluded:

'The standard gears give very good maximums, but with the torque available we feel that the optional Le Mans ratios and 4.55 axle are more suitable for competition purposes on our shorter circuits. The maximum in second gear then goes up from 56 mph to 72 mph at 7000 rpm, for example, and a 40 mph corner still gives 3900 rpm for acceleration. And a 0–100 mph time that is 11 seconds better should not be overlooked.

'The Twin Cam (one cannot use the letters TC, obviously) handles impeccably, like other recent models. There is over 150 lb more curb weight and the front wheels carry a slightly greater share of the total load than in the rocker-arm MGA. Still the extra torque is sufficient to produce oversteer in any indirect gear . . . In fast corners the tyres squeal but roll is very moderate, and the almost neutral (with light throttle) action of the rack and pinion steering is still as nearly perfect as in any machine we know . . .

'The Dunlop disc brakes and knock-off wheels appear to be partially responsible for the increased weight, but we liked them both. The brakes have no booster at all, which is surprising, but pedal pressure is exactly the same as on the MG with drum brakes . . .

'The new Twin Cam MG is a tremendous step forward for the firm. Designed primarily to regain prestige for the marque in production sports car racing, it should do just that. However, this is a car for the genuine enthusiast types, and we think the pushrod job is going to be just as popular as ever.'

SCI were surprised at their Castrol R-lubricated Twin Cam roadster's docility. They tested it at Lime Rock racing circuit first in standard tune as it came straight off the ship from England, then after attention from Ed Brown, who prepared the works Austin-Healeys for Sebring. At first the Twin Cam proved only as fast as a well-prepared 1600. When its engine had been set exactly to Abingdon specifications, fitted with a straight-through exhaust and mated to a close-ratio gearbox and 4.55 axle, lap times were reduced to 1 min 20 secs from 1 min 23 seconds. The 0–60 mph time was 9.7 seconds and standing quarter mile covered in 18.5 seconds. Top speed on the 4.55 axle was 115 mph and estimated at 120 mph with the standard 4.3.

Another MGA roadster tested by *The Autocar*, in this case the 1600 Mark II registered YJB 218, pictured in the London magazine's car park with other road test cars in July 1961: a Humber Hawk and two Mark II Jaguar saloons. The car park is still there today, shared with specialist magazines such as *Thoroughbred and Classic Cars*. Only the cars have changed . . .

Later when fitted with a competition clutch, stiffened springs and shock absorbers, lap times came down to 1 min 18.5 seconds with more performance to come with the possible removal of 'street' equipment such as bumpers, grille, silencer, interior parts and full-width screen, which would have taken about 200 lb off the weight.

John Christy, who tested the Twin Cam for *SCI* moved to *Sports Car Graphic* on the West Coast soon after and managed to test an MGA Mark II De Luxe in May 1962, masquerading under the title MGA Mark II Competition. This was the ultimate MG pushrod production roadster in terms of performance at the time, with full Twin Cam chassis modifications, close ratio gearbox, 4.55 rear axle and works hard top. The engine was standard MGA 1600 Mark II, the theory being that work could be done on it to meet whatever local regulations were in force in America once the car had crossed the Atlantic. Thus the attraction of the De Luxe was that all the Twin Cam chassis modifications could be bought for only $500 extra (about £200 including works hard top), ready fitted at Abingdon. Otherwise such modifications to a standard 1600 Mark II would have cost around $800 in America and might not have been fitted properly. 'In fact, we have a strong suspicion that there may have been some Twin Cam chassis laying about when they discontinued the double overhead camshaft engine,' said Christy, giving credence to the belief that the 1600 De Luxe was really a 1600 pushrod-engined Twin Cam with or without the close ratio gearbox, low rear axle and hardtop. At any rate, this rare car proved to be capable of 104 mph, and 0–60 mph in 12.4 seconds with a standing quarter mile time of 20.4 seconds, even while it was still brand new and stiff. Earlier estimates in *Road & Track* had credited the hard top with being worth an extra 5 mph on maximum speed over a billowing hood.

Another popular way of obtaining better performance from an MGA in the late 1950s and early 1960s was by supercharging. One of the most popular installations was by the American firm Judson, who marketed a do-it-yourself low pressure vane-type blower which proved reliable in use. Its 5.5 psi manifold pressure was enough to boost the power of the MGA 1500 tested by *Road & Track* in 1958 by 25 per cent. The car in question was fitted with a 'Continental kit' consisting of a bumper-mounted spare wheel which did wonders for the luggage accommodation but nothing for the aerodynamics, so the car's performance remained substantially as standard. However, *Road & Track* calculated that such a blower fitted to a standard car would have given it 105 mph, a 12.5 second 0–60 mph time and 18.1 seconds for the standing quarter mile. They also worked out that a supercharged fixed-head coupé would be good for 110 mph.

The fastest MGA road tested was undoubtedly the Bob Olthoff racing Twin Cam in the hands of Patrick McNally of *Autosport*. This hard top roadster, YRX 310, had competed successfully in long distance events (see chapter five) and had shown itself capable of beating even works Healey 3000s! It had the ultimate modifications allowed by Appendix J regulations (see chapter thirteen) returning 112.5 mph, 0–60 mph in 8.1 seconds and the standing quarter mile in 16.2 seconds on a 4.1 : 1 rear axle; McNally said the 0–60 mph time would have been better on its alternative 4.55 axle. He found the handling 'of a very high order' and said that it made an excellent road machine despite being a racing car.

Road tests of **MGB**s started in 1962 with an incredible 111.8 mph one-way run by *Motor*. The average of four runs in opposite directions was a good deal slower at 108.1 mph, but with a 0–60 mph time of 12.1 seconds and standing quarter mile of 18.7 seconds, the MGB proved itself considerably quicker than the MGA. Touring fuel consumption in the *Motor*'s car, a non-overdrive car registered 523 CBL, worked out at 28 mpg (with 22–24 mpg when driven hard), so its slippery shape was obviously paying dividends. Nevertheless, *Motor* said that it could do with a much higher second gear and slightly higher third gear for ultimate performance. In their opinion, the second gear had been kept on the low side to reduce the necessity of using the unsynchronised first gear.

The ride also excited some criticism: 'On indifferent, as distinct from really bad, surfaces and at intermediate speeds, the ride was much more shock-free than anyone accustomed to an earlier generation of sports cars would expect, but by no means as smooth and flat as in the best-sprung modern touring cars.'

Motor were totally complimentary on the steering, however: 'By use of a helical gear, the rack and pinion steering has been freed from kickback without flexibility or much frictional damping being perceptible, yet feel of the road is retained.'

They were quick to note that the revised interior allowed plenty of legroom for tall people and summed up by saying: 'No car can hope to please everybody and design compromises are very apparent in the MGB. A car of true everyday usefulness has been endowed with a lot of performance; verve has been blended with refinement to an extent which will suit any age from seventeen to seventy-seven; and, at a price which can be well below £1000, it offers sturdiness to outlast many saloons.'

Autocar could manage only 105 mph flat out in the same car with an average speed of 103.2 mph, although their acceleration times were virtually the same as those recorded by *Motor*. They were equally enthusiastic in general terms, however: 'There is no doubt that the new MG is a much superior car to its predecessor, the MGA, in all its forms. One cannot think of any aspect of this new sports car which does not show appreciable advantage in comparison with the previous model.'

On the power unit, *Autocar* said: 'It is significant that the new engine has lost the harshness but none of the low-speed traction of its predecessor, while at the upper limit of the range the engine has much more freedom to rev. Previously, 6000 rpm was regarded as a maximum safe limit, but now the engine may be taken up to 6800 rpm. This allows 34, 55 and 91 mph, respectively to be reached in the three indirect ratios, but it also permits an easy 70 mph in third gear, which is a very useful ratio for fast overtaking and main road cornering.'

They also liked the general feel, saying: 'Allied to the responsive nature of the car is its feeling of tautness. There is no scuttle shake, and the whole car feels immensely sturdy and rigid.'

First George Phillips, who had raced the MGB's ancestor at Le Mans in 1951, then John Bolster, were captivated by the MGB in their reports for *Autosport*. Phillips said:

'My acquaintance with the car was, unfortunately, all too short, but in the time it was at my disposal I must say I really fell for it. My very abridged test could hardly have been carried out under more adverse conditions—it was blowing a gale and positively pelting with rain. This at least gave me an opportunity to test the hood, and I am happy to say it was most effective. With the quarter lights open there was no sign of any leaks at all. I was also most impressed by the low level of the noise inside the car, the hood showed no signs of flapping and was very firm; also the engine and transmission did not encroach unduly—it was possible to hold a conversation with my companion without the necessity to shout while comfortably cruising at 95 mph.

'The driving position was to my liking and I found the seats very comfortable, giving all the support necessary. The rack-and-pinion steering was excellent; not too light and very sensitive. In spite of the high winds that were blowing, the car was in no way affected; doubtless the time spent in the wind tunnel had not been wasted.'

Bolster, who managed to wind up 523 CBL to 109.5 mph with an 11.4 second 0–60 mph and an 18-second standing start quarter mile time, said: 'The stability proved that the inherent handling characteristic is just on the understeering side of neutral. Any energetic driving methods, however, will translate this to oversteer with an ultimate rear-end breakaway. This is the type of response at which most British sports car designers aim, and so there is nothing new to learn for the man who first takes over an MGB.'

Road & Track hailed the MGB with the cry: 'Civilisation has come back to Abingdon-on-Thames.' They confided: 'Our styling experts (who really are) never had much good to say about the lines of the A. It was "corny, out-of-date in 1955, had poor surface development, etc." But there's no complaint over the fresh new look for the B. The worst we heard was that it's good but not very advanced or exciting. Perhaps this is true if you're comparing it to, say, a [Studebaker] Avanti, but everyone on our staff was enthusiastic over the appearance of the B, consultants notwithstanding.

> 'Our enthusiasm did not wane during 700 miles of driving. In fact, it grew stronger, and frankly this is the first British car in several years which created no arguments among the staff—even the Italian and German sports car owners forgot their private battle and admitted they liked to drive this new English job . . .
>
> 'A really worthwhile cockpit change comes via the new unit-construction which dispenses with the frame. There is, at last, ample pedal spacing for the average American shoe. The clutch and brake pedal pads are a little small (1.75 inches wide) but are spaced on 4.7-inch centres. Biggest improvement is accelerator pedal room—the space between the tunnel and the edge of the brake pad measures 6.1 inches. The pedals didn't satisfy some of our drivers; either the brake was too high or the accelerator too low; in any case it was impossible to heel-and-toe, which is unfortunate but could easily be corrected.
>
> 'The disc/drum brakes were absolutely without fault and despite there being no booster the pedal pressure was very moderate . . .
>
> 'Moving to the rear, the higher fenders [wings] should give more trunk [luggage boot] space, but volume is still skimpy and marred by the spare wheel and tyre being smack in the middle. Our thinking is that the gas tank should go somewhere else (maybe in the fender skirts like a Jaguar Mark X) and at least the wire wheel could be flopped over for more room.
>
> 'Our test car was a very early production model and yet, when we went over every square inch, the quality of workmanship and lack of flaws were remarkable. This is the best engineered, and best put-together MG we've ever seen.'

Performance figures on a tight new engine were pretty good at 106 mph, 0–60 mph 12.5 seconds and standing quarter mile in 18.5 seconds, which worked out much the same as those of *Car and Driver*, except that the East Coast magazine got the 0–60 mph time down to 10.6 seconds. Perhaps their car had an extra couple of hundred miles on it!

If anything, they were even more enthusiastic, capturing the MGB's fine points well: 'No MG has discredited the slogan Safety Fast, but compared with its predecessor the MGB is faster and certainly safer. With big disc front brakes and large drums at the rear, the MGB has more stopping power than it ordinarily needs, light, precise and quick steering at all speeds and improved driver comfort. A safer sports car would be hard to imagine.

> 'It is really not dissimilar to the MGA, yet somehow it seems improved in almost every respect. Its chief limitations are the retention of a rigid rear axle with semi-elliptic leaf springs and the lack of synchromesh on first gear.
>
> 'The lasting impression on all who drove it was that the MGB is an extremely easy car to drive well. Its behaviour is as well balanced as the MGA's

and it seems to be even more forgiving. It can be braked well into a corner, you can take the wrong line at the wrong speed, and make a number of other mistakes, yet the car will remain obedient to the steering wheel. Steering is very consistent, but the rear suspension reacts to unevenness in the road surface on corners by letting the rear end swing wide and thus the maximum speed at which corners can be taken varies markedly according to the quality of the surface.'

Bill Boddy used the overdrive on this *Motor Sport* road test MGB to good effect in 1965, recording 106 mph. But it wasn't all hammer and tongs. The car is pictured here at rest during a visit to a Vintage Sports Car Club race meeting at Silverstone.

Five months after the first spate of tests were over, Douglas Armstrong of *Cars Illustrated* tried 523 CBL with nearly 10,000 miles on the clock, but could manage only slightly slower performance figures than Bolster.

Armstrong found room, in a very thorough assessment which agreed with most of the points raised in earlier tests, to examine the MGB in great detail. He bemoaned the loss of the MGA's fly-off handbrake and the lack of a headlamp flasher, but considered that the horn push was far better placed in the centre of the steering wheel than on the dashboard. He also tested the car's aerodynamics by free-wheeling—and found that it went a long way, proving that the wind resistance was low!

Bill Boddy had a new MGB, 361 RJO, with overdrive for *Motor Sport*'s test in September 1965. He considered the overdrive well worth the £60 extra cost and recorded more than 25 mpg during the 50 mph speed limit period imposed by the then Transport Minister, Ernest Marples. He took performance figures on a test track, reaching 106 mph with a 0–60 mph time of 12.8 seconds and standing quarter mile of 18.5 seconds. After struggling with a rather stiff and 'high-set' gear lever, he said:

> 'It will be appreciated . . . that the MGB, while of handsome, much-improved, appearance, marred only by a rather short bonnet, bath-like cockpit, and recessed headlamps that could collect liberal quantities of snow, remains a sports car in the best British, rather antiquated, tradition . . .
>
> 'Old-fashioned this latest 1.8-litre MG may be, but it provides very fast, enjoyable, predictable fresh-air motoring for two keen people.'

So the world was beginning to consider the MGB rather old-fashioned, but loveable, by 1963; and these opinions were endorsed by *Car and Driver* in December 1964.

They appreciated that it was more civilised than the Morgan and less advanced than a Mini-Cooper S, but still considered that it was good enough to hook Americans. They said the ride was harsh, the handling fine (providing the surface was smooth), the appearance pleasing, the bumpers were dainty and in need of reinforcement for America, the cockpit was opulent with fighter plane efficiency, the instrumentation was fine, the locking glove box lid darned inconvenient, the seats were adequate and the top was a headache.

Autocar also managed 106 mph with their five-bearing MGB roadster pictured here cornering hard.

'There is a roof strut that runs laterally above the seats and a good bump can launch both driver and passenger into a skull-cracking collision with this length of iron. To anyone of six feet or more, this is a genuine hazard, even with the seat belt tightly clinched . . .

'The pendulum pedals are too high off the floor for efficient operation and we found the car devilishly hard to heel and toe . . .

'Excellent four-speed transmissions are no novelty today, and it must be difficult for BMC to justify the continued use of the present unit. It is unsynchronised in first gear, which automatically places it somewhere below the pinnacle of accomplishment in this field.'

They went on to complain about the low ratios of second and third gear and the way the transmission tunnel heated up, then added: 'There is an atmosphere that permeates the car that says "MG". No enthusiast can climb into the machine without being instantly aware that this is an MG. This impression gets massive reinforcement once the engine is turned on. There it is, the same exhaust note and virile mechanical clatter that has wooed enthusiasts since those giddy days following the war.' The performance figures were the same as those recorded earlier and the steering and brakes were unchanged, coming 'very close to nullifying the effects of the rear suspension. The MGB should maintain a strong position in the American sports car market for a number of years to come.' For just how long, *Car and Driver* could never have guessed.

Autocar found that the five-bearing MGB they tested in 1965 was slightly slower in direct ratios than the three-bearing car, although its overdrive helped restore maximum speed. The five-bearing car, BBL 966B, did 106 mph flat out (103 mph average) in overdrive top; 100.5 mph maximum in direct fourth gear (99.3 mph mean), 0–60 mph in 12.9 seconds and the standing quarter mile in 18.9 seconds.

The benefits of the extra bearings were most apparent between 1500 rpm and 4500 rpm. 'Even when revving the engine in neutral before driving off, one notices that what little harshness there was previously has gone. This may accentuate a general impression that the car is now less lively, although the performance figures are not markedly inferior. Standing start acceleration times are within a second of those of the earlier car right up to 70 mph, but from rest to 90 mph took 35.6 seconds—a full 3 seconds slower. The smooth, strong torque at low revs is more like that of a six-cylinder than a four.'

Motor returned virtually identical figures with the same car and complained about the awkward overdrive switch on the dashboard. *Cars and Car Conversions*, the successor to *Cars Illustrated*, tested an identical MGB, registered 667 UWL, soon after and commented that you needed a 'bootful of revs for much of the time if the full performance was to be enjoyed. Not that it is in any way inflexible; if you really want you can trickle along in traffic at 1000 rpm in top gear, which is almost good enough to be outstanding. But there is virtually no acceleration—not surprisingly—from this point unless you care to slot it down a couple. The power, in fact, arrives at the back wheels at something over 3000 rpm, and to hustle the car means that you really need to keep the engine speed above, say, 4000 rpm, which needs a pretty free hand with the gearbox.'

The introduction of the 70 mph blanket speed limit in Britain hampered *Motor* and *Autocar*'s maximum speed testing of the **MGB GT** in 1966. They listed only estimated top speeds following tests at the Motor Industry Research Association's track near Nuneaton. This banked track did not allow a long enough run-up for a car like the MGB GT to be driven absolutely flat out, but they reckoned its improved shape made up for the additional weight and the maximum speed would be about the same as that of the roadster. Acceleration times were slightly slower, at 13.2 seconds from 0–60 mph and a 19.5 second standing quarter mile for *Motor* and similar figures for *Autocar* on the same overdrive car, EOJ 221C. Fuel consumption worked out at between 21 mpg and 29 mpg depending on how the car was driven. In *Motor*'s opinion, BMC had 'greatly extended their potential sports car market. With a small back seat and a large platform behind it, the new GT can convey two adults, two children up to the age of about eight and considerable quantities of luggage over longish distances. For the true gran turismo, the additional human freight ought perhaps to be limited to one child or, say, to a child in a carrycot plus a toddler, since rear-seat legroom is a little limited even for children. The determined and enthusiastic private owner could modify the newly-created space in several ways to suit his own particular combination of bairns and baggage.

All this increase in carrying capacity has been achieved without any lessening in virility or sacrifice of the traditional MG virtues. Although the car is 2 cwt heavier than the open sports version, its performance is very little inferior, while the handling of the GT car, which has an anti-roll bar as a standard fitting, is a good deal better than that of an open car to which the optional anti-roll bar has not been fitted. More surprisingly, the vintage aspect of the MG character has not been lost: there is a purposeful clatter when starting up; the steering is direct and feels very positive (though rather heavy) in the best vintage way; and the straight-cut bottom gear emits a loud whine. An astonishingly smooth and flexible engine, a much reduced noise level and a taut, rigid structure justify the GT appellation and make long journeys effortless.'

Both *Motor* and *Autocar* worked out that the performance in direct fourth gear was slightly better and the maximum speed in overdrive fourth was slightly down—theories which were partly confirmed by John Bolster in *Autosport*, whose MGB GT, registered FOP 507D, recorded 103 mph flat out in direct fourth gear, 100 mph in overdrive fourth, and 98 mph in overdrive third, which provided almost exactly the same ratio as direct fourth. His 0–60 mph time was 12.95 seconds and standing quarter mile time 19 seconds.

In his opinion, the specification failed to reveal 'the very real personality of the car, which stems from its exceptional refinement and attractive finish.

Facing page: The suspension of *Autocar*'s MGB GT gets a thorough testing on this back road.

'The MGB GT can be regarded either as a two-seater with rather more luggage space than usual or as a family four-seater, the rear passengers being children. The driving position and the location of the controls are up to sports car

standards, nothing having been sacrificed to the utility role of the car. The driver's view, however, is disappointing, the wide screen pillars and swivelling quarter-lights causing a considerable blind spot. One misses the light and airy effect that one gets with Italian coupés.'

Cars and Car Conversions were equally impressed with their MGB GT, EOJ 240C, recording similar performance figures and saying: 'With less wind noise high-speed cruising is much more pleasant than with the open car (hood up, of course) and it really is a pretty civilised touring animal. The only thing we missed, the more so because it is now definitely a closed car, was some sort of interior light apart from that thing on the left of the dash which they call a map-reading light.'

Road & Track were as thorough as ever in their assessment of the MGB GT. They managed 105 mph with a 0–60 mph time of 13.6 seconds and a standing quarter mile of 19.6 seconds, and then devised a new way of testing the brakes. The results of repeated stops from 60 mph were alarming, as they recounted:

'If we ever thought MGs had outstanding brakes, perhaps it was because our tests weren't severe enough. The panic stop from 80 mph netted a respectable deceleration rate of 26 feet per second with good control in spite of some late rear lock-up: but the newly instituted fade test, not a drastic one, brought out the worst in the B's disc/drum set-up. They faded to the point of a 50 per cent (roughly) increase in pedal pressure by the sixth stop from 60 mph at 0.5 G, and on the last few feet of that sixth stop they were just about gone. They were also quite slow to recover from this faded condition.' Obviously the car needed different brake pads for racetrack use, although it would need an alarming driver to have to repeatedly stop dead from 60 mph in only a couple of miles.

As for the new body, they liked it. 'We had expected an MGB coupé right from the introduction of the car, so it seems a little late getting here,' said *Road & Track* in their 1966 test.

'Perhaps BMC hadn't really been serious about producing one until the current international Fastback Fad got under way. If so, their answer to the fad is not exactly a "me, too," and we're glad of that. Instead, the MG body designers and stylists have come up with a fairly original-looking shape that goes well with the basic B roadster . . .

'As for the jump seat itself, it could be best compared to that in the Austin-Healey: useless for adults, but as long as one doesn't plan to carry adults back there (well, one *could* sort of curl up) it should do nicely for a couple of small children and the tots will enjoy the cargo floor area as well. The driver of the MGB GT has benefitted too, as the windshield and side windows are quite a bit deeper than on the roadster and combine with a generous rear window at a useable angle to provide very good driver vision . . .

'As the car's performance isn't very wild it has less necessity than some for more sophisticated suspension linkage. The body structure does its part admirably—the B roadster has been one of the most rigid open cars around and

the coupé improves to the point of being Gibraltar-like . . .

'As an everyday, liveable and loveable car, the B is hard to equal. It starts readily if not instantly, down to o degrees F (heaven help you below that), runs smoothly at idle and low speeds, and has a general tractability that is legend with MGs. The major controls are handy, especially the gearshift and handbrake and even those who grow weary of manually shifted cars that really need to be shifted won't mind this job much. Heel-and-toeing is possible, but not especially easy. One staff member thinks BMC would be wise to offer an automatic transmission one of these days.'

Road & Track appreciated the headlamp flasher stalk on the steering column and bemoaned the lack of synchromesh on first gear but wound up saying the MGB GT could 'be more modern but it could be less too—long live the king.'

Needless to say, *Road & Track* were thrilled to test a Mark II roadster in 1968. 'The principle change is in the gearbox,' they said.

'It is marked visually by a straight gearlever instead of the bent one used before,

Another MGB GT, FOP 507D, endeared itself to John Bolster of *Autosport*, who liked its 'very real personality'.

For years, *Motor Sport*'s avid reader-
ship was treated to a different sort of
road test—by editor Bill Boddy's
motoring dog, a labrador which
probably travelled in a wider variety of
cars than any other member of canine
society. Here the motoring dog does its
back-seat driving in an MGB GT; she
was still going strong in the mid-
1970s, and now Boddy has her puppy
as 'motoring dog mark two'.

and it sprouts from an opening farther back on the gearbox tunnel—perhaps
a bit too far back, a criticism we almost never have to make. Shifting is much
the same as before—a bit stiff and notchy, but wonderfully precise—and the
new box not only eliminates the traditional first-gear whine but improves
general driveability by virtue of its better ratios . . . in short it's now possible
to drive an MGB like any other car, and it's a pleasant change.'

Road & Track's car which had air-injection equipment to reduce exhaust
emissions, was only fractionally slower than the earlier cars, recording 104 mph
flat out, with 0–60 mph in 12.1 seconds and an 18.7-second standing quarter mile.
Fuel consumption ranged between 21 and 27 mpg.

When *Motor* tested a Mark II roadster, SOF 365H, late in 1969, they were
surprised to find the MGB not only vintage in character but still competitive. They
said: 'Before our re-test of the open MGB we expected to find this ageing design . . .
to be completely outclassed by subsequent progress and perhaps no better than any
of several lively but quite ordinary family saloons. We are happy to report that our
expectations were, for all the important things, largely confounded. The MGB is still
a fast and satisfactory sports car. In performance it is still acceptably rapid . . .
moreover, in its responsive, accurate steering and well-balanced behaviour it can still
teach the young 'uns a thing or two. And despite running on relatively skinny tyres
the adhesion, especially on wet and greasy surfaces, was remarkable. But the best

feature of all is the price . . . which makes the MGB the cheapest openable sports car of its class.' *Motor* then went on to criticise heavily details such as the pedal layout, lack of an automatic stay on the luggage boot, glove box lock, finger-pinching hood irons, and ancient heater knobs.

Even automatic MGBs had a hard time with *Autocar*.

Motor also made an interesting observation about the engine. 'Although no increase in the original power output of the 1798 cc five-bearing engine has been announced, we suspect that through long-term development the 95 claimed horses are more muscular than before; certainly the performance figures suggest increased low-speed torque.' Their overdrive car did 108.3 mph flat out with an 105 mph average and a 0–60 mph time of 11 seconds. The standing quarter mile was covered in 18.2 seconds and overall fuel consumption improved to 23.7 mpg.

Motor's theory about improved torque was supported by *Autocar*'s test of an automatic MGB Mark II roadster, SOF 366H, in 1970. Normally automatic gearboxes reduce the all-out performance of such cars quite dramatically, but in this case the Mark II was not appreciably slower than the earlier roadsters with a 104 mph maximum, a 0–60 mph time of 13.6 seconds and a 19.5-second standing start quarter mile. In fact, *Autocar* were quite surprised by the automatic B. They said:

'In acceleration from a standing start, there is a definite, though not unacceptable loss. The torque converter's maximum stall speed is around 2000 rpm which precludes any wheelspin starts. That shows up in the 0–30 mph time of 4.9 seconds instead of 4.0 seconds; it is remarkable that the 10 mph increments

There's a strong technical side to road testing, of course, with all sorts of instruments being used to calculate a car's performance. Here *Motor*'s MGB GT Mark II manages 107.6 mph, measured by the fifth wheel behind its bumper at the Motor Industry Research Association's test track near Nuneaton.

all the way up to 70 mph are about the same as the 1965 manual car [tested by *Autocar*] which makes one wonder whether or not the automatic's claimed 95 bhp is not, in this case, from a more healthy team than the earlier car's. For comparison, here are the times in seconds from 40 to 90 mph, automatic first: 7.1 (6.0), 10.0 (9.0), 13.6 (12.9), 18.5 (17.2), 26.4 (24.1), and 39.0 (35.6). Over the standing quarter mile the automatic at 19.5 seconds is only 0.6 seconds slower than the manual car . . .

'Fuel consumption varies between a minimum of around 20 mpg driven hard to a typical figure for a fast cross country run of around 26 mpg. Our overall consumption of 25.5 mpg is, surprisingly, appreciably better than the earlier manual car's 22 mpg.' *Autocar* also noted that this outstanding application of an automatic gearbox in a sports car achieved very smooth changes, so it was a pity the car was no more popular.

The arguments of *Motor* and *Autocar* became even more convincing when they tested an overdrive MGB GT Mark II, VOF 844J, in 1970 and 1971. *Motor* managed a top speed of 107.6 mph (105 mph average), with 0–60 mph in 11.6 seconds and an 18.2-second standing quarter mile, and *Autocar*, although slightly slower, were still appreciably quicker than their earlier test GT.

Motor appreciated the minor changes inside the car, such as the interior light, and *Autocar* made an interesting point about the servo-operated brakes, which had come under such criticism from *Road & Track*:

'They are excellent, progressive and capable of achieving a 1G stop at only 55 lb pedal load; previously nearly twice the pressure had been needed for this result. This is thanks to the servo and the continuing improvement in pad and lining materials. Only after the tenth application from 70 mph in our fade test did they show any loss of performance.'

Cars and Car Conversions tried a Mark III overdrive MGB, a roadster registered AKO 181L, in 1972. Appropriately one of the testers was deputy editor, Clive Richardson, then owner of a 1967-model MGB. He wrote:

'On the road there wasn't a lot of difference apart from the obvious gearbox change and the smaller (steering) wheel. In some respects the wheel was a disadvantage compared with the massive early one. It made manoeuvring a heavier job, made the steering feel dead around the straight-ahead position and partly obscured the fuel gauge and oil pressure and water temperature gauge. However, the higher ratio improved high-speed cornering and made for less winding.

'The closer ratios of the all-synchro box certainly improved performance, gave a much quieter and more readily useable first gear, but the change was much more rubbery than on the early boxes and the overall transmission noise still high. Mind you, exhaust noise was almost too subdued . . .

'Certainly the B remains a very pleasant car—in fact even more palatable in its latest guise. But handling is getting dated, mainly because of the vast amount of built-in roll, and ride is choppy over bumpy surfaces. Yet in all there's not a lot needs doing to make the B good for another five years at least.'

Motor also gave a Mark III overdrive roadster, AOH 614K, a brief test in 1972, returning performance figures almost exactly the same as their previous cars, and complained only that the heating system still had its rotary knobs, the manual windscreen washers were completely out of date and there were still no sun visors. Of the improvements, they particularly liked the fresh air ventilation.

Car and Driver were one of the first magazines to test a rubber-bumpered MGB in 1975, and quite liked it, despite the changes in specification. They said:

'Visually, the added height is not *that* noticeable, but driving is quite another matter. There's been an appreciable gain in suspension travel which reduces the chances of bottoming. So rather than riding like a buckboard, the new B's ride is fairly compliant for a traditional sports car. The softness of the suspension and the raised centre of gravity does encourage a fair amount of unsporty body roll. Still, the car will weave and bob through corners like a giant-slalom racer after a few hot buttered rums. On the skidpan, the cornering capability of the new B is only 0.69G—about the same as the average American-built sedan . . .'

They squeezed this single carburetter emission car up to 90 mph flat out (with a 0–60 mph time of 13.7 seconds and fuel consumption of 21.5 mpg) and said:

'In general, the new MGB is a pleasant car. The fact that the speedometer needle will never see the last quarter of the 120 mph counter is its only real detraction. It is the lowest-priced "full-size" sports car available in the U.S., and it is 100-per cent MG. And to a lot of people, that still says *sports car*. . . . you can be sure that in years to come, the '75 MGB will find a special place in MG lore.'

Autocar tested an early version of the Mark IV rubber-bumper overdrive MGB roadster, TOF 558N, in 1975 and found that its performance had improved despite its weight increase. They said:

'The car is usefully faster in both acceleration and maximum speed. It has been suggested that this may be explained partly by the fact that the latest test car is on radial-ply tyres whereas our 1965 test roadster was on cross-plies. From a standing start, and in spite of a rising wind, the car reached 50 mph in 8.2 seconds where its identically-geared predecessor took 9 seconds, 60 mph came up in 12.1 (formerly 12.9), the quarter mile in 18.3 (18.9) and 80 in 22.7 (24.1). In overdrive the maximum speed was 105 mph mean (103.5 before) with a best leg of 111 mph on the MIRA banking. In direct top the car will rev beyond the peak power speed at its 104 mean, and just over-rev at its 109 mph best. With the hood and side windows down the car has more drag, the maximum in direct top dropping by 3 mph . . . overdrive engagement is better made with the help of the clutch.

'Overdrive is an option worth having these days, for obvious reasons. With fuel the price it is at present, and assuming at least a ten per cent saving in consumption, it would pay for itself (£102) in 37,000 miles.

'It is in the handling of the MGB that the biggest changes are to be found. Because of the extra ride height the car rolls quite a lot more than before, with a consequent and at first slightly alarming noticeable increase in roll oversteer, to the extent that we would suspect a detectable loss in overall roadholding. It is not entirely spoiled, since the basic stability that has always been such a splendid feature of the car is still there, but with any marked movement of the steering wheel there is now a twitchy response . . .

'One sympathises with any car manufacturer, British, European or American who tries to keep up with the caprices of Federal interference in design, but we do not see why the British and European MGB customer should have to put up with somewhat spoiled handling for the sake of transatlantic needs and production ease here . . .

'Summing up, it is obvious that the MGB more than ever needs some redesign. We feel that it would be bad sales policy for British Leyland either to drop the MGB in any of its markets since the MG name is still better known to the enthusiast, or simply let the car continue unimproved, since it is already far behind some of its international competitors. A new B is needed now . . .'

Late model MGB roadsters and GTs have been tested by British magazines.

Handling was much improved on the late model Mark IV tested by *Autocar* in 1977. They said:

'Thankfully the anti-roll bar modifications have now largely cleared up the problem (caused by the raising of the ride height)—though it must remain a mystery why Leyland did not provide them from the start. With the changes, the car has now reverted a good way back to its original levels of handling and roadholding.'

However, they added that 'the B has been overtaken by later designs in the handling/ride compromise. Newer cars have managed to combine the good handling with a higher all-round level of ride comfort than the MG's. Its ride is quite firm—hard if compared with saloons of similar performance—and would once have been thought typically sports car-ish if more recent cars had not proved otherwise. The harshness is especially noticeable on rougher roads, when the lever arm dampers and leaf springs get caught out from time to time over a succession of bumps.'

So far as performance was concerned, the 1977 test model, a GT registered NOF 480R, did quite well despite emission-inspired changes causing a series of flat spots on acceleration. The car recorded a best speed of 104 mph (99 mph mean) in overdrive top with 0–60 mph in 14 seconds and the standing quarter mile in 19.1 seconds with fuel consumption averaging 25.7 mpg.

Nevertheless, this test made rather depressing reading, but not so depressing as most of the comments on the MGC roadsters in 1967.

For a start, *Autocar* said the **MGC** lacked low-speed torque and had an engine that was reluctant to rev; its fan was very noisy; the fuel consumption was heavy and the brakes faded, not to mention strong understeer and low-geared steering that hampered rapid correction. The new all-synchromesh gearbox was good to use but had too wide a gap between second and third and an odd choice of ratios with overdrive. However the ride was an improvement and the finish was good.

With so much more power, performance of their roadster, KOV 259F, was considerably better than the B, but not so good as expected: maximum speed was 120 mph mean (121 mph best) in direct fourth or overdrive fourth, with 0–60 mph in 10 seconds and a standing start quarter mile in 17.7 seconds. Fuel consumption worked out at 17.5 mpg overall.

To *Autocar*'s testers the engine was something of an enigma. They said:

'It is smooth and flexible, but completely lacking in sporty characteristics. Whilst it pulls evenly from very low revs (below 500 rpm in top) there is very little low-speed torque and the engine seems reluctant to rev or develop much top end power . . . it also fouled plugs once or twice in traffic.'

However, the car was still good in a straight line. *Autocar* said: 'For maximum speed runs we took the MGC to Belgium and found it cruised very well at 100 mph with arrow-like stability.' The trouble started once you tried to take a bend fast:

'Apart from the low-geared steering there is strong understeer which makes the front end slow to respond. In the low gears there is enough torque to help the back round, but on a wet surface we found it very hard indeed to catch the tail if it got out of line, so we settled for a slow-in, fast-out (once it was straight) technique . . . it is better suited to the Routes Nationales than mountain cols.'

Motor were not quite so critical with their roadster, NJB 649F, and they also returned similar performance figures. However, they agreed generally with *Autocar*'s comments except that they did not find the understeer so difficult to handle.

John Bolster tested KOV 259F for *Autosport* and said that he thought that it might have been better with a V6 engine. He agreed with the basic points raised by *Autocar* and *Motor* and managed to 'get the brakes really smoking with some fading' at Snetterton motor racing circuit. His way of describing the handling was useful for anyone with his ability behind the wheel:

Both *Autocar* with KOV 259F (*above*), and *Motor* with NJB 649F (*left*), gave the MGC a thorough testing and were not very complimentary about their cars; comments which helped in-fluence many people against buying the MGC.

'By sharply flinging the machine into the sharper corners with full power on, it is possible to convert understeer to oversteer. The breakaway is sudden, while the rear axle indulges in some unexpected capers, which discourages the driver from repeating the manoeuvre. On wet surfaces the traction is good, but it is best to use some discretion on corners.

'For a young man who appreciates sporting characteristics and responsive handling, the MGB is a better car than the MGC, in spite of the considerably greater speed potential of the latter. These are people who formerly eschewed sports cars because of their discomfort and impracticability but who were attracted by their trim lines and sparkling performance. The MGC is just their car because it gives all the amenities of a high-class saloon and need never be driven in a sporting manner unless the owner is in the mood. To such prospective buyers, the rather heavy fuel consumption is abundantly justified by the smoothness of the six-cylinder engine.'

Surprisingly, Bolster, a renowned sprint driver, could only extract the same performance figures from KOV 259F as *Motor*.

Motor Sport had the car four months later and squeezed a little more out of it: the same 120 mph maximum, but a 0–60 mph speed of 8.4 seconds and standing quarter mile of 16.3 seconds with 20 mpg. They found it an enjoyable and tireless touring car but hardly a sports car. They endorsed the comments of the earlier road testers and said: 'On the face of it the MGC should have proved a real flier, almost a small version of a Jaguar E type. There was something missing, but just what we would not like to say exactly.'

The MGC came in for just as rough a time in the American specialist Press. Mike Twite, reporting from Britain in 1968 on a roadster registered KOV 260F, said in *Car and Driver*:

'Private owners have often made virile MGBs a reality by super tuning or engine swops. Unfortunately MG decided to try the same thing in the MGC and the job was botched . . .

'The big trouble with the beak-heavy MGC is trying to get it to go around anything . . .

'While the MGC is faster, the overall impression is that it's . . . well, lethargic. It's smooth and powerful so long as you're not interested in quick response, but once you shove down on the throttle, expecting a sudden surge of power, everything dies—that big anchor isn't about to pick up rpm quickly no matter how much you kick the throttle . . .

'Perhaps the only thing to come out of the MGC is the new four-speed gearbox. It's a brand-new unit (the only all-new component in the car) complete with a synchronised first gear. Yes, Virginia, a *synchronised* first on an MG. The throws are very short, very positive and it's impossible to beat the synchromesh into any gear. On top of that, it's the first MG transmission in history that doesn't sound like an air raid siren whenever things start moving quickly. We also tried an MGC GT equipped with a three-speed Borg

Warner automatic transmission. This option is intended primarily for the luxury/convenience oriented American market—at least that's what MG's PR-types told us. Between adding extra weight and robbing horsepower, the performance of the automatic version was noticeably less than a standard MGB . . .

'All in all, the MGC isn't an improvement on the B and it will very likely be a disappointment to MG fans who were expecting an all-new chassis and powerplant. Instead it's an evolutionary model that should point out once and for all the dangers of inbreeding.'

For the record, Twite recorded slightly slower than average acceleration figures and no top speed, and he warned that American versions of the MGC might have different performance figures in any case owing to the installation of smog equipment such as different intake and exhaust manifolds, sealed carburetters, air pump and different spark advance curves.

Road & Track found that their MGC, tested with smog equipment in America in 1969, was capable of 118 mph, with 0–60 mph in 10.1 seconds and a standing quarter mile in 17.7 seconds with its 3.7 : 1 rear axle. It was a roadster, with overdrive like all the MGC's ordered by California's British Motor Car Distributors. *Road & Track* were far less critical of their MGC than *Car and Driver* had been, considering it to be a six-cylinder smoothie rather than a sports car and rating the handling as decent although not particularly exciting.

'We would suggest that the car might be sharpened up for the American market with wider wheels (possible cast alloy ones instead of wires) and styling touches that make it more attractive than the B instead of less (ouch, that hood bulge). However, this roadster, priced at $345 over a similarly-equipped B, is a reasonable combination at the price and makes up what it lacks in refinement (when compared with its competition) with a liberal dose of performance of the kind that small-displacement fours can't deliver.'

Cars and Car Conversions found that they could cope with MGC handling in their 1968 test of an overdrive GT, KOV 258F, once they had got over the shock. They said:

'You soon learn to keep a very wary eye out for any damp patches on bends, for the front end loses grip before t'other and that's bad for your underclothing. The water will help you on the exit of a curve bring the tenacious SP41s at the back far enough out to require opposite for a brief power slide. In fact you learn very quickly to approach a twist at a lower speed than most cars—but leave it in Fine Style once your chosen path has been vetted (you, too, can be an astrologer). Driving a C in this style requires Charles Atlas biceps, very strong wrists and stamina, mainly because of the effort needed to hold it on course in the dry. When it's raining you'll still need strong wrists to keep the tail from dominating the scene. One of the car's party pieces is revealed when the surface is damp; select any side turning and emerge with a little too much right foot. The result is an MGC pretty sideways—without you having to operate the steering, which is heavy anyway.'

They went on to say that it was a car that takes a lot of getting used to, but it could be very good for long, fast, journeys, They could get only 115 mph out of their test car with 0–60 mph in 8.8 seconds on a 3.307 : 1 rear axle.

An MGC GT automatic, NOF 27F, tested by *Autocar* soon after did 116 mph average (117 mph best) with 0–60 mph in 10.9 seconds and the standing quarter mile in 18.2 seconds, supporting *Car and Driver*'s suggestions that the automatic was appreciably slower than the manual, unlike the MGB—although contrary to *Car and Driver*'s claim it was a little faster than the MGB GT. The fuel consumption of this automatic MGC GT was 19 mpg, a little better than *Autocar*'s overdrive roadster. They found the automatic GT a fast, but not exciting performer, far more like a saloon than a sports car. The transmission was smooth (unless it was used hard) and slow to kick down.

And so ended the sad saga of road tests involving standard MGCs. The **MGB GT V8** got much better reports in 1973.

Clive Richardson, by then deputy editor of *Motor Sport*, drove one registered HOH 932L as hard as he could to the South of France and back. At one point he averaged 121 mph for almost 100 miles with an overall autoroute average of 105 mph. In spite of this hard driving the overall fuel consumption worked out at 18 mpg with

Testers favoured the MGB GT V8 much more than the MGC. The car pictured here is on test with *Autocar*.

26 mpg being easily attainable with more normal use.

It's progress was startling. Richardson wrote: 'As a standard production "Q car" it reigns supreme, however, and left hundreds of amazed faces across the length of France. Often aggrieved faces, too, for the fashion in which this big-engined MGB disposes of Alfas, most Mercedes and BMWs and Citroens is remarkable . . . Straight-line acceleration from rest is impressive, but more important is the tremendous urge which the torque gives in the gears, reminiscent of a six-cylinder E type.'

His performance figures of 126–130 mph flat out with a 0–60 mph time of 8.6 seconds were impressive, but there were some points which he found depressing. They were chiefly the poor ride and excessive wind noise besides such often criticised details as the lack of door stays and key-operated glove box lid. Richardson summed up the feelings of many potential owners when he wrote:

'The car has some excellent attributes, but most of them are marred by some of its more dated features which I have tolerated in the MGB but find hard to accept in a car which is brand-new in price and performance concept, yet is wrapped in the same familiar package.'

Motor made similar comments to *Motor Sport* (obviously the smooth power of the V8 was appreciated and the stiffer rear springs were making themselves felt) and took comprehensive performance figures. They recorded 125.3 mph top speed, 0–60 mph time of 7.7 seconds and a standing quarter mile of 15.8 seconds with a car registered HOH 933L.

Autocar, whose performance figures were slightly down on those of *Motor*, were in full agreement over the shortcomings, particularly with regard to the high price, but considered that they were practically outweighed by the car's virtues. They said of their car, registered HOH 920L:

'All the MGBs are commendably tractable, and very easy cars to drive. They can be pottered gently without the need for critical use of gearchange points, and the V8 version distinguishes itself by being even more free of fuss than its smaller-engined brothers. Never before has a sports car in this class been as flexible and forgiving and so easy to drive smoothly, but then never before has such a smooth engine been offered beneath an MG bonnet.

'What is remarkable is that this marked increase in performance and flexibility is accomplished at little cost in fuel economy. Compared with the last MGB GT that we tested two years ago, the V8 gave 23.4 mpg overall, compared with 23.7 mpg overall for the smaller-engined car. While it would be possible to get a slightly better "touring" performance from the four-cylinder car, this is partially offset by the fact that the Rover V8 engine can run on three-star fuel, while the four-cylinder engine requires five-star, and we would expect that the same driver on the same journeys would get very similar figures in the two cars. When the considerable difference in performance is taken into account, this is a quite outstanding achievement.'

John Bolster gave HOH 932L another vigorous test for *Autosport*. He agreed that the suspension was hard and the ride choppy, especially at moderate speeds, but added:

'On the other hand, the roadholding is very safe indeed and entirely predictable, this being an easy car to drive fast on winding roads. There is really no difference in handling between this and the ordinary MGB, except that the tail can come round fairly smartly if one over-accelerates out of a sharp bend. The offside rear wheel spins very easily, due to propshaft torque tending to lift one end of the axle and depress the other, so a limited-slip differential might be a worthwhile extra.'

He managed 125 mph with the car, and a 0–60 mph time of 8.4 seconds with a 16.5 second standing quarter mile, and made the point that the engine was so quiet that the wind noise seemed more intrusive.

MGB-owner Fred Game, technical editor of *Cars and Car Conversions*, made the usual complaints about the cars when he tested a V8 registered HOH 901L, then said:

'Once I started to drive the car, most of the inherent faults could be forgotten, despite the unfriendly comments made previously. Really, I like the B, otherwise I wouldn't have bought one a couple of years ago, would I? In 1.8-litre form, an MGB is a smooth, fast touring two-seater, capable of covering large distances at high average speeds without reducing the driver to a quivering, overtired zombie. With the V8 urge the plus points remain, and in addition there is enough acceleration to outdrag most of the saloons that find it easy to overtake the four-cylinder device, a factor that might not sound important, but one that I used to find personally nauseating.'

Conversions

Because of its popularity and basic sound design, many firms have marketed conversion kits to improve the performance of MGBs and MGCs, and one firm has even uprated the V8. The first such conversion to be tested by the specialist Press was on an MGB driven by Patrick McNally for *Autosport* in 1964.

His Janspeed MGB had a simple £35 conversion involving a cylinder head skimmed 0.0060 of an inch, ports opened out and polished, combustion chambers reshaped and matched to a 39 cc capacity and a polished induction system. The results were well worthwhile: improved flexibility up to a 7000 rpm limit, similar fuel consumption to that of the standard engine, better starting, a top speed of 112.5 mph, and a 0–60 mph time of 10.5 seconds with a standing quarter mile of 17.8 seconds. One hundred octane fuel was vital, however, with the 10.3 : 1 compression ratio.

The Brabham conversion on a non-overdrive MGB tested by *Cars and Car Conversions* in 1965 improved the performance figures still further but did not offer

such good value for money as that of the Janspeed. The Brabham conversion had a 10.4 : 1 cylinder head, special manifold with balance pipe inside the twin inlet tracts to improve low-speed running, a single 45DCOE Weber carburetter and wilder camshaft. Two other non-standard camshafts were available with this conversion, one giving 114 bhp and the other 130 bhp. The cam as tested gave 'somewhere in between.' The car went well, without fuss other than the Weber carburetter's well-known sooner-or-later hot starting, right up to 115 mph flat out (113.7 mph mean) with a 0–60 mph time of 9.8 seconds and standing quarter mile of 17.5 seconds. The cost of this conversion with its special manifold, carburetter and camshaft would have been much higher than that of the Janspeed conversion.

A modified MGB complete with Mini-lite knock-on wheels goes on test with *Cars and Car Conversions* in 1967.

The Taurus stage one conversion tested by *Cars and Car Conversions* in 1965 was almost exactly the same in concept as that of the Janspeed and gave similar performance, but cost only £28.

The magazine also tested a Taurus Stage Two conversion on an MGB in 1965, similar to the Brabham conversion and costing four times as much as the stage one. It produced Brabham-style performance figures although the most noticeable increase in power was at the higher speeds, a full four seconds being knocked off the standard MGB's 0–80 mph time of 19.9 seconds.

It was with considerable interest, therefore, that *Cars and Car Conversions* approached a test of a works MGB, JBL 491D, in 1966 to see how it performed

A Nicholson-converted MGC like those road tested.

with all the modifications listed in BMC's tuning booklet. The car was exactly as it had returned from winning its class in the Targa Florio (see chapter five), with modifications as detailed in chapter thirteen. Apart from its full-race engine, competition clutch and close ratio gearbox, with uprated suspension, the car was mechanically standard.

'Bodily, apart from instruments, a roll-cage and a bigger fuel tank there were no changes, either,' said *Cars and Car Conversions*. 'Most of the dispensable items of equipment had been dispensed with in the interests of lightness, but a good many things can't be chucked out because of Group III regulations, and the thing was still complete with carpets, door-trim, dashboard and so on. All the bright bits inside were painted matt-black to eliminate dazzle, and there were cosy bucket seats for driver and co-driver/navigator/passenger or what-have-you.

'Having climbed in, you switched on and started her up—not with the key, but with a monster plunger-type switch. The car invariably started easily and promptly, hot or cold, and thereafter began to idle with the lumpiness you might easily expect from a wildish sort of car. We didn't expect it to be a nice car to drive in traffic, and it darn well wasn't, either—below 2000 rpm absolutely nothing happened, and the fire might as well have been out. Power started at about two-five, the lowest engine speed at which you could comfortably move off from, say, traffic lights, and with a sudden-death competition clutch this made the rush-hour in Oxford Street a good thing to keep out of. So we kept out of it. For the rest, town driving still wasn't all that nice. Not that the car was particularly noisy—it wasn't, and in fact didn't sound particularly hot—you only found out when other MGBs, attracted by the roundels, tried something! In top gear, 2000 rpm represented about 35 mph, below which you simply could not go in fourth—slower than this and you came down a cog or two.

'Things really start to happen at upwards of three-five, when you get the full benefit of all those extra horses, and the lumpy camshaft becomes definitely worthwhile. The MGB in standard form is a nice, spritely (no pun intended) sort of car, but its best friends couldn't say that it was anything of a flier. This was the difference—this thing went like a bat outa hell, if we may use the phrase and then simply went on going faster and faster until it ran out of revs. At least, it was the rev-counter which ran out of figures. It would go all round the clock in top gear, and once you get up around five-five it makes all the right noises. The suspension, which is set up to give a pretty choppy, hard ride at low speeds, takes hold and sticks the thing down with the proverbial glue-pot on each corner. It goes round all the swerves with no body roll at all . . .

'Fuel consumption? Who the hell cares!'

The performance figures recorded were: maximum speed, 120 mph (118.5 mph mean), 0–30 mph 2.5 seconds (4.0 seconds standard car); 0–40 3.8 (6.0); 0–50 6.0 (8.0); 0–60 8.2 (11.3); 0–70 11.0 (15.2); 0–80 15.0 (19.9); 0–90 20.5 (27.1); 0–100 26.1.

The engine work alone on this car would have cost £335 from a specialist tuner such as Bill Nicholson. However, for £75, he offered a conversion which went a long way towards giving the car such performance. It consisted of a modified and improved head and inlet manifold with twin 1.75-inch SU carburetters and ram pipes. An overdrive five-bearing MGB roadster tested with this equipment, a 4.3 : 1 rear axle ratio and lowered suspension, by *Motor Sport* in 1967 returned acceleration figures roughly midway between those of the works car and a standard roadster up to its 117 mph maximum.

When *Cars and Car Conversions* tested the same car in 1967 they managed to squeeze a bit of extra performance out of it, returning figures of 0–30 mph 2.0 seconds, 0–40 3.5, 0–50 5.6, 0–60 8.8, 0–70 12.0, and 0–80 18.5 with a top speed of 113 mph observing a 6500 rpm limit although 7000 rpm was possible. The only problem they encountered with what they considered to be an outstandingly sweet conversion was quite a bit of wheelspin.

Worn rear tyres handicapped acceleration times on a reader's MGB tested by *Cars and Car Conversions* soon after, but it was still impressive as one tuned exclusively for a typical clubman's needs: normal use during the week and competitions such as autocross and driving tests at weekends. The owner, a Mr R. E. Lowes, had asked Neal Davies Racing to modify the engine for good mid-range torque with a nice clean pick-up and good acceleration from 3500 rpm. He was not worried about top speed. To achieve these ends, Davis fitted a 10.1 compression ratio reprofiled and polished head with 45DCOE Weber carburetter and a free-flow exhaust system. Other specialities included a fly-off handbrake conversion and anti-tramp bars for the rear axle. The results were just what Mr Lowes wanted with acceleration times of 0–30 mph 3.8 seconds, 0–40 5.0, 0–50 6.9, 0–60 8.5, 0–70 11.8, and 0–80 16.1, which *Cars and Car Conversions* reckoned could have been improved quite a lot with more revs (they kept down to 6000 in deference to their reader's engine) and meatier back tyres for better grip.

When the engine of the MGB overdrive roadster, RGW 980F, that Clive Richardson drove when he worked for *Cars and Car Conversions*, finally wore out in 1972 he had it rebuilt by Janspeed. In its eventual form, it wound up with 0.0080 in overbore giving it a capacity of 1888 cc, with Special Tuning lightweight pistons and a 10 : 1 compression ratio head achieved without skimming by having the combustion chambers re-made to 43.5 cc to avoid the necessity of using leaded petrol.

A Special Tuning 714 half-race camshaft was fitted with bigger valves, twin 1.75-inch SU carburetters and Janspeed inlet and exhaust manifolds. After careful running-in, this balanced engine achieved 0–60 mph in 10 seconds and 125 mph with fuel consumption of 26 mpg.

There were few tests of conversions on the heavier MGB GT, but *Motor Sport*'s evaluation of a Nicholson GT published in November 1967 was interesting in that

The car that started the V8 Cult: the Costello GT, as tested by *Autocar* in 1972. The magazine was very enthusiastic about this car, which was simply an MGB GT with a Rover V8 engine, 3.07:1 rear axle ratio instead of 3.9:1 and a special bonnet with a wide bulge to clear the twin SU carburetters in their high Rover position. The test car had covered few miles but still managed 0–60 mph in 7.8 sec and 0–100 in 22 with a maximum speed of 130 mph. *Autocar* said the finish on the car was superb and the engine silky smooth; and it was far more pleasant to drive than their two Sunbeam Tiger staff cars of a few years earlier, which amounted to Sunbeam Alpines with V8 engines. The only drawbacks they could see with the Costello V8 were a high fuel consumption of 18.8 mpg overall and the high price of £2616 as tested.

the suspension had been improved. Nicholson softened the springs but kept the ride height the same with the result that its ride and stability were much improved. When *Cars and Car Conversions* tested another Nicholson MGB GT in the same month, it proved to be slower off the mark initially than their Nicholson roadster (probably because of its extra weight and standard 3.9 : 1 axle), but quicker at the top end. The performance figures were: 0–30 mph 2.6 seconds, 0–40 4.2, 0–50 6.5, 0–60 8.8, 0–70 11.9, 0–80 15.3, with 108 mph flat out observing a 6000 rpm limit because it was a reader's car.

Cars and Car Conversions were as wildly enthusiastic as ever when they tested the works MGB GT registered LBL 591E in Group Four trim in 1969. This steel-bodied car behaved like the works roadster they had tested earlier and had an 1820 cc engine with full Special Tuning stage six modifications, giving it performance figures with a 4.22 : 1 rear axle and standard ratio gearbox of: 0–30 mph, 4.0 seconds 0–40 6.0, 0–50 8.2, 0–60 10.9, 0–70 14.9, 0–80 19.9 and 0–90 22.8.

Tests of converted MGCs have been equally rare with *Autocar* trying a Nicholson Stage II MGC in 1968, *Autosport* a Downton version in the same year and *Cars and Car Conversions* the Chatham MGC V8 in 1978. *Autocar* were favourably impressed with the Nicholson car, which was fitted with a 10 : 1 compression ratio gas-flowed head with 2-inch SU carburetters, 14-inch wheels instead of 15-inch and stiffer springs with adjustable shock absorbers. The car was an overdrive roadster fitted with the optional works hard top which, according to Nicholson, reduced the top speed by 4 mph because the rounded shape adopted by the standard hood at high speeds was better aerodynamically. *Autocar* reported:

'Fuel consumption was virtually unchanged in spite of the lower gearing and the same is true of the MGC's delightfully relaxed and unfussy cruising ability. For the best high-speed handling, it was better to run with the adjustable rear dampers "done right up", though this made the car move stiffly with every irregularity in the road. Ride was more acceptable on the softest damper setting. Running on 32 psi front and 28 psi rear tyre pressures, steering is still on the heavy side but nicely direct with very good directional stability even in strong side winds. Handling is definitely much better. The car remains a marked understeerer but provided one is in the right gear, keeps one's foot down and the road isn't bumpy, the car will corner very fast indeed with the back end moving outwards slightly to counteract understeer in front. If however one lifts off during such cornering—only adviseable anyway on a closed track—the outwards lurch of the back is difficult to catch tidily with the low-geared steering. Wheels are easily spun in the wet and during our acceleration runs but without any tramp. Generally adhesion is very good.'

The figures recorded on this car were: 0–30 mph 4.0 seconds, 0–40 5.6, 0–50 7.6, 0–60 10.0, 0–70 13.8, 0–80 18, 0–90 23.1, 0–100 29.3 and 0–110 40.9 with a standing quarter mile in 16.8 seconds and 129 mph top speed (127 mph mean).

The Rover V8 engine installation in the Costello MGB GT.

John Bolster's *Autosport* test of the Downton MGC proved to be even faster with its Stage II conversion using 9.5 : 1 compression ratio and special inlet and exhaust manifolds. Despite very wet weather, Bolster cleared 130 mph and recorded 0–30 mph in 3.4 seconds, 0–50 6.5, 0–60 8.2, 0–80 13.9, 0–100 22.1 and the standing quarter mile in 16.5 seconds. Fuel consumption improved to 22.5 mpg.

The Chatham MGC V8 (basically a 1967 MGC roadster fitted with wide alloy 14-inch wheels and a high performance V8 similar to that used in the MGB GT V8, described in chapter twelve) was tested by the author for *Cars and Car Conversions* in August 1978 before he purchased it from its builder.

With a 3.7 : 1 rear axle, close ratio gearbox and low-profile tyres this 19-cwt machine turned in figures of 0–60 mph 5.8 seconds, 0–100 14.4 with a standing quarter mile in 14.5 seconds. Top speed was estimated at more than 135 mph. Since then I have driven it for more than 40000 miles on every conceivable kind of journey from delivering copy to the Post Office to lapping the Goodwood racing circuit and ploughing through London traffic jams. Its handling with stiff rear springs and magnesium wheels and flat tread 185-section tyres is astounding, more like a works MGB than an MGC. The standard MGC steering has been much improved by the lightweight road wheels which allow the use of a 12-inch steering wheel to effectively increase the ratio. A limited slip differential effectively controls wheelspin although acceleration cannot be exploited to the full from a standstill in the wet. It is possible to spin the rear wheels from 25 mph in second gear on soaking roads. The only problems encountered with the ultra-high performance conversion have been a high noise level in the intermediate ratios due to the use of straight-cut competition gears, a poor heater because the engine rarely gets warm enough to work it properly, and heavy fuel consumption at sustained speeds above 110 mph. Normally the car does 17 mpg while it is capable of more than 20 mpg with frequent use of overdrive top below 80 mph.

At the time of the *Cars and Car Conversions* test of the MGC V8 it used a Costello inlet manifold with a single Weber carburetter that had been developed for the Costello MGB GT V8 tested by *Autocar* in 1972.

This was an overdrive car fitted with the 3.07 : 1 rear axle ratio. Otherwise, apart from the engine, which was the same as that used in the twin SU carburetter 185 bhp Rover 3500 saloon, and a fibreglass bonnet, the car was the same as a standard MGB GT. Top speed was 130 mph (128 mph mean) with 0–60 mph in 7.8 seconds, 0–100 mph 22 seconds and a standing quarter mile in 15.8 seconds. Overall weight was 20.5 cwt (about 1 cwt lighter than a standard MGB GT) and fuel consumption worked out at 18.8 mpg. Apart from asking why British Leyland did not produce a car like this excellent conversion, *Autocar* made similar comment to those made in the next year on the MGB GT V8. It's a pity no one thought of dropping a hot V8 into the stiffer MGC shell in the late 1960s. Think of what the testers would have had to say then!

V

The MGA, B and C in Competition

ALTHOUGH works entries of the MGA, B and C have achieved notable success in international long-distance events, private entries have been few and far between. This is because long-distance events tend to be so expensive to compete in that they are beyond the scope of most amateurs, who have a hard time meeting the cost of travelling to far-flung British circuits, let alone flying their cars abroad with the masses of equipment needed for long-distance racing. The MGA, B and C have been more successful in international long-distance racing rather than in shorter events because of their weight and reliability. Light weight is of crucial importance in short-distance racing; reliability more important in long-distance events. However, the combination of strength and reliability has made the MGA, B and C probably the most popular car ever for club events, ranging from treasure hunts and trials to circuit racing. A majority of clubmen simply cannot afford to compete in fast, but fragile, cars.

The MGA made its competition debut three months before full-scale production started. These first MGAs were aluminium-bodied prototypes code-named EX182. John Thornley entered them for Le Mans in June 1955 because it was anticipated that production would start in that month and BMC managing director George Harriman was demanding success in competition at almost any cost. When it became obvious that production of the MGA would have to be delayed three months to allow tooling to be completed, Thornley got the entries, in the class for cars which were already in production, switched to the prototype class. This meant that the opposition—chiefly from works Porsches—was far stiffer, but allowed the EX182 cars to run with modifications not necessarily intended for production, such as oil coolers, lightweight bodies and 82 bhp engines.

As prototypes, they could have used far more streamlined bodies, but it was decided to stick to the ultimate production shape for maximum publicity. In this form, everybody could see what the new MGA would look like and hopefully rush out to buy a replica when they became available!

The engines were B series units with stronger main bearings and special cylinder heads developed by gas-flow expert Harry Weslake. Two 1.5-litre twin overhead camshaft engines were under development at that time by Austin and Morris, but they were not sufficiently advanced for use at Le Mans. Weslake's head had extra ports between the pairs of sparking plugs with an external balance pipe. A special camshaft was used with pistons giving a compression ratio of 9.4 : 1. This was considered the maximum because of the frequently poor quality of petrol supplied at Le Mans. Twin 1.75-inch SU carburetters were fitted. The gearbox was the same as that used on the production cars except that it had closer ratios, which Enever had discovered during tests earlier in the year worked best with a 3.7 : 1 rear axle ratio. The resultantly high gearing gave nearly 118 mph on the long Mulsanne straight, and he felt confident that the cars would last the race as similar modifications had been tested on Magnette saloons raced by drivers such as Essex MG dealer Dick Jacobs.

Four prototype MGAs were prepared meticulously for Le Mans under the direction of Alec Hounslow (who had been responsible for pre-war racing MGs), and Dickie Green (formerly of Aston Martin), who were both well acquainted with the demands of contemporary Le Mans events. The three race cars (the fourth was a spare) were to be driven by Californian-based Briton Ken Miles and British racing motor-cyclist Johnny Lockett; Northern club man Ted Lund and the Swiss Hans Waeffler; Dick Jacobs and Irishman Joe Flynn. In the event, the MGAs held positions around fortieth of sixty starters, until their pitmate, the Austin-Healey 100S driven by Lance Macklin was involved in the fearful accident when Pierre Levegh's Mercedes 300SLR collided with the British car and crashed into the crowd. Eighty-two people were killed and confusion reigned as Jacobs approached the scene on his next lap. It is believed that the shock of being confronted with such a carnage caused him to crash, wrecking the car and badly injuring himself. However, the other two MGs raced on rising to twelfth and seventeenth places, ahead of the rival works Triumph TR2s, and beaten in their class only by the exotic Porsche 550s and an OSCA. The twelfth-placed car, driven by Miles and Lockett, averaged 86.17 mph. It was a great debut for the new MGA, tempered only by the horror of the worst accident motor racing has experienced.

The MGA prototypes had been built with a view to running soon after in the Alpine Rally, but this event was one of the many cancelled that year in the aftermath of the Le Mans tragedy. Had they run in the Alpine Rally the cars would have been suitably geared down, the passenger doors unbolted and their small circuit racing screens replaced with a full windshield and wipers.

One of the few events not to be cancelled was the Golden Jubilee Tourist Trophy race in Ulster, and the three surviving MGs (Jacob's had been written-off at Le Mans) were entered. The two Le Mans finishers were fitted with the rival BMC twin cam engines and the third car (the Le Mans spare) was left in its original trim. Both twin cam engines gave trouble in practice and it was decided to go ahead only with the Austin engine. The Morris twin cam engine in one of the cars was replaced with a pushrod unit. The car which retained its twin cam engine (driven by Lockett and the Scottish ace Ron Flockhart) was also fitted with disc front brakes and bodywork modified for better air penetration. It proved to be practically as fast as the class-winning works Porsche driven by American stars Carroll Shelby and Masten Gregory before retiring with head gasket trouble. One of the pushrod cars, driven by Lund, retired with a split fuel tank, but the other, driven by Jack Fairman

The new MGA prototypes line up
for the Le Mans twenty-four hour
race in 1955 (*above*): from the left,
number forty-one to be driven by
Lockett and Miles; number forty-
two was for Jacobs and Flynn and
number sixty-four for Lund and
Waeffler. Much of the testing of
these prototypes, codenamed EX
182, had been done by Grand Prix
driver Ken Wharton, seen below,
reporting to John Thornley from the
cockpit of one of the cars. In the
race, Lockett and Miles finished
twelfth, Jacobs crashed badly, and
Lund and Waeffler, pictured *facing
page*, finished seventeenth with a
crumpled wing after spinning in
company with many other cars as
heavy rain swept the circuit.

and Peter Wilson, survived to finish twentieth, a lap ahead of the works TR2s. Once again the race was marred by tragedy, with three drivers killed in horrifying accidents.

The death toll was giving motor racing a bad name in Europe and BMC decided it was not worthwhile investing huge sums in building the type of sports cars which would have been needed to compete in the top events. 'To do anything notable in international sports car racing, we would have had to have built space frame cars and a 1.5-litre version of the twin cam engine.' said Thornley. This would have cost a great deal and all that would have resulted in terms of prestige would have been class wins. Bigger-engined cars such as Jaguars would have taken the lion's share of the spoils with overall wins in any case. It was decided, therefore, to concentrate on rallying and production sports car racing. Development was concentrated on the Morris version of the twin cam engine as it was more closely related to the B series unit.

The Le Mans cars were not used again except for one visit to Montlhery for a BMC mass record-breaking session where rally team leader John Gott covered 112.36 miles in an hour from a standing start. In a similar exercise, a production MGA driven by Ken Wharton covered 102.54 miles.

Five new competition cars were built by the works for the 1956 season, however. These were steel-bodied cars in virtually standard trim except for outsize fuel tanks, a variety of axle ratios, an oil cooler and no bumpers. BMC did not frown on their

North American subsidiary entering sports car races, well away from the European scene, so three went to Sebring for the twelve-hour season opener. The rest of the field, composed entirely of racing sports cars, was formidable. 'No production Porsche appeared, but a gallant squad of MGAs ran without hope of glory,' said *Road & Track*. Well, they might have had little hope of glory, but they certainly achieved some, winning the team award for drivers Kinchloe and Spitler, Ash and Ehrman, Allen and Van Driel, by finishing nineteenth, twentieth and twenty-second as more potent racing machines fell by the wayside. The event was won by a Ferrari driven by Fangio and Castellotti.

The two cars not used at Sebring raced in that year's Mille Miglia, with Abingdon proclaiming that it wasn't really a road race, more of a rally! Peter Scott-Russell and Tom Haig drove MJB 167 to second place in the limited price class behind a rather expensive Porsche Speedster with Nancy Mitchell and Pat Faichney third. The women's achievement provided great publicity for BMC as they were the first British girls to take part in the fast and furious 1000-mile road race. Pat said: 'At 2.27 am Nancy slowly moved down the ramp and then, with a roar, we were off, me clinging to my little hold-on bar for dear life, and in response to repeated bangs on the head, got lower and lower in my seat to avoid the wind. For the first three hours I really enjoyed life and was settling in, when down it came—the rain—in torrents and it never let up. We got wetter and wetter, miserable and more miserable as with every movement, the rain found a new entrance. To crown it all, Nancy got hungry. All she eats en route is oranges, peeled in quarter sections. You'll see just what I mean, if you try to peel one at over a hundred in the wet, and hang on at the same time!'

But hang on they did for a tremendously popular reception. Their next event in 1956, with the other four works MGs, was the Alpine Rally. They were a good deal more comfortable because the cars were fitted with hard tops, but not only out of sympathy for the drivers! In October 1955, following the Le Mans disaster, the French government banned sports cars from rallies on their roads. This was especially serious because most of the classic rallies, such as the Alpine, used French roads at some point. It was also short-sighted because Grand Touring cars, such as the fixed-head Mercedes 300SL, were still allowed in rallies. With their 140 mph performance and difficult handling, they were potentially far more dangerous than machines such as MGAs and Triumph TR2s. However, MG and Triumph had ingenious competition managers who discovered that by fitting the optional hard tops and sliding sidescreens, or wind-up windows, it was possible to get their cars re-classified as Grand Tourers, providing that at least 100 had been made in that trim. Hence the MGA's redesigned sidescreens.

Four of the cars in the 1956 Alpine team were painted Italian racing red—in an attempt to fool Italian level crossing keepers into giving them priority—and the BMC works team duly adopted those colours with a white top to make their cars cooler inside. Their fortunes were mixed in this event: Gott suffered from axle trouble and Jack Sears crashed near the end. But Nancy Mitchell and Pat Faichney, in the same car, MBL 867, they drove in the Mille Miglia, won a Coupé des Alpes and the ladies' award. A team of four were also entered in the Liege-Rome-Liege

MGAs were soon among the most competitive cars in club events in 1956. Peter Simpson, driving number nineteen, one of Dick Jacobs's cars, was challenging for the lead in the *Autosport* Three-Hour race at Oulton Park when he was delayed by ignition trouble and fell back to third place at the end. His team mate, Alan Foster, in number eighteen, had been 'dicing' three abreast with two other competitors when he put two wheels on the grass at the Cascades, missed a large tree and a marshal by inches, and slewed into the ditch as he tried to regain the circuit. Even then he tried to drive out of the ditch with the car at an angle of sixty degrees to horizontal. He didn't quite make it, despite violent wheelspin, sheets of mud from the rear wheels and steaming grass! The race was won by Fitzwilliam's MGA.

Rally in September, but were outpaced in what amounted to a really rough road race. Gott finished thirteenth and John Milne fourteenth.

The twin cam engine was still not fully developed, so the BMC works team concentrated their efforts on the Big Healey in an attempt to get more speed, once team manager Marcus Chambers was convinced that its chassis could be reinforced sufficiently.

The Fitzwilliam team

However, Thornley was still keen to see MGs doing well in European competition, so he had the Le Mans cars rebuilt for wealthy amateur Dick Fitzwilliam with pushrod engines and bodywork of standard appearance. Fitzwilliam always reckoned that he could make a good pushrod car go faster than any Twin Cam! With Robin Carnegie, he had won the *Autosport* club racing championship in 1956, using a standard MGA. This car was retained by the team.

Fitzwilliam entered the works-prepared cars in the Mille Miglia and the Nurburgring 1000-kilometres in May, but he was unable to get an entry at Le Mans in June because his cars did not form an official works team. It was an ambitious schedule, nevertheless, which could only have been undertaken with considerable works support. The two fastest machines, LBL 301 and LBL 303, were fitted with alloy bodywork and Dunlop disc brakes to race in the prototype classes with the other two in the limited-price classes. One of these, LBL 205, was fitted with a hard top to qualify as a GT.

The Fitzwilliam team finished the Mille Miglia more or less intact, with Carnegie thirty-first in LBL 303, six places in front of Tommy Wisdom's works Austin-Healey. Fitzwilliam struggled to the finish at Brescia suffering from a broken nose and concussion, and with the car's bodywork very battered after hitting a tree. However, Abingdon mechanics were on hand to patch up the car, and his wife, Doreen, drove it back to England! Later, the third driver in the team, Peter Simpson, told Chambers: 'Our most amusing incident was at a level crossing. Our team manager, John Keeling, told us that if we did come to a crossing with the barrier down, we should at least have a shot at getting under it. We only met one with the barrier down, and discovered that the A would just go underneath if John (Blacksley) and I both ducked our heads. We saw the train approaching rapidly, but scooted through very smartly indeed. We didn't care who won as long as it wasn't a dead heat!'

John Higg took second place in the limited-price class behind Wisdom with another private MGA, driven by John Sparrowe and Mike Reid, third.

All four Fitzwilliam cars presented themselves at the Nurburgring after hurried rebuilding at Abingdon and only two of them finished: Fitzwilliam and Hogg in the prototype class and Blacksley and Cuff-Miller in the GT category. Carnegie's car swallowed a valve and the fourth car, driven by Patsy Burt and Jean Bloxham, had oil pump trouble.

David Dixon drove one of the fastest MGAs in the *Autosport* production sports car championship in 1957. He is pictured here at Prescott in May.

Right : Stirling Moss, John Thornley and Syd Enever prepare for EX181's Bonneville record run in 1957. Moss is holding the small scale model of EX181 used in initial wind tunnel tests.

Below : Canadian Alec James (with the Maple Leaf background to his racing number twenty-nine) drove 'vigorously' in the first round of the *Autosport* championship at Mallory Park in 1959 in an attempt to keep Ted Lund (number thirty-two) out of third place. Eventually Lund squeezed past, but couldn't quite catch the winner, Jim Clark, in a Lotus Elite.

Their next race was the Rheims Twelve-Hour in which Carnegie again dropped a valve, but the never-say-die spirit of the team was evident as the mechanics replaced a piston and all the valves in one and three quarter hours before sending him off again. Hogg also had a rocker replaced and the team finished well down. As a gesture of support for the less-glamorous *Autosport* series, Fitzwilliam and Carnegie entered the grand finale, the Snetterton Three Hours, in October. Once again, they had engine trouble, finishing seventeenth behind MGAs driven by Ken MacKenzie, R J Rendle and David Dixon. Dixon and Alan Foster (entered by Dick Jacobs), had been competing in the championship all season with some works support. Their opposition was chiefly from AC Aces (Rudd's example won the three-hour race), Triumph TRs, Austin-Healeys, Morgans and other MGAs driven by men such as Reid.

A thinly-disguised works team of MGAs had been entered in the 1300 cc–1600 cc class at Sebring that year, too. They ran like clockwork for Miller, Leavens and Kieth to take twenty-third place, Ash, Ehrmann and Van Driel twenty-seventh, and Spitler and Kinchloe thirty-sixth, annexing the class award and the overall team prize. It was great publicity, although they were fortunate that the works Porsche Carrera of von Hanstein and Linge lost more than an hour with engine trouble. Later in the American season, MGAs driven by Harry Washburn, Sam Taylor and Sherman Decker achieved considerable success in SCCA racing and further afield from Abingdon, Ray Liddel starred in Canadian club racing and Bjorn Nassil in Sweden.

BMC had not abandoned the MGA completely in their official works teams. Nancy Mitchell took third place in the ladies' section of the Tulip Rally and Gott finished fourteenth with MJB 167 in the Liege–Rome–Liege Rally. Nancy Mitchell finished sixteenth in this event in OBL 311, and took the European Ladies Championship for the second year running.

Record Breakers

But the main works effort in relation to competition MGs had been devoted to record-breaking cars. One of the two prototype MGA chassis was used as the basis for EX179 which ran at Utah in 1956 with a modified version of the B type twin-cam engine which had been tried in 1955. In the hands of Miles and Lockett, and with Enever, Hounslow and Thornley in close attendance, it took sixteen international 1500 cc class records, from the ten miles at 170.15 mph to the twelve-hours at 141.75 mph. The same car was used, but with a 948 cc engine, to provide a great prelude to yet another Enever special, EX181, in 1957. This was an especially significant car because its shape was to form the basis for the MGB in 1962.

It used a highly-supercharged version of the 1957 twin cam engine, putting out 290 bhp at 7300 rpm, and a tubular chassis with MGA-style front suspension and de Dion rear. The driver sat as far forward as possible with the engine in the middle. With this highly-advanced car, Stirling Moss broke five international records at 245.64 mph that had stood since 1939 at just over 200 mph. Ironically, the holder was Goldie Gardner with the MGA-shaped MG record breaker, EX135!

Two years later, in 1959, world champion-to-be Phil Hill—who had started his racing career in an MG—took EX181 to six international records with the 1957 twin cam engine opened out to 1506 cc. In this form it gave nearly 300 bhp and propelled the missile-like car at 254.91 mph. These record-breaking sessions did wonders for MG publicity and encouraged the introduction of the Twin Cam in 1958.

Despite the efforts of enthusiasts including Fitzwilliam and Wing Commander MacKenzie, the pushrod MGA was being outclassed in club racing by new lightweights such as the Elva Courier, a car weighing 3 cwt less than the MGA, which frequently shared the same power unit. Peter Gammon's example led the *Autosport* championship for much of the season until Ian Walker gave the sensational new fibreglass Lotus Elite its competition debut. These two drivers were well in front of MacKenzie as the club season's big race, the Snetterton Three Hours, approached in October. But, with Gammon and Walker both succumbing to mechanical trouble, MacKenzie just scraped home to win his class in the championship and take third place overall in the race. His was the most competitive MGA on the track that year although the bulk of the fields were often made up by MGAs whose drivers included Gordon Cobban (later to become general secretary of the MG Car Club), Chris Tooley and the Octagon Stable of Geoff Dear, Jed Noble and Mike Reid.

The Twin Cam

The Fitzwilliam team interest had switched to Formula Junior, so Jacobs, whose MGs had been successful in saloon car racing, took over the unofficial works sports car mantle in 1958. Abingdon decided to give Sebring a miss and concentrate on the Twin Cam, with Jacobs receiving one of the first. This car, registered 1 MTW, was entered in the Tourist Trophy at Goodwood in September with Alan Foster and Tommy Bridger as drivers. Apart from the removal of air cleaner, full-width windscreen and bumpers, it was standard—'the only genuine production car in the race,' said *Autosport*. It was not homologated until the next month, so it was officially a prototype. In the event, the car ran so well that it finished third in the under two-litre class behind two works Porsches and fourteenth overall.

The works entered an MGA Twin Cam in only one event, the Liege–Rome–Liege Rally. Gott took PRX 707 to ninth place and used the same car again in the 1959 Tulip Rally. He also used another works Twin Cam, RMO 101, in the Monte Carlo Rally that year, and crashed. It was an unlucky car, crashing again in the Acropolis Rally later that year in John Sprinzel's hands. With a spot of mis-navigation in the Tulip it completed an unhappy competition career for the works Twin Cam. By 1959 the Big Healey had developed sufficiently to win international rallies outright, so the Twin Cam took a back seat.

Considerable attention was also devoted to a team of three works-prepared Austin-Healey Sprites for Sebring in 1959, although a trio of Abingdon-built Twin Cams were also entered by the US distributor, the Hambro Corporation. The

Twin Cams finished second and third in their class with Ehrmann and Seidel driving one finisher, and James Parkinson and Decker the other. It was all good publicity for the MGA, however, as the class winner was one of the fabulously expensive works Porsche RSKs driven by Taffy von Trips and Jo Bonnier. Sadly, by then, private customers were having difficulty making their Twin Cams go so well.

The best show in Europe was put up by Dick Jacobs, who entered two— 1 MTW and 2 MTW—in club events and the odd international. They won thirty places in thirty-two events, winning their class in the *Autosport* championship in 1959 and 1960. The cars were meticulously prepared by Jacobs with more than 2 cwt saved by attention to the bodywork and chassis. Foster drove 1 MTW in both 1960 and 1961, and Roy Bloxham, who owned 2 MTW, spent the first season in it before selling it to Jacobs and going on to other machinery. Tommy Bridger took over from him in 1960.

Hambros entered their Twin Cams again at Sebring in 1960, taking third and fourth places in their class, behind Porsches. Meanwhile, Bob Olthoff, who had won four races and taken fifth place in the Roy Hesketh six-hour race in

Dick Jacobs's MGA Twin Cams were among the fastest racing in 1960. Tommy Bridger is seen here leading Chris Lawrence's Morgan, Mike Parkes's Lotus Elite, Bill Moss's Marcos and Peter Lumsden's Elite in the Wrotham Trophy for GT cars at Brands Hatch on August Bank Holiday. Jack Sears won the race in an Aston Martin DB4GT from Parkes, with Bridger fourth.

MGA Twin Cam enthusiasts will never forget the exploits of South African farmer Bob Olthoff between 1959 and 1961. Olthoff bought his Twin Cam, the first to be assembled in South Africa, early in 1959 and finished fifth in its first event, the Roy Hesketh Six-Hour race in the March of that year. Four wins followed in races at South Africa's Grand Central circuit and at Lourenco Marques with a fourth place in the Rand Summer Handicap in January 1960 and third in class in the autumn handicap two months later. With these successes behind him, Olthoff rented out his farm and with his bride-to-be, asked friends not to buy them wedding presents, but to give donations instead towards the cost of a trip to Britain. When the newly-weds arrived in England, Bob could not get a drive in a British car, so he telephoned his father, asking him to ship the Twin Cam over to him. In those days, it cost only £50 on the weekly mailboat to Britain. Bob had also been unable to find a suitable job, but struck lucky when he toured Abingdon.

John Thornley found him work in MG's show car preparation department and arranged for him to start on the next Monday morning. When Bob failed to turn up for work, Thornley telephoned him at the Overseas Club in London, and it transpired that they wouldn't release the young South African until he had paid his bill! Thornley cabled him £30 and Bob started his career as a show car mechanic and ultimately a works driver.

Five placings followed in British club events between June 1961 and March 1961, before Bob took the Twin Cam to Germany for the Nurburgring 1000 kilometre race in May 1961. He took a creditable seventh place and next raced in Ireland, where he picked up two placings in July 1961. Numerous other placings, and one win at Goodwood in September, secured him third place in the 1961 *Autosport* championship.

Throughout this time his much-modified Twin Cam, at first bearing a South African registration, and later a Berkshire number, was used as his daily transport as well as a weekend racer. He is pictured here in the Twin Cam at the Nurburgring.

MGAs were equally popular as rally cars. This example is seen performing well at an event in the early 1960s.

South Africa in 1959, shipped his car to Britain, where it was modified to the limit of Appendix J rules and sprayed patriotically in the Springbok colours of green and gold. Olthoff, who received considerable moral support from Thornley and some assistance from the works, raced extensively in Britain and Ireland between June 1960 and December 1961, besides taking seventh place in the Nurburgring 1000 km and third overall in the 1961 *Autosport* championship. His car's modifications are detailed in chapter thirteen.

However, the works Porsches were generally much faster than MGAs, a situation that did not please Enever and Thornley. Soon after development was completed on the EX181 record breaker, Enever set about making a sports car to rival the German machines. This was EX186, which looked rather like a smaller version of a Mercedes 300SLR. It had a twin cam engine and de Dion rear suspension, like that of EX181, and was good for more than 140 mph, according to people who saw it. Although it was based on the MGA chassis, the BMC management would not allow it to race, in the wake of their Le Mans decision. It lingered on in the development department at Abingdon for a couple of years until one of the 1955 Le Mans drivers, Ted Lund, thought he had 'talked it out' for the French race in 1959. However, the BMC top brass stuck to their guns—it did not look like a production MG in any case—and Lund was disappointed. However, he had a Le Mans entry, so the factory built him up a Twin Cam for the event, using parts of the Fitzwilliam cars bodies salvaged from their rebuilds. A full-width competition windscreen was fitted and the car was registered SRX 210.

Lund shared it with Colin Escott, who had the misfortune to hit a stray dog on the circuit when the car was going well with only four hours to go. The crumpled bodywork led to overheating and they had to retire while placed fifteenth.

Lund had learned enough to be convinced that the car stood a good chance of finishing at Le Mans, so he bought it from the factory to make sure that BMC did not change their minds again. Abingdon continued to prepare it, though, and a bored-out 1762 cc version of the twin cam engine was fitted with twin 40DCOE Webers in place of the earlier 2-inch SU carburetters. New regulations meant that a full-size screen had to be fitted, so a coupé top was grafted on as that screen presented a better shape than the normal roadster screen. This top featured a fastback for reduced drag, but it still consumed more power, so the axle ratio was dropped from 3.9 : 1 to 4.1 : 1. Nevertheless, the car could still top 130 mph, and it averaged 91 mph for twelfth place and a win in the 2-litre prototype class.

Further improvements were made for 1961. The front was redesigned on the lines of earlier competition Triumph TRs, to reduce drag. This meant dispensing with the MG radiator grille. The wings were also cut back and another 1762 cc engine fitted. This gave 128 bhp at 5400 rpm and was good enough for 140 mph. Lund was soon lapping at more than 100 mph in the 1961 race (101.66 mph best lap) before a big end bolt gave way and he retired in the first hour. Olthoff, who had been looking forward to his stint as co-driver, never got the chance! A spare 1762 cc engine was fitted and Lund continued to campaign this car in club events until his retirement in 1968. It was then sold to Bob McElroy for historic racing with a 1622 cc unit.

Right : How the 'old girl' looked in the beginning taking first in class at Mallory Park on Boxing Day in 1963.

Below : Bill Nicholson and 286 FAC, by now sporting a hard top, contesting the Ragley Hall hill climb in 1964.

Facing page, top : Bill Nicholson

Facing page, bottom : 286 FAC as she looked in 1973 in full modsports guise with Minilite wheels.

One of the greatest personalities in MG racing is Bill Nicholson, who has driven his equally-famous MGB roadster, 286 FAC, in competition since April 1963. The car was a forty-fourth birthday present from his wife in the February of that year, when the former Jaguar development engineer decided to give up motor cycle trials riding. At the time of writing in July 1979, 286 FAC had scored 200 class and overall wins in international and club circuit races since Easter 1963, and made fastest time of the day eleven times in sprint races, with twenty class wins in sprints and hill-climbs. The car had covered 40,807.14 racing miles in Bill's hands, 10,106 miles on the road and 1,123.3 racing miles with other drivers. Major successes included first in class in the Colibri Trophy international race at Silverstone in 1963 and second in class behind a Porsche 904 in the Snetterton Three-Hours in the same year. Three firsts in class were taken in international races in 1964, at the Oulton Park Spring Cup meeting, the Phoenix Park Gold Flake Trophy meeting during which Bill took the class lap record, and another first in the Colibri Trophy. Porsche 904s and Ferrari 250LMs took most of the top awards in 1965, but Bill still managed second in class and third overall in the Martini Trophy at Silverstone, second in class in the Archie Scott-Brown Memorial Trophy race at Snetterton and second in class at the Guards Trophy meeting at Brands Hatch. More success came in 1966 with a first overall in the Oulton Park Easter Cup for marque cars and first overall in GT and Sports car events on the same circuit; third in class and sixth overall in the Ilford Films 500-mile race at Brands Hatch and second in class behind a Porsche 906 in the Guards Trophy race at Brands Hatch. The inevitable Porsche 906s were joined by Chevrons and Ford GT40s for opposition in 1967 with Bill's MG finishing third in class and ninth overall in the *Daily Express* Trophy race at Silverstone, and second in class and fourth overall in the BARC 100-mile sports and sports/racing car event at Snetterton. He also took first in class and second overall in the Aston Martin Owners' Club meeting's Monte Cristo Trophy race for GT and sports cars. Porsches and Ford GT40s were the chief opposition in 1968 with a fourth in class and twelfth overall in the *Daily Express* Trophy race at Silverstone, a third in class in the Zandvoort Trophy race in Holland during which 286 FAC lapped the works Porsche 911s and established a new class lap record; a first overall and class lap record in the Bardahl Trophy race at Silverstone, a

Cockpit of a racer ... 286 FAC.

first overall in the Clubmen's Championship race on the Silverstone grand prix circuit and a joint win in the Fred W Dixon Trophy championship. A fifth place in class behind four Chevron B8s and tenth overall in the *Daily Express* Trophy was the major achievement of 1969; sixth in class and twelfth overall in the *Daily Express* Trophy followed in 1970 with these events by then contested by Lola T210s and Chevrons. However, there was one more success at international level with a first in class and sixth overall in the BRSCC/AP Trophy Special GT and Modsports event.

At the end of 1970 it was decided to retire the 'old girl', as the Nicholson family called her, from international racing with Bill by then fifty years old. However at club level he was still doing well, winning the Dick Protheroe modsports trophy. He won his class again in this championship in 1971 with a first in class and sixth overall in the Clubmen's Championship at Silverstone in 1972. Bill and 286 FAC were outright winners in the Post-Historic Championship in 1973 and class winners in the MG Car Club Silverstone sprint in 1974. They won the two-litre front-engined GT car class in the Speed Merchants/*Classic Car* championship for post-historic cars by fifteen points in 1975. Major successes in 1976 included an outright win in the MG Car Club's Abingdon Trophy race at Silverstone, a class win and lap record at the international *Classic Car* meeting at Thruxton, another class win and lap record at Thruxton in the MG marque race and a class in the MG Car Club sprint at Silverstone.

Only three meetings were contested in 1977, with first in class and fastest lap at them all! They were all at Bill's home circuit, Silverstone: the SUNBAC Silverstone modsports race, the BMRMC modsports race and the Peterborough MC modsports event. Similar victories followed in the MG Car Club sprint at Wroughton, the MG Car Club's Abingdon Trophy event, and the Bentley Drivers' Club HSCC members' race at Silverstone in 1978. Bill was also proud to drive 286 FAC in the Birmingham street grand prix in that year, and by June 1979 he had won the Abingdon Trophy outright at Silverstone and taken first overall in the 750 MC event at Mallory Park.

Throughout the years, 286 FAC had changed its appearance innumerable times, running at one time on 15-inch Minilites, and at other times on 14-inch wire wheels. It has had all sorts of different engines with Bill eventually settling for a five-bearing crank in the interests of reliability. He says he is a firm believer in 'putting the car before the horse' in that he develops the chassis to its fullest extent before extracting more horsepower from the engine.

His chief chassis modifications (before trying skirts and an air dam for a grand prix-style 'ground effects' MGB!) centred on changed front suspension mounting points and rear suspension links. Weight has been saved wherever possible with alloy panels and a lightweight hardtop and windows, although Bill is insistent that the car's appearance should not be changed far from standard. All that and a love of breeding Alsatians for show keeps the Nicholson family from Northampton fully occupied ...

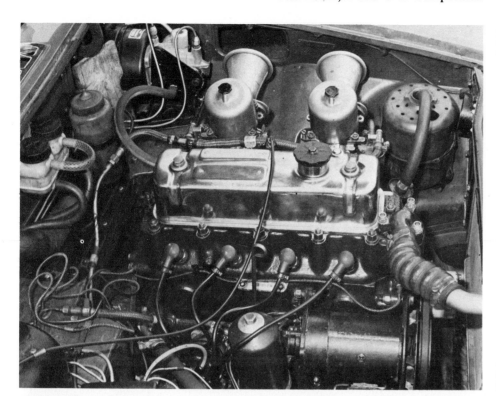

Left: The powerhouse of 286 FAC. Bill Nicholson prefers twin SUs to a single Weber.

Below: Nicholson and 286 FAC winning their event at the 750 MC meeting at Mallory Park in 1979.

De Luxe coupés

Perhaps the success of this car persuaded BMC to look again at the MGA for competition work. They built a pair of 1600 De Luxe coupés for Sebring in 1960. It was just as well, because a great rivalry had developed in the United States between MG and Sunbeam enthusiasts in SCCA racing. 'Talking point among the smaller car enthusiasts was the Sunbeam–MG rivalry, each marque having hundreds of vociferous supporters with the longer-established octagon contingent winning by sheer force of numbers,' said *Autosport*.

However, things were tense in the octagon camps as Paddy Hopkirk and Peter Jopp, Peter Harper and Peter Proctor, led their class in Sunbeam Alpines. Eventually they succumbed to tyre problems (they were running smaller wheels than the MGs), and overheating, and the De Luxe coupés driven by Americans Jack Flaherty and Parkinson, and British works drivers Peter Riley and John Whitmore, took first and second places in class ahead of Harper and Proctor. The Sunbeam crew reversed this result in 1962, though, Harper and Proctor finished a lap ahead of Jack Sears and Andrew Hedges, Parkinson and Flaherty, and Whitmore and Olthoff in De Luxe coupés.

The MGA also had a last fling in the BMC works rally team, as Stuart Turner took over from Marcus Chambers. Turner was more enthusiastic about MGs than Chambers and had a De Luxe coupé built using a 115 bhp version of the 1622 cc engine to contest the 1601–2000 cc international class. In January 1961, Don and Erle Morley won their class in the Monte Carlo Rally and took second place behind David Seigle-Morris's Austin-Healey 3000 in the GT category—no mean feat. Then this very successful car, 151 ABL, beat a team of new Triumph TR4s to win its class in the Tulip Rally for Rauno Aaltonen and Gunnar Palm. Gott took over for the Liege–Rome–Liege Rally, but like so many other cars, 151 ABL, succumbed in this very rough event.

The MGB

By then the works had turned their attention to the new MGB as privateers continued to race the MGA in all manner of events. Three works MGBs were built for the 1963 season, registered 6 DBL, 7 DBL and 8 DBL. They conformed to BMC policy in that they were not far removed from cars that virtually anybody could buy. All their specialised components were readily available from the Special Tuning department at Abingdon. At the same time international sports car racing regulations were being tightened up all the time, making it difficult to depart far from standard. As a result the works MGBs were too heavy to be competitive in many events, but scored in longer distance races because of their reliability, largely the result of long experience with the B series engine and meticulous preparation.

One of their few mistakes was right at the beginning of the MGB's competition career. Britain had a very bad winter in 1963 and heavy snowfalls prevented any proper circuit testing with the result that their engine ran the bearings. This was because the 1.8-litre units, although in similar tune to the 1.6-litre engine in

Facing page: Three MGA De Luxe coupés were prepared at Abingdon for a BMC North American entry at Sebring in 1962. Jack Sears is seen here leading Bob Olthoff during a shake-down run for the cars at Silverstone before shipping to Florida.

Three works MGBs, registered 6, 7 and 8 DBL, were prepared for competition in 1963. 7 DBL raced with standard-shaped bodywork and in long-nosed form at Le Mans (*pictured above*) while 6 and 8 DBL retained their 'normal' bodywork. 8 DBL is pictured on the facing page at Sebring in 1966.

151 ABL, used a different sump with, as it turned out, inadequate baffles to cope with the heavy braking needed on this tight circuit. The drivers of 6 and 7 DBL were Denise McCluggage and Christabel Carlisle, Parkinson and Flaherty.

On return from America, 7 DBL was prepared for British circuit racing, with better sump baffling, and further experiments were made in preparation for Le Mans. Alan Hutcheson took it to a class win at Silverstone and raced a works development car in *Autosport* championship races, eventually finishing a close second in class to Dickie Stoop's Porsche Carerra. Bill Nicholson also proved to be a close contender in another MGB, 286 FAC, bought for him by his wife as a birthday present!

The chief modification to 7 DBL for Le Mans was the fitting of an extended nose based on that of the record cars, and said to be worth 6 bhp. This used a much-reduced air intake, different wings with the lights lowered rather in the manner of the TT MGA, and a special bonnet. An additional fuel tank was fitted, with an extra-high 3.307 : 1 rear axle ratio, giving a top speed of 132 mph. In the event, Hutcheson ran into the sand at Mulsanne and spent eighty-five minutes digging the car out with his hands, helmet and passenger seat as other cars slid by six inches away. Nevertheless, with Paddy Hopkirk, he went on to second in class at nearly 92 mph, behind a prototype Porsche, but with the satisfaction of being the only GT to finish in its class.

Hardly any changes were made to 7 DBL for the Tour de France three months

later, proving what an excellent road car it was. In this road race-cum-rally, Andrew Hedges and John Sprinzel were holding down fourth place overall when they hit a rockface. Patrick Vanson and Roger Derolland finished seventh overall, however, in a new MGB bought just before the event.

Meanwhile, in SCCA racing, championships were simplified to include one for manufacturers in the GT class and one each for drivers of cars over and under two litres. Star attractions included Ronnie Bucknum in the Hollywood Sports Cars MGB, the start of many years of success in this form of racing.

Three more works cars were built for the 1964 season and registered BMO 541B, BRX 853B and BRX 854B, with 7 and 8 DBL being retained to complete the fleet as a fuller programme of rallies and races were contemplated.

The rally programme looked as though it might be as successful as that of the long-distance racing when the Morley twins took the much-used 7 DBL to a GT win in the Monte Carlo rally. The overall winner, however, was Paddy Hopkirk in a Mini-Cooper S, which scooped the lion's share of publicity, so when 7 DBL was written off by the Morley twins in the Scottish Rally and further disasters struck the cars in the Liege–Rome–Liege and the RAC rally it was decided to concentrate on the Mini-Cooper S. For the record, gearbox trouble eliminated works MGBs driven by Pauline Mayman and Valerie Domleo and David Hiam and Julien Vernaeve near Belgrade in the Liege, and engine trouble eliminated John Fitzpatrick and John Handley in the RAC.

One of the most versatile and successful MGB works cars was GRX 307D.
It is pictured here (*right*) in Monte
Carlo Rally trim for Tony Fall in 1966
and (*below*) at the Nurburgring during
its winning run in the eighty-four hour
Marathon de la Route.

Andrew Hedges retired with a blown head gasket in the Pyrenees during the Tour de France, but long-distance circuit racing proved far more rewarding. Ed Leslie and Jack Dalton finished an honourable seventeenth at Sebring with Jim Adams and Merle Brennan in twenty-second place before BMO 541B was fitted with a similar nose to that smashed on 7 DBL in the Tour de France. With this slightly more streamlined front it reached 139 mph along the Mulsanne Straight and ran with regularity to finish nineteenth overall at 99.95 mph. Hedges and Hopkirk were the drivers again and were beaten only by very special Porsches. Obviously results cost money!

Two more cars were built for the 1965 season, DRX 255C and DRX 256C, with 8 DBL retained yet again as a spare. It had become a tradition by then that at least one of the works cars was sold in America after Sebring to defray expenses, so 8 DBL was soon back in the thick of competition. DRX 256C was sent to Sebring, with an assortment of Austin-Healeys, for Merle Brennan and Frank Morrell to drive. Hurricanes and tornadoes were forecast, but the rain that the BMC camp had prayed for did not arrive until seven-and-a-half hours after the race had been under way. But when it came down it was fantastic: the tropical storm flooded the track eight inches deep in places and the fat-tyred racing sports cars had to crawl round at 25 mph in places where they had been doing 165 mph. One Ford Cobra started lapping a parking lot with its driver under the impression he was on the track. The BMC team were in their element as their skinny-tyred, virtually-standard, cars scythed through the floods, with Brennan and Morrell lapping the leading Chaparral three times during the one-and-a-half hour storm. Had the rain started earlier and lasted longer, a sensational result might have ensued. As it was, Brennan and Morrell finished twenty-fifth with another MGB driven by Brad Picard and Al Pense thirty-second.

As DRX 255C was being prepared for Le Mans, 8 DBL was entered for Britain's longest post-war race, the Brands Hatch 1000-mile, run in two heats. Although entered by Cambridge tuner Don Moore it was a fully-fledged works car with BMC drivers John Rhodes and Warwick Banks. The MGB proved to be ideal for this short-circuit marathon as tyre wear cut down the bigger car's speed advantage. Mechanical problems also afflicted a substantial proportion of the entry.

Rhodes and Banks took the lead on the first day at 400 miles and finished three laps ahead of a 4.2-litre Jaguar E type driven by Jackie Oliver and Chris Craft. Trevor Taylor and his sister Anita were third in the JCB-entered ex-works MGB, BRX 853B, with good performances put up by Nicholson and rallyman Andre Baldet in the perennial 286 FAC, and other MGBs driven by John Sach and Syd Enever's son, Roger, and John Ralph and A. Williams.

Rhodes and Banks circulated like clockwork the next day until they lost a few minutes with oil filter trouble. However, it was not enough to let the Taylors through despite their close challenge, and the works car ran out an easy winner by seven laps. The JCB car blew a core plug towards the end and lost nine laps—demoting it to seventh place when it could have had an easy second.

However, Ralph and Williams and Phil Cadman and Mike Donegan backed up well for eleventh and twelfth places overall. There could hardly have been a more convincing demonstration of reliability and speed with the overall win, first, second (Taylor) and third (Sach) in class, and four MGBs in the first twelve places.

DRX 255C, in almost exactly the same trim as BMO 541B the previous year, repeated the trick at Le Mans for Hopkirk and Hedges, taking eleventh place at nearly 99 mph!

One of the works cars was sent to the East Coast of America for the important Bridgehampton 500. Hopkirk finished a steady fourth behind three far lighter cars, a Porsche 904GTS driven by Herb Wetanson, and two Lotuses.

Much to BMC's surprise they found themselves third in the GT constructor's championship despite having entered only two of the twelve qualifying rounds and with much valuable publicity from the MGB's long-distance achievements. Turner's faith in the car was vindicated and a more ambitious official programme planned for 1966. Three more cars were built, GRX 307D, HBL 129D and JBL 491D, with the relatively ancient 8 DBL, plus DRX 255C, retained as part of the works team. It was necessary to have several cars, not only to cover for accidents, but because the machines were driven down to events where possible and frequently a spare car went along for practice. All the new cars were roadsters, like the earlier works machines, although the GT coupé had been introduced late in 1965. Some were even entered as GTs in races by virtue of their hard tops, but true MGB GTs were not used as works cars at this juncture because of the weight penalty. They were heavy enough as it was, the 1964 Le Mans car weighing 955 kg, 10 kg more than the winning three-litre Ferrari and only 20 kg lighter than a standard MGB because of its endurance equipment!

Tony Fall drove one of the new cars, GRX 307D, in the Monte Carlo Rally as a GT, but had to retire when a floppy oil cooler pipe chafed through on the steering column. Prospects looked brighter for circuit racing as sports car regulations were tightened up, making the MGBs, still substantially standard, more competitive. Le Mans was the exception, where they were to be outpaced so quickly that it was no longer practical to try to get an entry.

Two works cars were sent to Sebring, as official entries this time, for Hopkirk and Hedges, and a truly international team of Briton Roger Mac, Australian Peter Manton and American Emmett Brown. It was all part of BMC's policy of gaining as much national publicity and entering as many categories as possible. The Hopkirk car, 8 DBL, was bored out to 2004 cc to compete in the prototype class and the Mac car, HBL 129D, remained as a standard GT. They were joined by another MGB 1800 entered by Continental Cars for Albert Ackerley and Arch McNeill.

Hopkirk's car lost time with a broken rocker shaft and then led its class with one-and-a-half hours to go as all the other class-opposition retired, before it had the misfortune to throw a con-rod; the other works MGB sauntered home seventeenth.

May 8, 1966, proved to be a red-letter day for Abingdon when Roger Enever lapped Brands Hatch for six hours to take third place in the Ilford Films 500 in the works development hack, 2 GLL. Once again heavy rain came to MG's aid with the more powerful racing machines floundering in the very wet conditions. At one point, Enever and fellow works driver Alec Poole were up to second place and in the end were beaten only by a 7-litre Shelby American Cobra and a

Briton Roger Mac, Australian Peter Manton and American Emmett Brown raced a works MGB, HBL 129D, in the standard GT class at Sebring in 1966, finishing seventeenth overall.

Roger Enever in the works development hack, 2 GLL, complete with tax disc and RAC badge, chases Bill Nicholson in the Ilford Films 500-mile race at Brands Hatch in 1966. Enever pressed on in dreadful conditions to finish third behind a Shelby American Cobra and a Ford GT40.

4.7-litre Ford GT40. The organisers had thrown open the race, the previous year's 1000-miler, to racing sports cars in the hope of attracting a more glamorous field, and then amazingly an MG road car nearly beat the lot! Another way of looking at it was that it was some road car, even if it was equipped with a silencer.

Nicholson and Don Bunce were seventh in 286 FAC and other MGBs were driven by Mike Walton and Jerry Delmar-Morgan (ninth), Jean and Tony Denton (twelfth), Herbert Fernando and Ken Costello (fourteenth) and Bob Dewar and W Ramsden (eighteenth). Enever and Nicholson took first and third in class.

On the same day, far away in sunny Sicily, Timo Makinen and John Rhodes were cornering their official works car, the ex-Monte Carlo GRX 307D, on its door handles to take ninth place in the tough Targa Florio road race. They won the two-litre GT class and the entire GT category against all manner of exotic machinery with Hedges and Handley second in class with JBL 491D. It was a demonstration of the MG's outstanding handling as they had only 107 bhp and were fully road-equipped. Their spare car, incidentally, was the ex-Sebring HBL 129D, which covered the equivalent of two complete Targa Florios in practice.

JBL 491D went on to win its class and the GT category in the Spa 1000 km with Hedges and Julien Vernaeve at the wheel and not so much as an engine

rebuild. A week later, with more than 2000 racing kilometres plus road driving behind it, this long-suffering car burst a water hose and blew a gasket in the Nurburgring 1000 km. Hedges then took over GRX 307D for the Circuit of Mugello, an Italian version of the Targa Florio, and finished third in the GT class with Robin Widdows, behind two Ferraris.

BMC built one competition MGB GT, registered LBL 591E, pictured here in the Targa Florio in 1968. Otherwise they raced roadsters with hardtops in GT events!

GRX 307D and 2 GLL, which had also completed 10,000 miles at 100 mph as part of a Shell publicity campaign, were then entered in the eighty-four hour Marathon de la Route at the Nurburgring. This was officially a rally, a replacement for the Liege–Sofia–Liege, which was upsetting holidaymakers too much. But, in reality, it was a very tough circuit race with a highly-complex scoring system that evened out cars remarkably well. Hedges and Vernaeve had GRX 307D, by now equipped with a battery of four Lucas Flamethrower lights, and Enever and Poole were together again after Brands Hatch. Enever and Hedges both found the same patch of fresh, loose, gravel and crashed on their first and second laps respectively. Enever's car was not badly damaged, but Hedges managed to clear the ditch and land in a field. Both extracted themselves and hobbled back to the pits for repairs and heavy penalties. Slowly they fought their way back into contention in the race and were third and fourth overall before the leading Volvo retired on the second morning;

Top and bottom: Private entrants continued to race MGBs in long-distance events, particularly in America, in the early 1970s.

Facing page: Bristol racing driver John Chatham bought a large quantity of works parts, including three light-weight MGC bodyshells, when Abingdon decided to concentrate on the Mini-Cooper and Austin 1800 rally cars in 1969. He built up one of the shells to works circuit racing specification, and registered it VHY 5H, before racing it in the Targa Florio in 1970. 'It seemed a good idea at the time,' said John, years later, 'but things like Porsche 908/3s were a bit too quick for the old MG. Even when they had only three wheels . . .' Apparently the Finnish driver Laine had just overtaken Chatham when the British driver saw in the distance a Porsche wheel flying high in the air. Slowing down, expecting to find a pile of debris from a smashed car round the corner, he saw only an empty road. He drove on cautiously, expecting to find Laine's wrecked car at any moment, only to discover that when the Finnish ace lost a front wheel, he accelerated to 140 mph, which lifted the Porsche's nose, and drove on to the pits for a new wheel!

one day later, a Lotus Cortina, which had been harrying them, had to retire and rain came to their aid once more. The leading Ferrari crashed in a downpour and the MGBs took first and second places, only for Enever to crash, too. However it took more than just a couple of shunts to finish such a veteran and Poole took over to fight his way back to second place, only to break a half shaft. Hedges and Vernaeve hammered on, however, to win the marathon outright. The battered and buckled GRX 307D was the only GT to finish among fourteen survivors; a fantastic feat. MG might also have had the team award had the private entry of Wolf Kniese and George Bialas not broken a fan belt half way. Works cars always carried a spare taped to the bonnet stay . . .

Comprehensive repairs were undertaken and the same two works cars then finished second and third in class in the Montlehery 1000 km behind a Porsche Carrera 6! Meanwhile, enthusiasts were racing MGBs everywhere, some with success in long-distance events. Holden and Underwood drove their MGB 650 miles from Sydney to Surfers' Paradise in Queensland, won their class in the local twelve-hour race, then drove back to Sydney.

The MGB GT and Lightweight MGC GT

Meanwhile the works built yet more cars for 1967, an MGB GT, LBL 591E, in the hope that they could get it homologated in time for GT racing, and another roadster, MBL 547E. GRX 307D and DRX 255C were retained.

Ever-tightening regulations had eliminated the Big Healey from long-distance racing, leaving Abingdon without a contender in the 2–3-litre class unless an MGB was bored out to 2004 cc, which was rather dodgy and hardly made the best use of the capacity limit! Extensive knowledge had been gained over the years with the Big Healey's three-litre unit, which could be made to give a reliable 175–200 bhp at the flywheel. So when development started on the MGC in the winter of 1966, six new MGC GT shells were ordered for competition use as it had been decided that there was more future in publicising the standard shape than continuing to enter roadsters with hard tops in the GT classes. The standard GT shell was very heavy, however, and Abingdon cars were constantly coming up against lightweight competitors, so it was decided to join the enemy and built real lightweights like their own. Therefore the new works shells were built with steel underpans and alloy superstructures and skins. Seeing as they would have to race in the prototype classes, at first anyway, they were also fitted with wide flared arches to cover the large alloy wheels they intended using.

These shells were difficult to build, however, so the steel-bodied GT was made ready for Sebring. Because this body shape had not yet been homologated, it had to run in the prototype class, so it was decided to get as much as possible out of it and a 2004 cc engine was fitted. To keep it looking as standard as possible however, the relatively-narrow wire wheels were fitted. With racing MGs, it was a question of extracting as much publicity as possible as it was unlikely that they would win the race outright. In fact, the only bodywork modification to the GT was the fitting of a massive double-decker bus-style snap-action filler cap, which was virtually

standard wear at Sebring, to save vital seconds and make refuelling safer.

This left Abingdon without a car to run in the GT category, so, ironically, GRX 307D was prepared for this class with standard bodywork and a hard top! Hopkirk and Hedges had LBL 591E and Makinen and Rhodes GRX 307D. In the race, each car finished third overall in its category, the GT winning its class and the prototype beaten only by two seven-litre Ford Mark IVs which came first and second in the race overall. The MGs' overall positions were eleventh for the Hopkirk car and twelfth for Makinen's machine.

The MGC had not been announced when the Targa Florio was to be run, so a 2004 cc engine was fitted to the first of the GTS cars, registered MBL 546E. This meant that it could be listed as just a special MGB GT. Under the skin, however, it had the MGC's floorpan and suspension, extra axle location, and Girling disc brakes and adjustable telescopic dampers all round. In this form, with SU carburetters in place of its normal Weber, and 150 bhp rather than 137, it finished ninth overall on the road. It was excluded from the official race results, however, because it had finished more than ten per cent down on time to its class winner, the Porsche 910/8 driven by Paul Hawkins and Rolf Stommelen, which also won the race outright. It was a thoroughly disappointing journey for the BMC team, especially as the brand-new MGB hard top roadster, MBL 547E, driven by Hedges and Poole was written off when it hit a tree while leading the GT category comfortably.

Abingdon were then instructed to concentrate available resources of Austin 1800

Stalwart club competitor Barry Sidery-Smith chases Derek Grant in the Red Rooster during an MG Car Club race in 1974.

development (they had always been up to their ears in Mini-Cooper rally work) and it was left to a variety of MGBs to continue upholding the model's honour in club racing. The most successful driver in this sphere was Nicholson with 286 FAC, who also prepared many of his competitors' cars. He won ten races in 1967 with his nearest rival in an MGB, Royston Ashford, taking six. Other notable drivers in these cars were Bunce, Barry Sidery-Smith, Peter Brown, Vic Gardner, Jean Denton and Gabrielle Koenig. However, Abingdon found time to work on MBL 546E during the winter and it was duly prepared for Sebring as a proper MGC now that this model had been launched. LBL 591E was also prepared for Sebring again, with Minilite wheels this time, but not so wide as to need bodywork modifications.

At Sebring, Hopkirk and Hedges finished tenth overall, the highest placing there by an MG, winning their class and coming third overall in the prototype category behind the inevitable Porsches. The MGB GT driven by Americans Garry Rodrigues and Richard McDaniell and Canadian Bill Brack, finished eighteenth overall and fifth in class.

The MGB GT was then driven to the Targa Florio for Hopkirk and Hedges and finished twelfth overall—three places behind the position achieved by the lightweight the year before. It was placed second in the sports car category (despite being a genuine GT!) and retained its overall position. Wild enthusiasm had always greeted this road race—the last such classic in the world—but the regulations were enough to put anybody off. Various English club racers also entered the event, including Peter Brown in the JCB lightweight roadster, with Tony Fall as co-driver.

Barry Sidery-Smith in an MGB GT V8 and Anthony Binnington in a 1962 MGB roadster race neck and neck at Brands Hatch in an MG Car Club event.

They had failed to qualify for the Monza 1000 km, but had better luck this time. In the race, they crashed, stopped for chassis repairs, crashed again and still managed to finish twenty-fourth with a place in the general classification!

They went on from there to compete in another old-time road race, the Circuit of Mugello, first run in 1914. They were joined by Enever and Poole in the veteran black 8 BLL and Mike Garton sharing Jean Denton's MGB. Poole threw a rod almost immediately after the start but the JCB car ran perfectly to take fourteenth overall with fifth in class, and Garton and Denton fifth in their class.

Then the works came back on the scene in their official capacity, preparing two GTSs for the Marathon de la Route, MBL 546E for Hedges, Vernaeve and Fall, and a new one, RMO 699F, for Enever, Poole and Clive Baker, who had driven a Sprite at Mugello. MBL 546E was lying third after sixty-seven hours when, because of a miscalculation, the front brake pads were down completely, wrecking the discs and calipers. Repairs cost them a total of twenty-five penalty laps, heartbreaking when they had been catching the leading Porsches and eventually they finished in sixth place only twenty-eight laps in arrears. The other car retired with engine trouble.

The two GTSs were sent to Sebring in 1969 for Hopkirk and Hedges and Brack and Craig Hill. The BGT was entered for Gerry Truitt and Logan Blackburn. In the event, the Hopkirk car finished fifteenth, Truitt's twenty-eighth and Brack's limped in thirty-fourth two places behind a private MGB driven by Park and Colgate. BMC had decided to concentrate on saloon car rallying and sold the remainder of their MG sports car racing stock to Bristol MG and Austin-Healey specialist John Chatham. He built one of the GTS shells up into a works-specification car for the 1969 Targa Florio. 'It seemed a good idea at the time; there were only three other cars in the over 3-litre sports car class and we reckoned we might cover the cost of the trip with a bit of prize money,' said Chatham. However, the MGC, registered VHW 5H, proved totally unsuited to the tortuous circuit and failed to make the official classification despite the efforts of Chatham, who had won a record number of club races with an ex-works Austin-Healey 3 litre.

He turned one of the three shells he had bought into a road car and built the other up as a modified sports car. Chatham fitted this car with one of three all-alloy experimental engines (the works cars had used Healey-style alloy heads and cast iron blocks), but suffered a woeful lack of reliability in 1972 and 1973 although it lapped Silverstone once in 1 min 5.4 seconds, a very fast time. 'We could have made her lighter,' said Chatham, 'But, although this shell had been gutted before purchase, it was so beautifully made that we hadn't the heart to hack it about.'

As one of the few champions of the MGC, he also built yet another shell, a roadster this time, up to works specification and it was raced in club events by Derek Grant in the early 1970s and Steve Bicknell and Matthew Bracey in 1979. This is the 'Red Rooster' described in chapter thirteen.

Meanwhile the MGA Le Mans coupé had reappeared in historic racing and squadrons of MGAs, MGBs and the occasional MGC continued to contest club races, with some success in production sports car events. MG T series exponent Gerry Brown was one of the most formidable drivers in this branch of the sport.

Today, MGAs, Bs and Cs with the occasional V8 have flourishing championships, with Bill Nicholson, at the time of writing sixty years old and his car among the front runners. The MGB GT V8 had even competed in international rallying in the hands of Michael Pearson. In America, British Leyland's Quaker State racing team have wiped up countless SCCA races with the MGB and although works participation is at an end interest in competition in MGAs, Bs and Cs has never been higher.

Facing page, top: Michael Pearson drives his ex-works prototype left-hand-drive MGB GT V8 in the RAC Rally.

Facing page, bottom: MG enthusiasts Malcolm Beer (modified V8) and Barry Sidery-Smith line up for an MG Car Club race at Brands Hatch.

VI

Strengths and Weaknesses: Part One

THE MGAs, Bs and Cs are extraordinarily strong cars but they are as susceptible as any other to corrosion; it just takes longer to cause real problems than on other cars. The MGA used to be considered virtually impregnable because of its massive chassis. The bodywork, especially around the sills and in the door posts, frequently showed signs of rust after five or six years, but there was always the thought that there was a chassis underneath it all. So it was a case of bodge up the body and blast off down the road. Today, however, the results of that bodging are showing through. Twenty-five-year-old MGAs are crumbling at the chassis under apparently sound bodies. This frequently happens in seemingly good restorations where a decent job is made of the body with little regard, other than a coat of black paint, to the metal underneath.

Whereas almost everything else on the car was of good design, the way in which the body was mounted most certainly was not. The space between the sills and the chassis sidemembers is an open invitation to accumulated mud and debris thrown up from the front wheels and down the rear wings by the back wheels. The mud that lodges there holds moisture and corrosion starts; now that roads in many countries are heavily salted in winter, spring and autumn, this process is accelerated. The doors, bootlid and bonnet last quite well because they are made of alloy, but even this rust-free material is prone to corrosion caused by dampness, and particularly salt.

The only cure for such corrosion, and it is very common in MGAs, is replacement of the parts affected, which can be many.

When inspecting an MGA, first pay attention to the bottom of the front wings; it is one of the most common mud traps. Then check the door pillars by simply opening the doors and seeing if you can move them up and down. The door shut plate and the area immediately behind it are also particularly susceptible to rust. Then get down on your knees (or flat on your back) and check the petrol tank and its straps, the battery carriers, the exhaust and the brake pipes for signs of corrosion. One, or all of them, are frequently in need of replacement, as are parts of the boot floor. The sills can be checked for corrosion at the same time, and on the fixed-head coupé, look at the joint where the top meets the body. Body flexing can start cracks here, with resultant rot. Other areas of potential trouble that can

The MGA's body was of entirely separate construction to that of the chassis. A body unit is being lowered onto a completed chassis on the production lines here at Abingdon. In a similar manner, the body of an MGA can be lifted off, although with considerably more difficulty on an old car!

be easily checked from the outside include the parts of the wings where the lights are mounted, particularly around the sidelights. It is important also that the chrome is in good condition, as this can be very expensive to replace.

Now you have a chance to straighten your back it is worth delving inside the car to see what the floorboards are like. If they need replacing the new ones must be a tight fit and varnished or painted on both sides to keep out the moisture. Then, while you are delving inside the car, attack the chassis inner side members with a screwdriver or punch. These members are frequently much thinner than they might appear and are absolutely vital to safety. In common with other areas of the chassis which corrode, such as the cross member joints, the chassis side members are repairable and the Rubery Owen industrial giant can straighten the chassis with the original jigs; but it's a major job, to put it mildly!

Should the chassis be at all suspect, its worth checking for signs of accident damage, particularly around the suspension mountings; MGAs can survive tremendous punishment.

Providing the chassis is sound, the sills and door pillars can be repaired with the body on the car. With patience, the wings can be removed quite easily as they are bolted on. Once they are off, the inner wings and vulnerable door pillars are readily accessible.

Similar problems beset the MGB and MGC, although attacks of terminal rust have manifested themselves at an earlier point with many cars as none of them have a chassis to rely on. With these younger models, the sills are of paramount

This MGA fixed-head coupé is undergoing a total restoration at Brown and Gammons works in Baldock.

Right: A typical case of corrosion in the outer sill of an MGA. Complete replacement is the only way to repair the damage.

Facing page, top: Door shut faces are equally prone to corrosion on the MGA. This is a rear view of a replacement shut face.

Facing page, bottom: Front view of the MGA replacement shut face.

importance. They literally hold the front and back of the car together, with the transmission tunnel and propeller shaft. On really badly rusted roadsters it has been known for them to break in half along a line at the back of the seat pan. The GT examples suffer less from this highly dangerous condition as they have the hefty steel roof to help hold them together, with the permanently-fixed windscreen pillars.

Trouble with the sills of an MGB (and the MGC) can crop up with any cars over four years old. Corrosion of this type occurs in younger cars, but not often and it is difficult to spot. Again the fault is in the design. Water and mud penetrates the box formed by the outer sill and the side members which provide much of the car's strength. The trapped moisture eats its way out through the outer sill at first. If this sill panel is not replaced immediately and the inside of the sill exposed for treatment, the result can be rapid, and very expensive, rot. It's the most important area of the car to inject with a rust-proofing agent. It is also of prime importance when repairing the ravishes of rust in this area to make sure that enough metal is replaced. Always insist on the proprietary kits in which the sill roots are included if there is any danger of rust in the bottom of the front or rear wings. It's no good just replacing the centre section of the outer sill if this is the case as the repair is too weak and merely cosmetic.

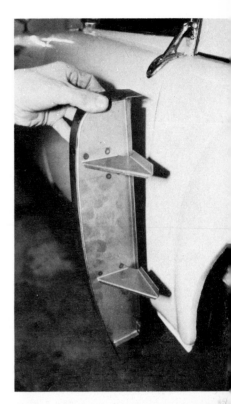

The other major areas of corrosion in the MGB and MGC are in the front wings, the rear wings, the petrol tank, battery boxes and outer areas of the floor. Inner parts of the floor survive remarkably well as accumulated oily gunge protects those areas from corrosion.

Trouble strikes all over the front wings, which, fortunately, are detachable like those on the MGA. Mud collects on a shelf between the inner and outer wing and paint bubbles and pin pricks appear on top of the wing about a foot forward of the windscreen just outside the bonnet edge. This is the first sign of rot in the wings. Further corrosion occurs in the inner wing in the same area and around the lights, in the same manner as on the MGA. More corrosion can appear around the bulkhead at the back of the front wings as mud and debris collects, although this cannot be seen until the wing is removed or a piece falls off! It happens because mud and debris accumulates in this region, having penetrated the front wing's inner splash guard.

At the same time rot attacks the rear wings, which are not readily detachable. The first signs here are usually around the wheel arches, where the inner arch joins the rear wing. This shows itself in paint bubbles and pin pricks like those on the front wings, at a point about an inch from the edge of the wheel arch. Other corrosion points on the rear wings are at the top where they join the rear shroud or roof.

Petrol tanks, luggage boot floors, battery boxes, exhaust systems and brake pipes suffer from the same trouble as those on the MGA, but the MGB and MGC have a special problem with their steel doors, particularly on earlier cars.

Flexing, slamming and general mis-alignment cause characteristic splits in the skin up to six inches long at a point immediately below the quarter light's rear edge. This can be repaired without dismantling, but in extreme cases a new door skin can be needed. The bottom of the door usually needs replacement by then in any case.

Other rusty problems that rear their head with the MGB and MGC (sometimes at a very early stage) are an accumulation of water behind the chrome strips running along the car's sides. This can lead to a marked deterioration in the paint's finish and ultimately the metal behind the strip around its fixing points. The rear valence under the bumper bar is also a noted point for corrosion.

The way to stop all this rot is by comprehensive repairs if the car is already affected, followed by dedicated maintenance. It is best to use original-pattern steel parts for repairs although fibreglass wings can be fitted quite successfully to the MGA, B and C. Fibreglass does not rust, but the dreaded tin worm can still strike underneath so this property is of little value as the outer wings still have to be removed for repairs to the inside; fibreglass can also detract from the value of a car when originality is of great importance.

Steel wings are more rigid unless the fibreglass panels are so thick that they weigh practically as much.

The real value of fibreglass is in non-standard parts such as Sebring-style wings and works bumper valences, where the equivalent parts beaten from metal would cost a small fortune and add little to the value of the car as they are non-standard in any case.

There is also a problem of inter-reaction between the aluminium (invariably used for such special parts in metal), and the steel chassis or monocoque, so if you are thinking of fitting such components to your car, use fibreglass. The only exception is in some competition categories where fibreglass bodywork is against the regulations when aluminium or steel was used originally.

Once the car has been restored to good condition (see chapter fourteen) it is a case of keeping it like that. It is well worth while introducing anti-corrosion agents to the sill areas of the MGA, B and C; such treatment can be very effective at stopping internal corrosion providing the dose is repeated every couple of years (or more frequently if so advised by the manufacturer). One good way of getting into the box section of the sill is by removing the interior panelling behind the seats and forcing in the anti-corrosion agent through the hole you will find in the steel pressing.

Blasting off excesses of mud and salt with a high-pressure hose is also well worth while. Alternatively, or in addition, have the car steam cleaned underneath after the worst of the winter is over. It is essential to repair any loose or cracked underseal, which is frequently made worse by the steam cleaning.

Another system which seems to work well is high-pressure oil blasting under-neath every time the car is serviced. This has the effect of building up a protective barrier between the metal and accumulated road debris, which has been notably successful on my own MGC V8. This gunge is then steam cleaned off at least once a year and the underseal repaired. When applying oil in this manner it is essential to use fresh supplies—it only takes a pint or so—as old sump oil contains impurities that can be just as corrosive as a saline solution! With the MGA, particular attention should be paid to keeping the chassis clean and well protected.

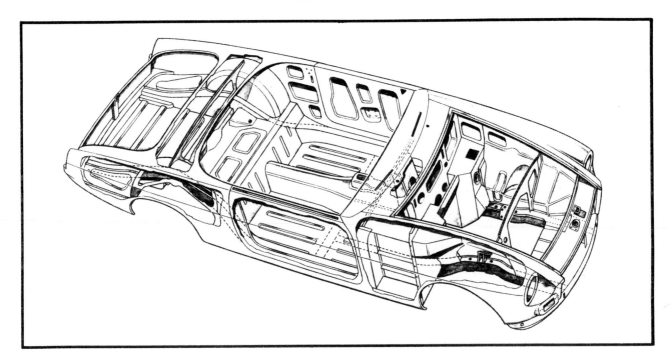

The MGB (and MGC) body/chassis shells were built as one unit. This sectional diagram of an MGB roadster shell shows the areas where corrosion can strike. MGB GT and MGC shells were of similar construction.

Careful maintenance of the paintwork and chrome obviously pays dividends as it does for the interior. The same applies to the chrome strips along the sides of the MGB and MGC. Should they be giving trouble with corrosion, remove them and treat the damaged paint at an early point rather than late when the whole car will need a respray. It is possible to have the chrome strips removed and their mounting holes filled in, but the car does not look so good if you do.

Door splits on the MGB and MGC can be repaired by silver soldering and lead filling after a hole has been drilled at the end of the split to relieve stress. Fitting a wide-based external mirror at this point can prevent this condition recurring; at least that's what BMC found out! Splitting doors are most frequently caused by mis-alignment and slamming the door. Initially, the hang of the door can be checked by careful examination of the chrome strips on the car's side. Slamming the door when it is mis-aligned causes the very rigid quarter light frame to put stress on the door skin, with the resultant split. A loose-fitting hard top can also accentuate this problem by applying pressure to the top of the quarter light frame.

To rehang the door, remove its interior trim and loosen the three Phillips head screws at the bottom of the front hinge and at the top front hinge. Then carefully close the door, which should then be lifted until the chrome strips are in line with the rest of the trim. Then re-open the door and pack cardboard on top of the sill so that when the door is partly open—enough to give you access to the screws—it is supported in the new position while you tighten up the screws. This method, used by Martin Bentley of the MG Owners' Club, works well, although he points out that you will probably need an impact screwdriver to loosen the screws in the first place! MGs are generally very well screwed together and present few problems compared to those associated with cars designed in a similar era.

VII

Strengths and Weaknesses: Part Two

THE mechanical and electrical components of an MGA, B and C are likely to present fewer major problems than the body and chassis. Most of them were intended for far heavier BMC saloon cars and commercial vehicles, and they had an excellent reputation for durability. Even in the MG's advanced state of tune (for a B series engine), 70,000 miles or more can be expected from a three-bearing engine before attention to the bores is necessary; the five, seven-bearing and V8 engines are good for more than 100,000 miles. The Twin Cam unit is the most pernickety, but when updated to its eventual production form and carefully-maintained, is far less troublesome than its reputation would have everybody believe.

All the pushrod four and six-cylinder engines sound 'tappety', but they are intended to have wide clearances, so beware of any that are unnaturally quiet. Valve trouble can result from clearances that have been reduced too far. Timing chains have been known to stretch, adding to the general din, but not often. If the car's engine is really noisy, check for bearing wear; the oil pressure should be at least 50 psi at 50 mph in top gear when everything is warmed up. A test drive to check this is far better and quicker than just letting it tick over until the oil and water are hot.

The V8 engine is an extraordinary one: it rarely runs at more than 45 psi hot and frequently drops to 5 psi on take-off and tick-over with no seeming ill effects! Beware of anything resembling the tick of a loose tappet, on this engine, or any misfiring. A ticking from a hydraulic tappet can be the cam follower tapping the camshaft, with resultant expensive repairs if this condition does not receive immediate attention. Plug leads frequently fall off the side-mounted plugs on the V8 and cause it to misfire; it's easy enough to replace the offending plug lead, but if the misfire persists, check everything, including the compression. The high-compression engine in my V8 ran with a slight misfire for 1000 miles before it was discovered that this condition was caused by a broken piston (which, in turn, was caused by temporary enforced running on low-grade petrol). Oil level is also of crucial importance in this engine, which, in common with similar low-pressure American V8s, has an exceptionally small sump. It is essential to change the oil at approximately 4000-mile intervals if bearing wear is to be minimised.

The Twin Cam runs at the same pressure as the other B and C series engines,

Ron Gammons (left) and Gerry Brown, who specialise in all things MG, at work in their engine-building shop.

but it should be rather quieter at the top end. It is unlikely that any Twin Cams are still running with chrome piston rings and most of the early engines have been updated to the lower compression ratio (see chapter two).

Fuel consumption with the Twin Cam should never exceed 20–25 mpg under normal restrained driving conditions as this would indicate an excessively-lean mixture (another sign is white powder inside the exhaust pipe—pale grey is better). If the mixture is too weak, piston trouble can be imminent. In contrast, the other four-cylinder MG engines are capable of returning well over 30 mpg, especially if the car has an overdrive. V8s and MGCs run up to 25 mpg. An oil consumption of up to 400 miles per litre is common with the Twin Cam, even in good condition, with four times this figure for the other cars. The V8's oil consumption can rise to 400 miles per litre if it is driven really hard.

All MG engines should be relatively oil-tight, and the under bonnet area generally clean; suspect any car that is a mass of gunge under the bonnet and remember that it can take eight hours to remove the engine before you face the time and expense of working on it.

The same strictures apply to the gearbox and overdrive, as the engine has to come out in a unit with them for attention that cannot be administered from inside or underneath the car. Avoid any car that has been hacked about underneath so that the gearbox can be removed on its own; these are dangerous because the structure will have been weakened.

The gearboxes made without synchromesh on first gear before 1967 often have not much synchromesh on second or third either after as little as 20,000 miles.

This is no serious matter if you are accustomed to using such a gearbox, but a decided handicap if you prefer strong synchromesh, so try the box if you are thinking of buying the car you are inspecting. Poor synchromesh means that the gearbox will ultimately need attention, although these units can go on for many thousands of miles in this condition. All these gearboxes are prone to whine in first or reverse gear, because of the square-cut gears, but this noise should not be really excessive.

The later, all-synchromesh gearbox on the four-cylinder MGBs and MGCs should have decent synchromesh and be smooth and quiet; pay particular attention to the gearbox on the V8 model as the great torque of this engine can play havoc with the gearbox bearings, causing them to fail in as little as 25,000 miles with hard driving. For ultimate reliability, the only real cure for a V8 is to fit the noisy competition straight-cut gearbox or the expensive five-speed Rover SD1 unit (see chapter thirteen). The standard gearbox is really the V8's Achilles heel.

Overdrive, where fitted, should function reliably, quickly and smoothly; should this be giving any trouble other than that reminiscent of clutch slip (the rev counter suddenly soars out of relation to the speedometer needle) these units are often remarkably easy to repair. But should it feel as though the clutch is slipping when the overdrive is engaged, without the characteristic sound of tortured clutch plates, the engine and gearbox might have to come out to change the unit (which can also be expensive).

The automatic gearboxes fitted to MGBs and MGCs should present no problems (the MGB's installation is remarkably smooth) but if they do, it is highly advisable that you seek the advice of specialists. Even main dealers can be extraordinarily ignorant when it comes to malfunctions in automatic gearboxes and frequently suggest total replacement at great cost when only a small amount of attention is needed. Automatic gearboxes and their torque converters, are usually far more liable than their manual equivalents, but are like the mysteries of the Orient to many garages, who seldom have the right equipment for testing them in any case.

Rear axle trouble with an MGA, B or C is most unusual and do not panic over a restrained 'clonk' when the drive is taken up, with a similar noise when the car is reversed. These axles are made with generous tolerances which give a degree of backlash. Should there be much clonking, it is important to find out whether or not it is being caused by the propeller shaft's universal joints, or whether they are contributing to the clonking. The best way to do this is to put the car on a garage's ramp and check to see if there is any play in the universal joints and make sure the centre spider is not moving in its yokes. Any such wear is easily remedied and should be eliminated before further checks are made on the rear axle. These checks are more important on the MGC and V8 where the axle has to absorb more power and torque than with the four-cylinder cars. Hub wear is unlikely to be above the average for any car and should be checked in the normal manner by supporting each wheel individually and trying to rock it.

Braking should be progressive and smooth on all models. There are few problems with the braking on any model except the Twin Cam. Do not worry too much about slight scoring of the discs, although they should be replaced if there is

Plate 1 The MGA and one of its immediate predecessors, the MG TC.

Plate 2 Ted Lund's Le Mans fixed-head coupé.

Plate 3 Two of the most adventurous MG enthusiasts ever: Norman and Pat Ewing, set off from South Africa's Kruger Park on a trip to the Arctic Circle during which their daughter was born.

Plate 4 MGAs are still as popular as ever in club racing. This example is driven by Londoner Roy McCarthy.

Plate 5 The MGA 1600 Mark II roadster.

Plate 6 The last MGA Twin Cam made, owned from new by Mike Ellman-Brown.

Plate 7 *below left* The magnificent nose of a Belgian MGA Twin Cam shown at the MG Car Club's Silverstone weekend in 1978.

Plate 8 *below right* Cockpit of the Twin Cam.

Plate 9 Don and Erle Morley take their works MGA 1600 De Luxe coupé 151 ABL to a great class win in the 1961 Monte Carlo Rally.

Plate 10 Owners have been trying out their own ideas on MGs since they were first made. Some have been quite tastefully customised such as this MGB.

Plate 11 *right* Every model of MGA, B or C is popular at MG Owners' Club meetings.

Plate 12 *facing page* The MGB roadster; a classic in its own lifetime.

Plate 13 *overleaf* Bill Nicholson and 286 FAC.

Plate 14 High and low: two MGBs, one of which has been lowered to the original ride height by specialists Brown and Gammons of Baldock.

Plate 15 *right* A practical way of pepping up the B series engine: a Brown and Gammons stage one conversion.

Plate 16 *facing page* Alan Hutcheson and Paddy Hopkirk take the long-nosed MGB registered 7 DBL to twelfth place at Le Mans in 1963 despite having spent eighty-five minutes stuck in a sandbank at the end of the Mulsanne Straight.

Plate 17 The *Autocar* road test MGB GT.

Plate 18 The man behind it all: John Thornley with his faithful MGB GT, registered MG1.

Plate 19 Model in suspension: a 1979 MGB GT V8 built by John Chatham Cars in Bristol, pictured in front of the city's famous suspension bridge.

Plate 20 Underbonnet view of a 1979 Chatham-built MGB GT V8.

Plate 21 The Hopkirk and Hedges
MG GTS at Sebring in 1969.

Plate 22 The tragically short-lived
MGB GT V8.

Plate 23 The brutal, aggressive MGC.

Plate 24 The Red Rooster, the fearsome lightweight MGC road/racer driven by the author and owned by John Chatham Cars.

Plate 25 Typical concours line-up at an MG Car Club weekend.

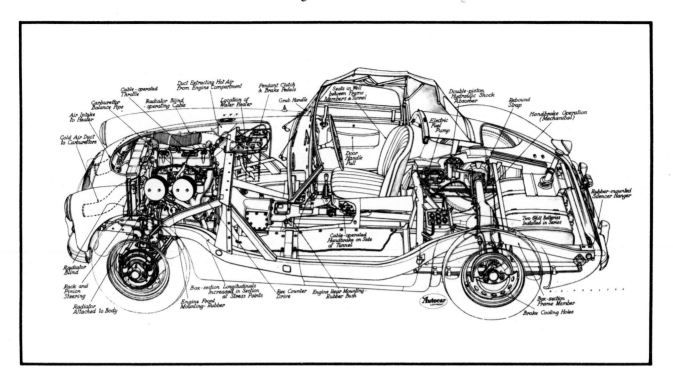

too much scoring; and the MGC with its larger front brakes is famous for squeal, which can be very difficult to eradicate. Should there be any brake judder, check the suspension joints for wear first; then check the discs and drums for accuracy. No more than 0.005 inch of run-out on the discs is permissible and they must be of constant thickness. The drums must revolve truly and you will need gauges and micrometers normally found only in a garage or dealer's to carry out these checks. Another, very rare, cause of brake judder can be loose steering arms. To avoid breakage of these cast items through overtightening of the bolts which secure them to the brake backplates, the bolts are of an exact depth. This means that with a proper washer in place they cannot be tightened too much, but they can come loose! It is worth checking these for tightness if the front brakes judder, particularly on one wheel only.

Exploded diagram of an MGA roadster.

Further clonking at the back of the car can be caused by the failure of the automatic slave wear compensators. These must be kept clean and well lubricated.

The Twin Cam brakes can present special problems. The rear discs rust badly and replacements can be difficult to obtain. So are the Dunlop master cylinders, which are out of production at the time of writing this book. The only cure if the rubbers cannot be replaced on this unit is the substitution of another similar, but non-standard, cylinder.

Handbrakes on the Twin Cam and De Luxe are not so efficient as those on the drum-braked MGs and need meticulous adjustment to ensure reasonable efficiency. The brake hoses on all cars need careful checking to see that they are not chafing on suspension components, particularly shock absorbers.

Autocar
copyright

Exploded diagram of an MGB roadster.

Pay particular attention to the brake and petrol lines where they run under the jacking point beneath the right-hand seat on the MGB and MGC. On my own car, admittedly much lower than standard, rough road driving resulted in the petrol lines and rear brake circuit wire chafing through. Next time the brakes were applied, the brake light bulbs short circuited and a spark from the bared wire next to the petrol line set fire to fuel weeping from the scraped piping. Apparently this happened when the car was travelling at speed as the fault was not discovered until a comprehensive check was carried out to see why the fuel consumption had risen. It was then that a patch of burned underseal revealed that the air passing under the car had blown out the flames! Keep a close eye on the front of the fuel tank, also, for signs of leakage. The tank can rust through where its top is fitted to the boot floor with a resultant loss of petrol adjacent to the exhaust system and rear axle. The tank can be repaired with fibreglass, but a replacement, although expensive, is desirable to minimise the chances of rupture should the car be subject to a rear-end impact. Inspect the underside of the tank for scrapes and bangs. Hard-driven cars seem to take a lot of punishment in this area . . .

Mysterious braking problems can be caused by the servo, where fitted. Losses of brake fluid accompanied by a brake pedal needing very hard application means that the servo is absorbing fluid from the braking system. This can be cured by fitting new rubber seals, but can also be caused by failure of the valve at the engine end of its vacuum pipe. Brakes which lock on can be the result of a sticking piston in the servo or dirt in the master cylinder. The engine pinking under load and curious emissions of white smoke have also been traced to faulty servo units

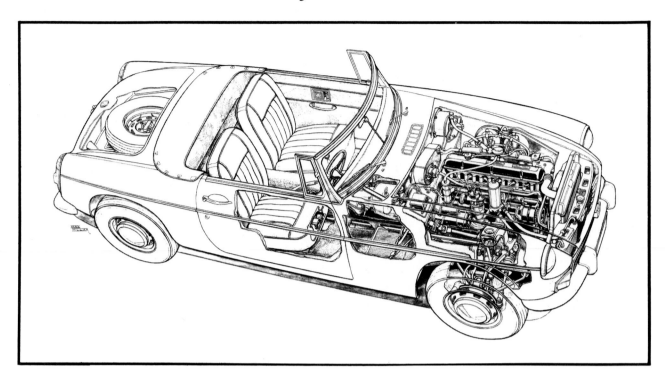

absorbing brake fluid and transferring it to the combustion chambers!

The front suspension is particularly prone to show signs of wear on old or high-mileage cars. This condition can easily be checked by jacking up the car under one of the wishbones (not under the centre of the car, as the suspension medium—coil springs or torsion bars—then absorbs wear), and rocking the road wheel, then repeating the trick on the other side. At the same time, check kingpins for wear by levering the wheel up with a bar placed under the tyre, check the steering rack for any wear and be particularly vigilant with the MGC as spares are in very short supply and expensive, because they have to be specially made. The same qualifications apply to the MGC's kingpins, and fitting new kingpins on any of these MGs needs a special reamer in any case.

Front shock absorbers on all MGAs and MGBs wear quickly and have to be replaced as a unit, which is expensive. Check by bouncing the car and seeing how well they control the rebound. Leaks in the shock absorbers are too difficult to be cured by the average home handyman. As ever, the MGC has to be different. It has telescopic front shock absorbers and they last much longer and work better than those on the other cars! They cannot be repaired however.

The rear suspension gives little trouble other than that normally associated with leaf springs and lever arm shock absorbers. The same comments and tests as those made on the front shock absorbers apply to the rear shock absorbers on all MGAs, Bs and Cs. Check the spring leaves for settling and hairline cracks and the U-bolts for tightness. Loose U-bolts can cause some alarming whipping at the back of the car.

Exploded diagram of an MGC roadster.

Wire wheels, where fitted, particularly on American-registered MGs, need careful checking for loose or broken spokes. Simply run a pen round the spokes and listen for irregular sounds and at the same time look for tell-tale signs of rust at the point where the spokes are threaded through the wheel centre. American MGs are more prone to wire wheel trouble as the pneumatic tyre changing apparatus in general use there is so powerful that it can put too much pressure on the rim. Different, and far safer, machines are marketed by firms such as Dunlop, who make the wheels. This apparatus is in general use in Europe. Nevertheless, with wire wheels it is more desirable to have tyres changed by the old-fashioned method with tyre levers. They are old-fashioned wheels after all.

Expect trouble also when tubeless tyres are used for the first time on rims that before had only tubed tyres. Dirty or superficially-rusted rims can lead to imperfect sealing and resultant flat tyres. Also make a point of jacking up the car and checking old wire wheels for true running.

Don't think that all untoward noises on an MG are expensive and difficult to repair, however. A curious boom from the exhaust in mid-range does not mean yet another replacement for the fragile system. It can simply be caused by misalignment of the bracket between the pipe and the bellhousing. And a swishing noise through the gearlever does not necessarily herald the replacement of the gearbox as on many cars. The noise frequently disappears when a new gear lever knob is fitted with a rubber insert in the hole where it fits on to the lever!

VIII

Common Problems

THERE'S no substitute for a workshop manual and a handbook for the car when it comes to keeping the MGA, B or C running. Workshop manuals are readily available, and while handbooks for some cars can still be obtained from British Leyland for many models; the MG Owners' Club can provide them for others. However, these books were written for the owners of cars in their first flush of youth or for people with considerable practical knowledge, and some specialised tools. A lot of MGA, B and C owners do not fall into these categories, so tips on how to keep the cars running and how to do some of the major, and expensive, jobs at home never go amiss. They are invariably the results of hard-won experience!

A lot of big jobs can be done with the engine still in the car; the head can be lifted, the sump dropped, the big ends split and the pistons withdrawn through the bores with the block. With the radiator off, the water pump and timing gear can be removed for attention.

However, for bigger jobs, such as removing the crankshaft, changing the clutch or attending to the gearbox internals, it is necessary to remove the engine and gearbox as a unit. It is quite a straightforward job although it can take a day each way. One of the basic things to remember is to support the front of the car about a foot higher than normally possible on axle stands.

You will need this clearance to manoeuvre the gearbox tailshaft out of the car. Should you be working in a low-roofed building where the front of the engine might meet some obstruction such as a beam, raise the back of the car to a similar height, with the front facing an uncluttered area about half as long as the car, so that the engine can be extracted on a horizontal plane. If there is not room for this in a lock-up, do it with the nose pointing into the door, then remove the car so that you can work on the engine and gearbox inside the lock-up.

The reason that removing the engine is such a long job is that so much preparation is needed. You can make the job easier by first draining the coolant at the drain taps on the radiator and block, disconnecting the battery and removing the bonnet. The radiator can be lifted out as one unit with the oil cooler and pipes if fitted, and the top and bottom water hoses (always disconnect them from the engine end, there's no need to take them off the radiator for engine removal). Disconnect the petrol lines and plug their ends to prevent either petrol spilling if the car's tail is in the air, or dirt getting in if the nose had been lifted. It's not absolutely necessary to remove the air cleaner and carburetters on the MGB and MGC and with the B and C series engines leave the inlet and exhaust manifolds in place. They make useful location points for hoisting apparatus. On the other hand, if you are using a proprietory lightweight gantry and hoist with nylon ropes, remove every possible ancilliary from the engine and gearbox before extraction (even the cylinder head) to make the units lighter and easier to manoeuvre. Mark the propeller shaft and flange before disconnection as it is surprisingly easy to get it out of balance if it is reconnected in a different position.

The engine will be easier to handle if you remove the oil filter bowl first and if the disconnected exhaust pipe is tied up out of the way. Tuck all the other loose ends out of harm's way, too, taking special care with the water gauge's sensor tube. Once broken, you are almost certain to need a new combined oil and water temperature gauge, tubes and sensor as there are very few people who can repair them.

With a jack, stands or hoist, you need to take the engine's weight before removing the engine mounts and don't forget the earth strap. Make sure you reconnect it also when the engine is returned to the car, or the engine will earth through something else, which could lead to very dangerous fireworks when you try to start the car!

After you have removed the odds and ends from the gearbox end, the unit can be removed, but you will find that the gearbox is a close fit in the transmission tunnel, so you must expect to spend some time freeing it. If you like, you can remove the gearbox extension first; this will give you more room for manoeuvre.

Once you have removed the engine and gearbox for any reason, always examine the clutch on manual models. MGA, B and C engines and gearboxes are pretty reliable units and it might be years before you have to repeat the job: so there is little point in returning the unit with wear on the clutch linings which would mean that everything has to come out again to attend to them. Never try to economise on the flywheel either. If a slipping clutch does not receive immediate attention, the flywheel will probably be scored, which means that it must be replaced or new clutch linings will last no more than a couple of thousand miles. You can have the flywheel skimmed, but this makes the clutch action sharper and there is always the risk of hot spots being left by the machining, which can reduce the clutch life to no more than a few thousand miles. For this reason, lightened flywheels must be checked meticulously.

There are no short cuts with major engine work, but there is always the decision whether to buy a guaranteed unit or to rebuild the existing engine. There are advantages in taking either course. Most exchange engines, including those of the manufacturers, carry a warranty. However, it can be cheaper to carry out a bottom overhaul even if the top has been overhauled with the engine in place only recently; it is possible to improve on any exchange unit by having existing components balanced before re-assembly. Balancing ensures a much sweeter-running engine which will last even longer than a normal unit.

Exchange gearboxes fall into similar categories; guaranteed units cost more than simply repairing the worn synchromesh on early gearboxes, for instance. Gearbox overhauls are usually beyond the scope of all but the most skilled amateurs, but it takes only about six hours to strip and overhaul a box with worn synchromesh on second gear, which even allowing for the cost of parts, is a considerable saving on the price of an exchange unit. Overdrives should always be exchanged as a unit, because they are very specialised devices.

Much corrective work on overdrives can be carried out without removing the engine and gearbox. The amount of oil, or type of lubricant, can be critical with an overdrive. They won't work properly, if at all, if there is insufficient oil or additives, such as STP (excellent in the engine) have been used. If the overdrive is quick to engage but slow to disengage, or it slips out, particularly on bumps or corners, suspect a low oil level. If it suddenly ceases to function, particularly with the popular Triumph or late model MGB gear-level switch, the most likely cause is electrical. With the gearlever switch, there is sometimes a tendency for the wiring terminals inside the gearlever cap to touch, blowing the fuse covering the overdrive. This can also account for a hot top to the gearlever!

The earlier dashboard switch gives little trouble other than rare occasions when the wires fall off. Therefore, with these switches, any electrical fault is likely to be elsewhere and it can usually be identified by sudden lack of overdrive. To check the electrics on the gearbox, remove the tunnel cover, engage top gear, switch on the ignition and the overdrive: you should hear a click from its solenoid. If it doesn't click, make sure the single wire to the solenoid is not broken and that it is attached to a switch at the front of the gearbox (you can see this from inside the car). Check that this switch is tight, but do not over-tighten because its body is made of alloy.

If you find that wriggling the lever in third or fourth gear position produces an occasional click, the cause is probably a loose switch. Should you still be unable to operate your solenoid, remove it for examination. Connect its wire to a battery pole, put a nail in the end of the solenoid and touch the casing on the other battery pole: the nail should pop out! If it doesn't, you'll probably need a new solenoid, but if it didn't click when it was on the car, suspect swarf on its plunger inside. Dismantle the solenoid and clean everything meticulously.

Should the solenoid be burned out, its wiring has probably been chafed somewhere, which means that you must replace that as well as the solenoid. If everything else fails, get the overdrive pressure tested before you remove everything from the car, then try one more test: the fault could be a sticking sliding member inside the overdrive which can sometimes be cured by letting in the clutch with a bang at about 40 mph on the over-run. This measure should only be used with due regard to other traffic, however.

Overheating is another common ailment with the MGA, B and C that is easily cured by the home mechanic. The most common cause is a faulty thermostat and the most common problem with the thermostat is getting it out! There are two possible reasons for this difficulty: either jointing compound has been used to seal the water outlet covering the thermostat, in place or there has been corrosion between the housing and the studs. In the first case, you should try tapping the elbow gently upwards with a rawhide mallet or a rubber hammer; for corrosion, try applying copious quantities of penetrating oil as well.

It may be necessary to cut away the elbow and fit another. In this case, use new studs and smear them well with grease on re-assembly, avoid jointing compound like the plague and rely on the thermostat housing gasket.

Another common cause of overheating, on the V8, is failure of the electric cooling fans: this is frequently traceable to the switch (by-pass it until you can get another) or sometimes, in damp weather, to bad connections including the fuse box contacts.

Fan belts sometimes break, too; pieces can wrap round the pulleys with serious results and it is very easy to blow a head gasket with the subsequent overheating. The gaskets are most likely to blow between cylinders three and four on the B series engine: always watch compression readings here with special vigilance.

Burnt exhaust valves can also cause overheating and manifest themselves in lack of power, lumpy running and low compression readings. Don't drive a car long in this state, it is quite easy to crack the cylinder head. Broken piston rings, especially on high-compression engines, can have a similar effect. Make sure that the cylinder head bolts are tightened to exactly the right torque after the head has been off: if they are not tight enough you can blow a gasket and overheat; if they are too tight the studs can pull out.

Poor water circulation can be caused by a blocked radiator core or worn water pump, and results in overheating; the water pump shrieks when it is on the way out. Never drive the car far in this condition as the unfortunate pump can let fly with disastrous results. Low oil pressure can lead to serious problems with bearings and show up as well in overheating, but may not always be caused by anything more serious than a faulty oil pressure relief valve spring. One of the most likely reasons for the engine rattling between 1000 rpm and 2000 on the way up, is that the big ends are on the way out; if the rattle is on the way down between 2000 rpm and 1000, it is likely to be caused by the little ends.

Battered and choked exhaust systems can also cause overheating and valve trouble, and the exhaust system on the MGB, particularly on the chrome-fronted models, has a very low point under the seats. Keep a careful check on this vulnerable spot, particularly with old cars on which the springs might have settled. If your daily journey involves constant abuse for this point of the exhaust system (the office car park ramp is a favourite obstacle), don't worry too much. Just replace the middle box with a piece of straight pipe. It doesn't make much difference to the exhaust note and gives a lot more clearance. You can save yourself a good deal of money also by replacing only the worn and rusty parts of an MG's exhaust system rather than all of it. They don't last long anyway (except on the V8, which seems to be made from better material) so any saving here is noticeable. Unless you can afford one of the top-quality stainless steel systems, just buy pattern silencers or a piece of pipe to cover whatever hole the exhaust gases are blowing through.

Handbrake cables are a perennial source of trouble on the MGA, B and C. The linkages are prone to wear to such an extent that you cannot take up all the slack by adjustment at the lever.

Bad vibrations are often the source of great mysteries on MGs. If you can localise the vibrations to any particular corner, they are probably caused by nothing more serious than a wheel out of balance. Some tyres are much more difficult to balance than others and sometimes their balance changes as they wear. A strong vibration that affects the whole car can be caused by the propeller shaft being out of balance. Carelessly-daubed underseal is a common cause of this complaint.

A shrill shrieking from the V8 on acceleration with vibration through the steering wheel is caused by worn engine mountings allowing the torque to force the exhaust manifold onto the steering column. These cast manifolds have frequently given problems with cracking, and can be very difficult to locate. They also cost a lot, so there is a good case for having a bespoke extractor manifold made to replace them. Vibrations through the brake pedal can be caused by disc run-out and calls for replacement of the discs.

One of the most annoying noises is a grating squeak when the steering wheel is turned, and most people automatically suspect the column's top bearing. Too often the squeak is caused by the horn contact on cars with a central horn button which can be cured by adjusting the contact to the best angle for operation and smearing it with Vaseline.

Knocks and rattles from the front or back or just one corner are commonly caused by worn suspension parts, particularly the shock absorbers. Always check the bolts securing lever arm shock absorbers and the levers for tightness on their splines before replacement. Low-speed clonking in the front suspension of MGAs and MGBs is often mistaken for kingpin wear, according to the MG Owners' Club's excellent *Yearbook*. It points out that 'there is a spring which collects stones, bits of tar, etc. When the suspension goes down, the stone flicks out, Clonk! Check your suspension and clear these gremlins out. The noise may well be cured. Also check the rubbers at the point where the wishbone is pivoted on the cross member.

The low and exposed fuel pump on the MGA, B and C is often the cause of breakdowns. A sharp tap with something like a screwdriver handle can get it going again, although sometimes only for a short time. If it needs a tap frequently, to get you home, remove the right-hand battery cover and hit its casing with the screwdriver or jack handle while in motion as the fuel pump's clicking stops and the car hesitates. It helps to have a co-operative passenger for this task! Loose connections can also cause intermittent fuel pump trouble, so check these at the same time. The usual cause of fuel pump failure apart from old age is lack of maintenance: the unit should be kept clean and the points should receive attention every 6000 miles.

The wrong sort of attention can be a cause for more expensive trouble with wire wheels. When fitting a wheel it is vital that the hub nut is tightened when the wheel is off the ground. Over-enthusiastic hammering can lead to the wheel centre belling out as its conical mating faces are forced into the hub. Then the heavy-handed hammerer hits the wheel even harder and makes the problem worse till everything is ruined. If this violent operation is carried out with the wheel on the ground, the tension of some of the spokes can be affected with subsequent trouble all round the wheel.

The reason for having such a heavy hammer with wire-wheeled cars is to loosen the hub nuts, which are automatically tightened as the car is driven away because of the way in which the threads are arranged. However, these right- and left-handed threads assume that the car is to be driven forwards immediately the wheel is refitted. Don't reverse away too quickly from the scene of your wheel change or you might loosen the wheels enough to damage the splines!

IX

The MGA, B and C Abroad

THE United States has always tended to take the lion's share of MG sports car production since the war, particularly that of open cars; other export markets, chiefly in Europe, Australia, New Zealand and South Africa, have also favoured the open car. Following British Leyland's aggressive marketing policy with the hard top Triumph TR7, there has been little choice for buyers; the MGB GT having been dropped in America in 1975 and Europe in 1976. The curtailment of GT exports has done little harm to the MGB, however: it still continues to outsell the TR7 at the time of writing, doubtless because it is an open car.

There's more to a mystique than that, however: so why have the Americans, in particular, been so loyal to the MG for so long? Long-time MG enthusiast John Christy described it very well in *Motor Trend*:

'From 1923 to the present, the products that have rolled out from the doors of the old Morris Garages and later, Abingdon-on-Thames, have been alternatively praised and damned, eulogised and slandered, under and over-rated—often with good reason on either account. In all the years during which MGs have been built it is likely that ninety-nine out of a hundred of them have been driven harder and with more enthusiasm than the builders ever thought possible. Such treatment engenders praise for the cars that can seemingly absorb the punishment and criticism because the treatment inevitably results in things falling off. But MGs have always been that way and remain so to this day.

'The comment one hears about MGs in many ways recalls those made by US Navy people concerning British wartime ships: often uncomfortable, wet, bluff and straightforward almost to the point of crudity—but they got the job done. So it is with the MG: blunt, strong and, by today's standards of sophistication, almost crude, they accomplish their purpose in a manner both surprising and admirable. Where other, more complicated cars accommodate themselves to the road, the MG fights back gamely and tenaciously—and usually wins . . .

'In an MG, a freeway is one long interminable, boring drag strip without end. This part (of a test course) left us with the feeling that a warning

Right: Thomas Studer lives for his rare left-hand-drive MGB GT V8, visiting MG Car Club meetings in Britain as often as possible from his home in Switzerland.

Below: Steve Glochowsky's 1973 harvest gold MGB roadster fitted with an American fibreglass hard top.

buzzer should sound in an MG, after one continuous run of fifty miles on a freeway at which point you have five minutes to find an offramp and some sort of thoroughfare with turns and speed variations. If ignored—BOOM!—you're vapourised and the car goes off looking for someone more appreciative.

'What MGs are all about are the mountains and the tighter, twistier the road and the higher the altitude, to about 7000 ft, the better. From about 3000 ft up the MG comes into its own and doesn't begin to suffer altitude bronchitis like ordinary cars until the 7000 ft level is reached. There is some loss of power, but very little compared to your average V8 family sedan . . . where more prosaic machinery is huffing for breath and tip-toeing around, the MG is up on the step and motoring.

'The GT is, of course, at home anywhere and is handy in the hill country, but the roadsters really come into their own in that milieu, especially at night with the hood down. If you've been used to riding around in cars with solid roofs, you suddenly discover there's a whole big world out there. You not only see it and hear it, you smell it, and in that sort of country, the sort of country where the MG is most at home, the air is so clean it stings your nose. And you know without looking that the farmer over there is growing corn and the house on the hill has a hardwood fire going on the hearth. It's an experience that is getting increasingly harder to find these days.'

Christy wrote those words in 1972 when there were other open sports cars on the road and the great American convertible was not yet dead: in its last years the MGB has had few competitors and it is easy to see why it is so beloved of hair-in-the-air Americans.

There was more competition when the MGA was introduced in 1955, but it mattered little. MG sports cars had established a great reputation with the preceding T series and the MGA sold in large quantities in America, and other export markets, for the same reasons as the MGB does today. It is a great, durable, fun car. Sales of the 1500 cc MGA totalled 48,431 in America against 5722 in other export markets and only 2687 in the United Kingdom; the equivalent figures for the Twin Cam were 1035, 583 and 360; for the 1600, 25,219, 2658 and 2172 and for the 1600 Mk II, 6468, 1431 and 596.

Many of these MGAs were used as road cars during the week and for racing at weekends. It also became traditional for at least one of the works cars that had been raced at Sebring to be sold in America to help defray the cost of the trip. So it came as a great thrill for one of those wandering Australian MG enthusiasts, Ian Prior, from South Blackburn, Victoria, to discover an ex-works car in need of loving care and attention in Florida. He wrote in the North American MGA Register's newsletter:

'It was like one of the TC-in-a-barn stories which you hear about but which never actually happens to you. Well this time it did. Pam and I were travelling around the USA, enjoying the fabulous scenery and meeting many very hospitable Americans afflicted with that MG bug, when Art Floyd, our genial host in Titusville, Florida, took us to see a Y special he was building. Just out of interest, he showed us what appeared to be a rather battered and rusty MGA Twin Cam coupé in the yard of a body shop next door. The penny dropped as Art explained that this was no ordinary coupé, but in fact an MG works-entered Sebring car. You can imagine all the mental arithmetic and scheming going on in my mind while I inspected the car. Push-rod motor, Twin Cam chassis, five-inch Smiths chronomatic tacho, adjustable shocks, right-hand drive, extra cooling ducts, hole for the roof light, lightened here and there, etc.

'Is it for sale? Maybe, was the reply, but sanity prevailed—what with three Ts at home and a very limited budget to complete another eleven months of travelling. After all, we had only just started, and what treasures might we find in England? Unbeknown to me, Pam was also scheming, but said nothing. Thinking much, but saying little, we ventured on to California where we met up with MG folk from the Los Angeles club. We told them about the Sebring car, and it was their enthusiasm which prompted us to make the decision to buy it.

'It is one thing to buy a car, and yet another to get it home. After completing our circum-navigation of the US—some 18,000 miles in 100 days, we arrived back in Titusville, Florida, and began our inquiries into the freight business. The closest port with services to Melbourne was Charleston, North Carolina, 400 miles to the north. It was quite a simple matter to hire a 30 ft truck for the journey, but it was with great difficulty that we hoisted our most prized souvenir into the back. We only had to contend with one road block on the way . . .

'My research into the car's complete specification and history so far shows that GHD 100148 is an ex-works MGA coupé which competed with great success in the 1961 Sebring 12-hour race. One of two, especially built at Abingdon in late 1960, it came first in its class for GT cars up to 1600 cc, and fourteenth overall, completing 175 laps of the 5.2 mile course. Carrying number forty-four, the car was driven by two Americans, James Parkinson and Jack Flaherty. The sister car, number forty-three, driven by Peter Riley and John Whitmore, completed 173 laps, finishing sixteenth overall and second in class . . .

'After the race, the team cars were offered for sale by a local MG dealer. GHD 100148 was purchased by Richard Robson, who campaigned it in sports car racing for the following few years until it became uncompetitive. It was then registered for road use in February 1966 and used until 1969 when it was crashed by Robson's girlfriend. During this period it had been kept in good condition and was resprayed just before the crash. I have been told that it "went like the clappers" doing 50 mph in first, and 75 in second. With only 50,000 miles on the clock, the car was left out in the weather, slowly deteriorating while a buyer was sought. Finally, in 1974, a friend of Robson, Don Loftus, purchased the car for $100 but it remained out in the weather, slowly rusting away until we rescued it from certain death.

'In its present condition, the car needs a full rebuild as the front is badly knocked in and the demon rust has removed the sills and door pillar assemblies, leaving the doors hanging on for grim death. Fortunately, most of the original bits and pieces came with the vehicle, which makes it a feasible project to restore to its original 1961 race condition. Hopefully it will be complete by the National Meeting in Easter 1980.'

Today, the MGA has been elevated to the status of an antique, many being restored with the sort of enthusiasm shown by Prior. MGBs still tend to be considered as everyday sports cars, though. Fewer have been used as weekend racers, because of the increasing specialisation in circuit racing. They are popular cars for off-road club events in America, though, with many enthusiasts using them for autocrosses and gymkhanas.

The vast majority of MGBs exported to America (the total is expected to pass 340,000 in 1979) have been bought by everyday users, not necessarily interested in motoring clubs. A far higher proportion of these enthusiasts are to be found among the home buyers (100,000 forecast by the end of 1979) and people in other export markets (40,000 in the same period). It was fascinating, therefore, to read

From the left: American MGB Association publicity director Steve Glochowsky, with co-chairmen John Giannasca and Rick Horan. And the girl? Miss MGB at the 1978 Chicago Auto Show.

the reasons in a *Road & Track* survey of 1968 as to why the average American bought an MGB. More than half gave their primary reason as styling, with handling, price and reliability roughly equal in terms of precedence. GT owners, as expected, said that they bought their cars because they were looking for a 'sports car with GT comfort.' These sales accounted for roughly one in seven of the MGBs sold in America, emphasising the overwhelming popularity of the open car. Roughly one in three MGBs exported to other countries were GTs, however, but nearly half of the total number of MGBs sold in Britain were GTs. Weather must have something to do with that.

Road & Track then tried to analyse the incredible MG tradition and concluded: 'Previous ownership, not anticipated as a frequent reason for buying a popular sports car, was given by nine per cent of the owners—reflecting that MG is, after all, the pioneer in the American sports car market. The final—and perhaps the most telling—question is "Would you buy another of the same make?" Seventy per cent said that they would; nineteen per cent said absolutely not, eleven per cent weren't sure. Half of those who "will not" intend to go to more sophisticated and expensive cars, like Porsches, stating that they are satisfied with their Bs as far as they go. Bad service, outdated engineering and unreliability were quoted by those not intending to buy MGs again.'

Such reports were treated with great respect by British Leyland and several years later John Thornley told me that great efforts had been made to improve service, which had improved reliability in its wake. The all-synchromesh gearbox had not had time to make an impact on the readers surveyed by *Road & Track* in 1968, and would have done a lot to alleviate the complaints about outdated engineering. That, and the way the MGB's rivals have fallen by the wayside have contributed to the model's incredibly consistent sales record in America. The younger generation appear to be just as likely to buy another as their elders have been, as Steve Glochowsky, publicity director of the American MGB Association, told me:

'As long ago as it was, I can still remember that white MGA I saw when I was four years old. This was the first MG I had ever seen. At that early age, I knew I wanted to own an MG.

'Just less than twenty years later, I fulfilled that dream. While MG was celebrating its fiftieth anniversary, I decided that it was time to go ahead and buy a sports car, after all those years of desire. But what I read in the automotive press made me take a good hard look at the new 1975 model, which had just undergone major modification resulting in decreased handling and performance.

'After driving a 1975 MGB, I decided to look at used MGBs. Looking at used cars was something I thought I would never get into. But after seeing a dozen or so MGBs, I bought a harvest gold 1973 roadster. It was a peppy car that handled nice and tight, and its appearance was in good order.

'Shortly after purchasing this car, the American MGB Association came into life. This was just what I was looking for. The club had just started, and

Left: A typical South African club scene with the Twin Cam of Peter and Dot Jack in good company at the second National South African gathering in 1976.

Below: The MGA Type Owners' Club of Holland are among the model's keenest supporters. This pristine example was owned by their chairman and secretary, Bram Hoogendijk.

Above left : The Ewing answer to all those who say you can't pack much into an MGA.

Above right : In Norway in the shadow of Mount Bispen.

Right : Their MGA, 'Midgy' visits its ancestral home at Abingdon. Their daughter Jane was by then ten days old and occupying a carrycot on wheels.

Norman Ewing, chairman of the Johannesburg centre of the MG Car Club, is one of the marque's keenest supporters. In 1970, he set off from South Africa for the Arctic Circle with his wife, Pat, then five months' pregnant, in his MGA roadster. They planned that their child should be born in England and took everything they needed with them: a tent, two sleeping bags, a stove, lighting, sufficient clothing to appear well dressed for a two-week trip by sea, two spare wheels, tools, fifty spools of film, baby clothes and so on. Incredibly, they managed to pack it all into the hard top roadster except for the spare wheel, which was carried on the boot lid. Norman had just spent two and a half years rebuilding the car.

Their daughter Jane was born in Derby and during their year-long trip to Europe, they covered 28,000 miles and added a pushchair to their luggage. That was carried on the bootlid with the second spare wheel, and Norman claims to have been the only MG driver to have lapped the Nurburgring with a wife, child and pushchair! The European trip took in countries as far away from South Africa as Norway before the Ewings returned. Norman is still driving the same car today, with 161,000 miles on the clock, but now Pat has her own MGA coupé. This immaculate Old English White car was formerly owned by George Tuck, MG's publicity manager from 1929–39. His car was maintained at the factory from new in 1960 until he sold it to the Ewings in 1974. With 128,000 miles behind it, it still goes 'incredibly quickly,' says Norman, whose other MGs include a ZB saloon and a TF.

Left: The Ewings far from home on the Swiss border near Mount Blanc.

Below: Susan Tuck with the ex-George Tuck coupé before it was sold to Pat Ewing.

New Zealand MG enthusiasts lead a very active sporting life. Here John Durry puts his immaculate MGB through its paces at an MG Car Club gymkhana.

I was proud to belong to such a group of enthusiasts, plus getting in at the beginning and getting a low membership number. Later, of course, I was to become the club's publicity director on both local and national levels, becoming addictively active in the AMGBA.

'When MGB ownership was a reality, I plunged into learning more and more about my car. Initially, I learned through books and magazine articles. When the AMGBA came about, my fellow members, and some mechanics I did not know of previously, taught me even more about my car. This is most important, as you never stop picking things up when you are constantly getting together with fellow enthusiasts.

'Through the AMGBA, my car was involved in rallies, concours events, tours and gymkhanas. On a less formal level, there is many a time when a few members will just impulsively get together, and just take the cars for a ride somewhere. If one of the cars had a CB radio in it, something like "You MGs are lookin' good" would undoubtedly be heard. As much as I enjoy an MGB, it is all the more enjoyable to have other MGBs and their drivers in your company!

'Nineteen seventy-eight was a banner year for the AMGBA. Two major events were held that year. Just before those events, though, disaster struck me. While on my way home from an AMGBA Chicago chapter meeting, my car was demolished in an accident. If I had been sitting in the car at the time, I would not be here today, so it could have been worse for me. But there I was, planning two major AMGBA events, and I was without an MGB. Nevertheless, the events went on, and I was fortunate enough to have MGBs at my disposal.

'As soon as I had finished those events, my enthusiasm drove me to search for another MGB. I was rather discouraged at having all my efforts in restoring the 1973 car ruined by an incompetent driver, so I ordered a new 1979 MGB, just the way I wanted it. However overdrives are hard to come by, here in the colonies, these days. The dealer, at the time of writing, still has not received the car. My fellow members, in the meantime, were searching for good used MGBs for me.

'I'd look at them and walk away, as I didn't want to go through another restoration. But then I ran across a low-mileage, chrome-bumpered, dual SU carburetted 1974 roadster. It was one of the last US specification cars to be built that way, in beautiful teal blue with autumn leaf interior. This car did not need much work. Suddenly, my patience had been restored. In fact, this MGB was even nicer than my first one. Today, this car is my pride and joy. For the past three months, I have found myself pampering the car even more than I did my '73! Like a new car, everything is in excellent working order, but this car offers the performance and handling I had been accustomed to in my '73.

'Being without an MGB for a while makes you appreciate the car even more. The car's whole personality is unmatched by any other car. Just look at the car and it says "drive me." Even when you don't want to drive the car, it wants to go. Here in Chicago, we get some dreadful winter weather. But after a couple of miles, the heater comes on real strong. With the fibre glass hardtop on the car, and the heater going well, its downright comfortable in there, despite the elements outside.

'In the summer, when we get the other side of the coin, top-down cruising puts me in a state of ecstasy. This top-down joy is why I have never bought a GT. I like to look at them, but no matter how hard you try, you just can't get that top down! And as far as the roadster goes, I like its lines even better than the GT's pretty form. But, one day, I hope to own a GT, as well as my roadster.

'I don't know what I would do without MGBs, and I am lucky enough to have hundreds of friends who would say the same thing. The car, and the club, have both provided me with the ultimate joys of motoring.'

So there you have it, the MGB is rapidly moving into a similar status as that enjoyed by the MGA, a ready-made classic and a way of life. Steve Thompson summed it all up with a magnificent tribute to the MGB in *Car and Driver* in 1978. He wrote:

'The MGB is the Morgan of the Seventies. Wedging yourself behind the wheel opens mental doors to rooms you'd almost forgotten, behind which lie surreal images of flashing wire wheels, skinny tyres, cloudless days enjoyed in wide-open cockpits and hoarse, raspy exhaust notes. The images, you find, persist, and they're what have driven men to spend long hours in devices other people might consider mere transportation. That's why MG still sells a basically

One of the rarest MGs of all, the 1600 Mark II De Luxe, affectionately called Albatross by its owners, Len and Ruth Renkenberger, editor and secretary of the North American MGA Register. Outwardly it appears as any other Mark II MGA other than for its Twin Cam wheels. The chassis is substantially the same as that of a Twin Cam except for seat belt anchorages.

unaltered product after fifteen years, and is also why, in an era of wistful imaginings, that product is selling better than ever.

'Sports-car trendies hate the car and all it stands for. Britain disgraced. Stone-age technology. A dismantled society, devoid of a future in a Giugiaro-shaped world. Little, excruciatingly peculiar curvy convertibles with breathless ancient engines and creaky suspensions have no place in any wedge-shaped, rear-engine, independently-suspended scenario they can imagine.

'For pretty much the same reasons, even British car freaks are embarrassed by the dowager MGB. Like a senile old grandmother who was once the sweetheart of the promenade, she is tolerated, even amusingly pointed out to friends, but she smells too much of rosewater and denture paste to get too close.

'The trendies and Anglophiles are both wrong. The new MGB is as fun a car as it was back in 1963, when it was big news to a world used to drafty tops, side curtains and bare interiors. Only now, because it has survived the purges of the market, it stands almost alone as an open-air sports car.

'Yes, it is too high. Yes, it is too narrow and ugly. Yes, it still has an awful top, and yes, yes, it still goes slow. But it also makes any drive down any two-lane country road a relaxing, peaceful delight. Who cares if Volkswagens outcorner it?

'A lot of the many people who buy new MGBs have reverted to the ways of old hot rodders in circumventing the car's emissions and safety-related millstones, and with a modest-to-healthy investment, the car can be given positively remarkable sparkle. Even with its solid rear axle, complicated windjammer top and weird rubber nose, it has, after all, survived many other "better" sports cars.

'There is a reason for that, and you can see it in the eyes of anyone you take along for a drive on a sunny afternoon. Because the MGB is inexpensive, relatively unassuming, and firmly established as a real sports car in the minds of millions who don't even know why, it makes for not only a lot of fun, but a superb undergraduate course in sports car-think. Lack of speed, cornering grace and all, I hope it lasts another fifteen years.'

What a pity . . .

X

The Men Behind the MGA, B and C

CREDIT for the extraordinary success of the MGA and MGB must go to two men, John Thornley and Syd Enever, who with a lot of help from a handful of friends managed to achieve so much. Both Thornley and Enever spent virtually all their working lives with MGs. Enever even pre-dated them, joining Morris Garages straight from school in Oxford as an apprentice in 1920. By the time Thornley joined as a junior executive in 1930 after three years as an accountant in London, Morris Garages had spawned the MG car company, and was producing sporting machines at Abingdon. Their leader was Cecil Kimber, the general manager of Morris Garages whose influence could be seen in every MG made up to the MGA. Enever progressed through MG's experimental department to specialise in designing record-breaking cars, notably Goldie Gardner's famous pre-war EX135. Thornley started off running the MG Car Club and carried on as service manager before becoming a Lieutenant Colonel in the Royal Army Ordnance Corps. He rejoined the company in 1946 to become service manager again, and successively sales and service manager and assistant general manager until he was appointed general manager in 1952 soon after the MGA story started.

Immediately after the war, when MG was still part of the Nuffield Organisation, H. A. Ryder was the director in charge of Abingdon. He followed the official line of strong disapproval of racing, which had been curtailed in 1935. To men such as Ryder and Nuffield, racing was a waste of money. But it was the lifeblood of others, such as Enever and Thornley; they often talked of the cars they would like to build and so needed little encouragement to give what 'under-the-counter' help they could to people racing MGs. Enever and Reg 'Jacko' Jackson, MG's pre-war racing chief (then in quality control), managed, for instance, to give a bit of surreptitious spare-time help to Gardner, with the post-war record-breaker, EX135.

When S. V. Smith took over from Ryder, this love of competition could come out into the open a little more, because he was not so rigidly against racing. It was most evident when *Autosport* photographer George Phillips, who had raced a special based on the T series—Abingdon's current production sports car—landed himself an entry at Le Mans in 1951. Naturally he approached Abingdon and asked if they could build him a special car worthy of the great race. There wasn't the time, nor the money to build a completely new car, but Enever seized the chance to try out some of his ideas.

Using Gardner's EX135 body shape as a basis, he sketched out a streamlined body to replace the T series car's chief handicap, it's square-rigged body which limited speed.

Harry Herring, one of MG's craftsmen in the body shop, turned Enever's design into the reality of a quarter-scale model which was tested in the Armstrong-Whitworth windtunnel. This was normally reserved for planes, but Armstrongs were good friends of Enever from war-time days. This project was code-named EX172 and found a measure of approval from Smith and MG's managing director of the day, Jack Tatlow. This car succumbed to mechanical trouble in the race, but not before it had shown that it could lap faster than any other MG special. Enever knew that with some modification—such as sitting the driver and passenger much lower—he had the basis of a wonderful new MG to replace the T series. He was a man who worked all hours and rarely stopped thinking of his cars of the future. It was in the back room of his home in Oxford that he sketched the new chassis frame that was to be at the heart of the MGA.

Everybody at Abingdon was delighted with it and Thornley, who, by then was in charge, made haste with the design to show his new boss, Leonard Lord of BMC. Austin and the Nuffield Organisation had been merged in 1952. It was then that big company politics proved troublesome. Lord recognised the need for a new sports car to replace the ageing T series, but regretted to inform Thornley that he was three days too late. BMC could introduce only one new sports car at present, and he had already decided to go ahead with the Healey 100 designed by one of MG's competitors, Donald Healey. Lord's decision was influenced by the fact that the new car, to be called the Austin-Healey 100, would use a quantity of redundant Austin power trains and that the MG T series was still selling well despite its antiquity.

The disappointment at Abingdon was almost as intense as when Lord—as Nuffield's right-hand man before the war—had curtailed racing. However they had an unparalleled reputation for getting on with the job without grumbling and gave the TD a facelift to prolong its life as the TF. Development chief Alec Hounslow and works manager Cecil Cousins, a dominant figure who had been MG's first employee, were instrumental in this. Enever consoled himself with designing yet another record car, EX179, using a chassis he had put aside at the time he was developing EX175. It was built along the same lines as EX135 except that it used a prototype MGA chassis and blown TF engine.

Meanwhile BMC were developing their B series engine and Lord, who believed firmly in the principle of promoting competition within his ranks, got the Morris (or Nuffield) and Austin designers to produce a twin cam head for it. The version designed by Gerald Palmer at Cowley and developed by Morris Engines at Courthouse Green in Coventry, was more closely related to the standard Austin B series engine, so it eventually gained BMC acceptance over the rival Austin twin cam.

Enever's department were working on these engines when Thornley at last gained Lord's approval for the MGA in 1954. The T series sales were wilting in the face of opposition from the Austin-Healey and Triumph's rival, the equally-modern TR2.

Soon after, the two twin cam engines were tested in the MGA prototypes for future use (see chapter four) and it was decided to fit the pushrod B series engine and gearbox to the production car rather than the Morris-based XPEG engines of the TF and EX175 prototype. Thus Thornley got his car and Lord found another home for his Austin mechanical components.

At this time, William Lyons, at Jaguar, was capitalising on his successes in sports car racing and Lord decided to get in on the act. Most of the remaining racing men in BMC were still working at Abingdon, so he decided that a competition department should be set up there. The Healey Motor Company had remained a separate entity from BMC, the Austin-Healey being produced by Austins on a royalty basis, although the Healey family continued to do development work.

The well-respected Marcus Chambers was hired to run the BMC competitions side from Abingdon. This involved the potential use of all cars produced within the group. Enever and Hounslow gave assistance, but were left free to deal with MG production problems and their very specialised and highly-successful record breaking cars. They really were the best at this game, although Donald Healey enjoyed some success.

Enever's next great project in the record-breaking field was EX181, another superbly-streamlined car using the Morris prototype twin cam engine in blown form. It achieved great success in 1957 and 1959.

Meanwhile the tragedies that hit sports car racing in 1955 (see chapter four) put Lord and BMC off circuit racing and Chambers concentrated on rallying. The MGA soon proved to be rather underpowered in pushrod form as the competition in international rallies became more intense. At that time, in 1956, Austin-Healey production was moved from Austin's works at Longbridge to Abingdon, and the little Berkshire factory became the biggest in the world specialising in sports cars.

These years, from 1952 when BMC took over, to 1957, were the most dramatic for Abingdon, according to Thornley. 'Up to 1952, Abingdon produced 250 vehicles a week all-out. By 1956, it was producing 1300 from very much the same floor space. When we were producing 250 T types a week, I suppose we possibly employed 550 to 600 people all up, of which, perhaps, 200 were the irreducible minimum of admin. That meant that you had around 400 work people and foremen. By the time we were building 1300 vehicles a week, we had 1300 employees and made some play of "one vehicle per person per week: match that anybody else if you can." But, of course, we bought the vehicle in such enormous chunks that it wasn't very highly labour intensive.'

This was also a period of intense change at Abingdon as 'producing the car in large chunks'—essentially assembling power trains into near-complete body-shells—left them more exposed to enforced switches of production than when they virtually hand-built cars such as the T series.

'On the design side, we did everything first and presented it as a *fait accompli*,' said Thornley. 'Why I didn't get kicked all the way from here to

The men who thought in octagons: Thornley and Enever with their MGA.

Birmingham and back, I cannot imagine, but I did this constantly.

'There were major confrontations as a result, but no recriminations for having done so. By the time it was done they were always very delighted.

'The major confrontations were concerned with threats to close the plant down and shift production elsewhere. I fought a number of battles on these lines.

'On record breaking, we took it to the point where it would have been foolish to cancel and step back, and I then went forward and said I want £5000 to go to Utah and that sort of thing. We did a lot of skating on thin ice one way or another. What an exciting life it was!'

The MGA and MGB were designed as a team effort with Thornley making suggestions and his trusted lieutenants, such as Cousins and Enever, combining their own ideas with his. Thornley said:

'There were perhaps a dozen of us at admin level, and probably three dozen of artisan level—highly-skilled chaps—who were the nucleus of the MG Car Company. I never had to give them instructions, I just suggested that something might be done. It was marvellous, an almost unbelievable spirit prevailed amongst that lot. It was something that nobody understands today. It was implicit trust all round.'

In this way the MGA Twin Cam was born as a *fait accompli* with Thornley encouraging private entrants to race it when Chambers became more enamoured with Austin-Healeys; and when Thornley was wondering how to follow up the MGA, Enever had only to look to his EX181 record breaker for inspiration, knowing that his boss would see that his efforts received recognition. Enever worked in a similar way to Thornley, when it came to the subtle handling of staff. In moments of inspiration, he would rough out what he wanted and pass on the sketches to his draughtsmen and designers. They, in turn, looked at the problem in great detail. Wooden models were made of body shapes, for instance, from which further 'pretty pictures,' as Enever called them, were drawn up. After consultation with Thornley, these efforts were submitted to Lord for his comments. Sometimes the process was repeated involving outside specialists, such as Italian styling firms or Harry Weslake the great cylinder head expert. But all the time, Enever—and indirectly Thornley—kept control of design work on the MGA and MGB.

Enever was particularly keen on ensuring that his new sports car had a really rigid bodyshell. He went to great lengths over this with the MGB and it was here that Thornley proved to be so good at backing him up. One of Thornley's main problems was to produce the car at the right price, and it seemed that the initial cost of tooling up for the MGB's shell would be too high; therefore, he agreed a more acceptable tooling cost with Pressed Steel and paid them slightly more for each shell delivered! With hindsight, BMC would have done better to have had the implicit trust in Thornley which he showed in his staff.

Throughout his time at Abingdon, Thornley tried to increase the selling range of MG sports cars: hence the MGA coupé, based very closely on Jaguar's XK 120 fixed-head coupé—a more luxurious version of the basic roadster—and ultimately the MGB GT. This bodystyle was based on that of the hatchback Aston Martin DB 2/4, the sort of sports car to which Englishmen in particular had long aspired but few had been able to afford. At the time that Thornley made the following quotes to *Motor* in 1966, the MGB GT had just been launched and the MGC was under development:

'I think progressively the sports car is achieving a broader base, a wider appeal in the public's mind; if we take this latest thing of Syd's, the MGB GT, I think we're moving into a market that even he and I didn't suspect when we first dreamed it up. We've produced a motor car now in which no managing director would be ashamed to turn up at the office and therefore it makes new inroads in that direction. When the MG addict acquired a wife and family he was driven out of a two-seater motor car—now he can at least go on until his kids are seven, eight, nine, provided he hasn't got any more than about three. With the GT we have reached beyond anything we had previously thought of as a market—we're getting a very much wider acceptance . . .

'From the design and construction point of view, I'd like to see the universal acceptance of the GT-type of motor car with a stressed top. If we could design with a stressed top, we could get a lot of weight off the bottom half of the structure.'

At this point, Enever interjected: 'It's not all to do with speed—there are still many youngsters who want an open car just for short journeys at reasonable speed.'

During the 1960s, Thornley was one of the first to note—with dismay—the way in which insurance companies discriminated against sports cars. The loading of premiums against such charming (and safe) cars as MGs caused the owners' age group to rise. Many young men and women simply could not afford to run them any more. But Thornley was not a man to sit back and moan about this; with his characteristic energy, he set about producing a car that would appeal to an older, and better-off, buyer. Thornley and Enever were not alone in their search for such a solution to the problem of the sports car's changing appeal. The Healey family were just as keen to find something to replace the Big Healey, the sales of which had lagged far behind those of the MGB, partly because of the insurance problem.

One of the Healey's biggest design handicaps was the weight and bulk of its BMC C series power train, a six-cylinder version of the B series unit. But Enever looked at its contemporary rivals (see chapter three) and reckoned it was possible to reduce its weight dramatically and make the engine smaller. As ever, Thornley gave him full backing and BMC instigated design studies on higher-powered versions of the Big Healey and MGB. The Healey was to be powered by a four-litre Rolls-Royce engine that was being used in Austin's top saloon car and the MG by a lightweight version of the Healey's three-litre engine.

By that time, Jaguar had joined the BMC camp and, upon consideration, it seemed as though the Rolls-Healey would be too close to Jaguar's E type market besides presenting considerable problems in meeting looming American safety regulations. Lyons had more sway than Donald Healey and so a decision was taken, therefore, to sink everything in the MG project. 'We were still aiming to produce a poor man's Aston Martin,' said Thornley, 'and if it hadn't been for the BMC hierarchy mucking up the engine we would have very nearly got there.'

Enever did his best to make the MGC handle properly, but the bulk of the redesigned C series engine was too great, even if everything about the concept was right. A 125 mph MGB GT would have been a world beater as the Japanese equivalent, the Datsun 240Z, was to prove in 1970; there was the added bonus that MG had an open version as well.

Thornley, who retired in 1969, remembers those last days at Abingdon with regret. He feels that with their magnificent record they should have been able to have designed more parts of the car to suit their requirements, rather than having been forced to accept major components that were unsuitable.

At this time, Enever was also experimenting with various V8 power plants from within the BMC group. Coventry-Climax and Daimler V8s were fitted to MGBs but never went into production because there was either no home for them in current saloon cars or their future was limited; and the Rover V8 engine that eventually went into the MGB GT came into the parent company a year too late.

Even as the MGC was about to go into production, BMC were about to be taken over by Leyland. But this merger, including Rover with their new V8, was not completed until 1968. Several months of turbulent upheaval among the hierarchy followed with Abingdon wondering what its fate would be. Had this merger taken place a year or so earlier, which would have been quite possible, Thornley and Enever might have landed their ideal engine, the Rover V8.

As it was, it was left to special builder Ken Costello to fit it to an MGB to show what could have been. Costello's project obviously had such potential that in 1971 he went to Donald Stokes—who had taken over control of British Leyland— to ask for guaranteed supplies of the components he needed for his car, particularly the engine.

Stokes, who had brought Triumph into British Leyland, is frequently said to have favoured this marque, long one of MG's greatest rivals. In this case, he certainly did Triumph no favours in that Costello did not get his engine and Abingdon was told to get on with producing the MGB V8 as quickly as possible. Money was short, so the conversion had to be as simple as possible. Enever was in his last year at Abingdon, but as influential as ever, and so the V8 went only into the more rigid GT shell.

The MGC roadster shell would have been stiff enough to take the V8, but its tooling had long gone. Enever and Thornley might have retired by the time they saw their desired car receive such acclaim, but their hearts were still at the works. As ever, Thornley adopted a more vocal attitude than Enever, saying that he felt there was a lot of behind-the-scenes manoeuvring over the use of the V8 engine. British Leyland management had been taken over almost entirely by former Triumph men, who naturally favoured their own projected sports car, the TR7. They did everything in their power to make it succeed, to the detriment of its chief rival, the MGB. The MGB V8 was such a good car that it could not be allowed to dominate the mass sports car market. Therefore it was priced at midway between the bespoke Costello cars and what it could have been made for: £1800–£1900, around £500 more than a four-cylinder MGB. In this way, British Leyland visualised a reasonable profit from a relatively small production run, rather than a higher profit from far larger production runs. The reasoning behind this was that the V8 engine was needed in large quantities in any case for Rover saloons and Range Rovers, which would have suffered had the MGB V8 been too successful.

Most of British Leyland's resources available for investment in sports cars were taken up by the TR7 project. This car followed Thornley and Enever's long-held philosophies in that it was designed with a stressed roof from the start, but no similar provision was made for an open version. The styling was also controversial, lacking the timeless elegance of Enever's record breakers. 'Fashion, gimmicky fashion,' Thornley told MG historian Wilson McComb in *Autocar*. 'A bloody silly wedge flying into the ground, apeing Formula One, I suppose, and trying to look like a latter-day boy racer. Absolutely no chance of lasting long enough to show any sort of return on invested capital.'

The task of selling the TR7 was made much more difficult by constant industrial trouble at Leyland's huge new plant in Speke on Merseyside. This hit supplies and quality badly while the traditionally excellent labour relations at Abingdon gave the MGB every advantage the TR7 lacked: good quality and supplies allied with classic styling and the fact that you could still buy it in open form. As a result the

MGB and the men behind it seem to have hung on long enough to allow a new generation of Enevers and Thornleys to produce a successor.

That's a long way off, but after years of neglect, there is a renewed enthusiasm for MGs among the top men at British Leyland. William Pratt Thompson, managing director of the Jaguar Rover Triumph specialised cars division, which includes MG, told Philip Turner in *Motor* in 1979:

'The MGB is now the legend in its own lifetime that I guess the Beetle became and it occupies a unique position with its classic sports car ride. It hasn't the sophisticated suspension of the TR7, but it does have that old-fashioned solid feel of a well-made car. There continues to be a very strong demand for it, and if we could we would increase the production of MGBs, but we're really restricted by the supplies of engines. I intend that the MGB keeps on going. I want to improve it; I think it wants a bit more performance, but we have plans in that direction.'

Wishful thinking . . .

XI

The Interchangeability of Spare Parts

THE MGA, B and C were built basically from BMC saloon car components, which would seem to be a godsend to people trying to run them on a tight budget or seeking to improve their cars' performance by fitting parts from more powerful machines. It is surprising, however, how few parts are directly interchangeable! The B series engine used in the MGA and MGB has always been more highly-tuned than in almost any BMC saloon and the Austin 3-litre saloon which used the same engine as the MGC is even more difficult to find than the sports car.

Many components are interchangeable among individual models in the MG range and some of the smaller items with the Austin-Healeys made at Abingdon, so there's more scope for swopping parts about in this sphere. The MGB V8's engine, apart from its induction and exhaust systems, is virtually the same as that used in the big Rover saloons and the Range Rover, making the construction of MGB V8s a practical proposition (see chapter twelve).

However, to get back to the MGs made since 1955: the B series engine was used in various capacities between 1500 cc and 1800 cc in the Austin A50 saloons and commercial vehicles; the Metropolitan 1500 (marketed by Nash in America), the MG Magnette ZA and ZB saloons, the Wolseley 4/44 and 15/50 and all Austin, Morris, MG, Wolseley and Riley variants of the Farina-bodied medium-sized saloons, Austin petrol taxies, and some Austin and Morris commercial vehicles produced between 1959 and 1967, plus other 1800 cc British Leyland saloons and commercial vehicles made between 1967 and 1978. Engines with the capacity of 1489 cc, 1622 cc or 1798 cc are basically the same as those used in MGAs or MGBs and usually share the same ancillaries; the chief differences are that the MG sports car engines had higher-performance cylinder heads and different camshafts, carburetters and exhaust systems. The mark one version of the MGA 1600 and the Twin Cam shared their engines with no other car.

Clutch units are generally interchangeable among these cars, but the gearboxes on the MGA, B or C are not shared. Many of the earlier BMC saloons had steering column gearchanges and later ones did not use the MG's gearchange extension. In the same way, although rear axles are of similar design, they are frequently of a different track, although final drives made between 1955 and 1967 are widely interchangeable. The same applies to final drives made after 1967, but

Left : John Chatham with a car he built entirely from interchangeable spare parts, his first new MGB GT V8 of 1979.

Left : The B series engine is fitted in varying stages of tune to many BMC vehicles.

Right : Wheels are popular items for swopping around, but look carefully before you leap in with an offer: these Cosmic alloy wheels are of use only for an MGC as they have five stud fixings.

Above: Speedwell's Monaco hard top
was a popular fitting on early MGBs.

Right: The authentic Abingdon works
hard top fits both MGB and MGC.

the pre- and post-1967 components are not interchangeable.

Of the smaller, and frequently more difficult to obtain, components, instruments and all manner of minor fittings are shared with Austin-Healeys and MG Midgets, and even some body parts, such as over-riders, with BMC saloons.

There is far more scope for changing parts around among individual MG sports cars. All major MGA body components are interchangeable, with the exception of the doors and windscreen, which differed in design between the fixed-head coupé and the roadster. It's quite easy to turn a Twin Cam into what amounts to a 1600 De Luxe by fitting a pushrod engine—a popular conversion over the years—but extremely difficult to turn a pushrod MGA into a Twin Cam! The Twin Cam's special parts, such as wheels and brakes, let alone the engine, are very difficult to find. It is quite feasible, however, to rebuild a wrecked Twin Cam using a pushrod car as a basis providing you have the special wheels, brakes and power train. This had happened in a number of instances.

In addition, it is not too difficult to fit an MGB engine to an MGA for added power and flexibility, or if, simply, that is the only compatible power unit available (see chapter twelve).

Among MGBs, major mechanical components can be interchanged on cars built between 1962 and 1967: it does not matter whether they have a three-bearing or a five-bearing engine, providing that either the bottom half is changed or preferably, the entire unit is replaced. However, it is not possible to fit the later, all-synchromesh, gearbox or post-1967 rear axle to earlier cars as considerable changes were required in the floor pan. It is quite feasible, though, to fit an all-synchromesh gearbox in place of an automatic gearbox in an MGB, or an overdrive gearbox to a non-overdrive car providing related components, such as the propeller shaft, are available. Overdrives can be fitted to non-overdrive gearboxes, but various internal parts have to be changed as well.

Body parts are widely interchangeable among the MGBs (and MGCs) except in the areas affected by the fitting of rubber bumpers in 1974. It is impractical to fit early body panels to a rubber-bumpered car to make it look like a chrome-fronted machine because of extensive sheet metal changes in the body construction under the new bumpers.

A Rover V8 engine can be fitted into any MGB (or C) providing the MGB shell is strengthened if it is a roadster; pre-1974 model year cars require slight surgery to the engine bay (see chapter twelve) whereas later cars, whether roadster or GT, shared the same engine bay as the MG V8. It is not wise, however, to mate the standard MGB clutch and gearbox to a V8 engine; special parts are required to ensure reliability (see chapter twelve).

Many body parts can be exchanged between the MGB and MGC with the exception of the bonnet from the MGB to the MGC. V8 conversions can use the standard MGB bonnet if they have the special MG V8 inlet manifold and carburetters, or a Holley or Weber carburetter conversion; otherwise they have to use a modified bonnet to clear the higher-mounted carburetters used on the standard Rover engine. MGB and MGC steering and gearbox components are not inter-changeable (much to the chagrin of MGC owners!) and the MGB rear axle ratio is

One of the most attractive hard tops for an MGB or MGC was the Bermuda type with windows in the top used on this racing model.

too low for road-going MGCs. Automatic MGCs can be fitted with MGC manual gearboxes if one can be found. Fuel tanks (which are frequently the subject of corrosion) are not interchangeable among MGBs or among MGCs unless the shape is the same as that of the old component. In the same way, interior parts are not directly interchangeable unless their appearance is identical, although different style interiors can be fitted complete with a bit of cunning adaptation.

In the same way, older cars can be quite easily adapted to take later-style rear lights and so on, but windscreens are not interchangeable between MGB and MGC roadsters and GTs.

Wheels are readily interchangeable, providing they have the same offset and width, among MGAs and MGBs, but not with the MGC: that had either five-stud Jaguar hubs against the four-stud Austin/Morris fixing or because of its weight, it had the heavier wire wheels. There are some Jaguar wheels, however, which will fit the MGC with spacers at the rear (see chapter twelve).

MGB and MGC hard tops are readily interchangeable, as are soft tops and tonneau covers, except with cars fitted with late-style seats from the 1977 model year. Antiroll bars are interchangeable among MGBs and MGCs providing all the fittings can be obtained and the rear anti-roll bar from the MGBs made from the 1977 model year onwards can be fitted to earlier rubber-bumpered models to improve handling.

Late-model MGB radiators with electric cooling fans can be fitted to earlier MGBs and to MGCs providing the appropriate polarity is observed with the electrical system. MGBs made from the 1968 model year, and all MGCs, had a negative earth system and alternator against the positive earth and dynamo used on earlier cars.

The main rules to observe when obtaining spare parts for an MGA, B or C from another car is to check, first, that the parts are of identical appearance, and, second, that their specification is compatible, before purchase.

The lightest wheels normally available for the MGB (or the MGC in five-stud fitting) are Minilites made by Tech Del.

XII

Modifications

ORIGINALITY has become all important with classic cars nowadays, and if you want to preserve the value of your investment, it is wise to keep it as close as possible to the maker's original specification. As John Thornley often said: 'The most profitable line of approach is first to make sure that the car is as the designer intended it to be. Most times, that is not a bad starting point.'

But although that is sound advice, driving an MGA, B or C can be frustrating in that they are cars designed for the mass market and as such there will always be ways of improving them to suit individual taste. Not all modifications need detract from the value of the car and those made by racing enthusiasts are a good example. There are a few modifications that the tourist can benefit from, too.

To improve the performance of the B series engine there were several stages of works-approved tuning. Stage one involves the polishing and matching of cylinder head ports and manifolds to give an extra 3 bhp; stage two involves swapping camshafts as well and gives more power lower in the engine's range, with a further 3 bhp as the reward, but not quite so much punch over 5000 rpm. This is about as far as most people will want to go with a road car and yields a total of 100 bhp with the 1800 cc engine. Similar work can be carried out on the MGC engine.

Stage three, gives up to 120 bhp, and involves additional work on the valve gear, a different camshaft, bigger carburetters, with the option of head machining and different pistons and con rods. These modifications mean that the engine needs more frequent overhaul and they are chiefly done for competition. Stage four involves extensive modification to the engine for at least 120 bhp, stage five includes the substitution of a Weber carburetter, and stage six additional work for 130 bhp. This is about as far as most racers go, although some are now obtaining more than 150 bhp with extensive modifications. Again similar modifications can be made to the MGC engine.

More equipment is becoming available for the V8 engine now, although the easiest way to improve its already impressive output is to fit high compression heads and different carburetters—either a Holley with Offenhauser manifold, or Weber with Costello/Traco manifold—with the Holley conversion as the much cheaper.

The modifications that can be made to this engine are far-reaching, practically

Bill Nicholson's B series engine pictured in 1967 with a stage six conversion using a single Weber carburetter.

A Downton stage two conversion on a C series engine, using two SU carburetters.

The Downton stage three conversion
on a C series engine with three SU
carburetters.

doubling its power without supercharging or turbocharging, which presents formidable difficulties with the MGB and MGC as there really isn't enough room under the bonnet for such bulky equipment.

One of the first things to do to the V8 after fitting better carburetters is to change the con rods. Stronger Oldsmobile items are readily available in America, but almost unobtainable elsewhere, so Europeans have to fit Carrillo forged steel rods. Unfortunately, these are expensive, but worthwhile as the standard V8 rods are not strong enough to take much extra power. The crankshaft is very strong, however.

The oil temperature on this engine is critical and should never exceed 110 degrees Centigrade. Therefore it is worth fitting an oil temperature gauge, and possibly an uprated oil pump.

Standard pistons, which are available for a variety of compression ratios between 8.5 : 1 and 10.5 : 1, are strong enough for most applications, although Venolia high performance pistons are better for racing. They are also very expensive, like the forged con rods.

Early V8 cylinder heads had rather small valves and a noticeable improvement can be obtained by fitting the later Rover SD1 heads.

Camshafts available for the Rover or Buick V8, range from mild to wild. At

The Holley four-barrel carburetter using an Offenhauser Triumph TR7 V8 manifold fitted to a Rover SDI engine in a Chatham conversion.

The Weber/Costello/Buick conversion fitted to the Rover V8 engine in the author's MGC V8.

'Mike the Pipe' tubular exhaust manifolds fitted to a Rover V8 engine in an MGB.

The works front valence as fitted to the Le Mans MGA prototypes.

The Chatham works-style valence fitted to the MGC V8.

least five camshafts are readily obtainable, three for use with the standard hydraulic tappets and two for solid lifters. With suitably improved carburration, ignition and exhaust systems, 7000 rpm can be used safely with the best of the hydraulic tappet cams, and with other modifications, 8000 rpm is obtainable with solid lifters. It is also worth updating the older Rover V8s with SD1 hydraulic tappets (and matching valve springs) so that they can be taken beyond 6000 rpm.

A variety of carburetters, and even fuel injection, are available for the V8 from tuning specialists, but before fitting such items to an older V8 it is wise to uprate the ignition by substituting a Mallory Dual Point distributor, which gives a much better spark. Later V8s have better distributors in any case.

Generally, with such tuning it is best to fit an oil cooler if the car does not have one already, and the hotter stages of race tuning require a competition clutch and flywheel, too.

One of the easier engine swaps for improved performance is fitting an MGB unit to an MGA. There are a variety of ways in which it can be done, depending on which combination of engines, gearboxes and starter motors are available. If you intend to use a three-bearing MGB engine with a complete MGA gearbox the engine needs to retain the MGB clutch, and it is essential that the clutch plate has the same number of splines as the input shaft of the MGA gearbox. This might be nine or twenty-four splines. The front cover of this gearbox must be changed to that of the MGB type and the MGB clutch release mechanism must be fitted.

If the MGB clutch and gearbox are to be used with the MGB engine, it will be found that the rear mounting of the gearbox is completely different, so the rear extension of the MGB box must be removed and replaced by the MGA extension. It's a good idea to fit the MGA speedometer drive gear to the output shaft as well, so that it reads properly.

The same factors apply when using the five-bearing MGB engine, but this unit has a larger crankshaft bush, so either the appropriate gearbox input shaft must be fitted with an MGA gearbox or an adaptor bush made.

It must be realised also that the MGB starter motor is bigger than that of the MGA and will not fit the housing in the MGA cockpit floor. This means that you either have to fit the MGA starter motor and hope that it is strong enough to turn over the new engine in cold weather or modify the floor. The floor needs extensive modification in any case on early MGAs as their starter motor was in an entirely different position. Further problems that will crop up are that the exhaust systems are much different, so that it is necessary to rework the MGB system to fit; retaining the MGA system with the MGB engine reduces its power to MGA standards. The MGB water pump needs more room, too, so it is necessary to remount the radiator 0.25 inches or so further forward. You can fit the MGA water pump to the MGB engine, but this is inadvisable as its smaller capacity risks overheating.

Fitting a V8 engine to an MGB or MGC is rather more complicated and involves replacing the gearbox for reliability, but it is quite a feasible project. It is also necessary to change the rear axle ratio on the MGB and is definitely not recommended for the MGA with its more confined engine bay.

The Chatham rear valence fitted to the MGC V8.

The best V8 to fit to an MGB or MGC is, not surprisingly, the Rover or Buick all-alloy 3.5-litre unit. Even with ancillaries, this weighs only 6 lb more than the B-series engine and at least 200 lb less than the MGC's engine; other readily obtainable engines, such as the all-alloy Daimler 2.5-litre V8 and the Ford Zodiac V6 have been fitted successfully to MGBs, but neither makes such a good conversion as the Rover or General Motors engine. MGBs made before the 1974 model year and MGCs need minor surgery in the engine bay and their steering racks re-mounting to accept this engine, which is similar to that used in the MGB GT V8. All MGBs made for the 1974 model year and after have incorporated these modifications so that they are even easier to convert. With the older models, it is necessary to cut the corners above the transmission tunnel off the main bulkhead, weld plates over the resultant holes, make small indentations in the inner wings to clear the new exhaust manifolds and, with the MGB, remove the front radiator mounting. The steering rack is re-mounted one inch lower to clear the V8's sump and special engine mountings with spacing washers are welded into place. The V8 engine's sump has to be remodelled to clear the front suspension cross-member with the MGC shell. New sheet metal mountings have to be made up for an MGB V8 radiator, mounted well forward in the nose.

Problems with these conversions are few and centre chiefly on the engine mounting rubbers, gearbox, exhaust system and rear axle. The mighty torque of the Rover V8 (especially in its 185 bhp saloon car guise) can lead to trouble with engine mountings and gearboxes after about 30,000 miles. The left-hand-side (viewed underbonnet) engine mounting rubber is liable to collapse and with right-hand-drive cars cause the exhaust manifold to vibrate on the steering column unless an adaption of the Morris 1000 or Mini engine stay is fitted; standard MGB V8s also suffer from these problems on occasions. None of the standard four-speed MG or Rover gearboxes seem adequate for the engine's power. Therefore it is recommended that the standard gearbox is fitted with works straight-cut competition gears by specialists or replaced with one of the new Rover SD1 saloon car five-speed gearboxes. Both units can cope with the torque without problems. The disadvantages are a pronounced whine in the intermediate gears with the straight-cut gearbox (music to many enthusiasts' ears) and high cost with the Rover five-speed box. The straight-cut box has an additional advantage in that its change is fantastically fast and smooth. Unless the car is intended for competitions, it is best to fit the MGB with the MGB V8 rear axle ratio of 3.07 : 1. The lowest overall gearing practical for road use in my MGC V8 (which is fitted with 14-inch wheels as on the MGB) has been found to be 3.03 overdrive top, 3.7 direct top, 4.0 overdrive third, 4.88 direct top, 6.48 second and 9.06 first. These ratios are achieved by using the BMC straight cut gear clusters with a Laycock competition overdrive and MGC 3.7 rear axle. Fuel consumption is relatively high at around 17 mpg but acceleration is extremely good up to a maximum of around 140 mph; higher overall speeds and better fuel consumption can be achieved with higher gearing at the expense of acceleration. Little, other than violent wheelspin, can be achieved by lower gearing on road wheels.

Standard MGB GT V8 carburetters and manifolds can be fitted to the Rover engines without interference with the bonnet line although the alternative carburetters that can be used—Holley or a backdraught Weber—are preferable. Standard V8 exhaust manifolds have a reputation for cracking and are very difficult to obtain, so custom-made tubular extractor manifolds are recommended. The standard MGB GT V8 exhaust system works very well with V8 conversions and it seems pointless to fit anything else for road use. The best carburetter conversion to fit to the V8 is an Offenhauser manifold with a four-barrel Holley; good results are possible with the Traco/Costello manifold and a Weber twin choke carburetter, but tuning is more difficult and the engine more like a racing unit in its peaky response. All necessary parts, including carburetters, radiators, engine mounting plates and gearboxes, can be obtained.

One of the most dramatic improvements that can be made to an MGA, B or C is in damping and the reduction of unsprung weight. Lever arm shock absorbers have to be retained on the front of the MGA and MGB because they form part of the basic suspension, but stiffer dampers with competition valves can improve stability at the expense of ride. Telescopic shock absorber conversions, such as those marketed by Koni, are particularly effective at reducing rear axle hop and MGC owners are fortunate in that these adjustable dampers can be fitted all round. In conjunction with alloy wheels and modern low-profile tyres to reduce unsprung weight, dramatic improvements can be made in roadholding. The widest wheels that can be fitted to the MGA, B and C for road use have seven-inch rims and require minor modifications to the steering arms for clearance. These arms have to be heated up and bent in slightly (with consequent adjustments to the tracking) or filed down a little at their extremities to clear such wheels. The wings have to be stretched a couple of inches out at the front or flared and the rear wings treated in a similar manner with the MGA or simply jacked out an inch with the MGB or MGC. Wider wheels require extensive alterations to the wheel arches and the fitting of

Sebring-style wings on the MGB and C. There is little point in fitting wider than seven-inch wheels for road use as wet weather handling is inferior with such 'cotton reels'.

The MGC also benefits from the fitting of fourteen-inch diameter wheels, rather than the standard fifteen-inch, now that fourteen-inch tyres that can stand up to its extra weight and performance are readily available. These smaller wheels reduce unsprung weight on the MGC and the resultant lowering also improves handling. Ground clearance and gearing are reduced, of course, but the ground clearance is still quite adequate providing the springs and dampers are in good condition and the gearing is a matter of choice.

Fourteen-inch wire wheels for the MGC are readily available, but fourteen-inch bolt-on wheels present problems. The best available with the right offset for this five-studded hub (the MGA and MGB have four-stud hubs) are made by Minilite and cost a lot because they are cast from aluminium or magnesium.

Further improvements to roadholding can be made to the MGA and MGB by fitting a front anti-roll bar if it has not already got one; and fitting a rear anti-roll bar to the 1974 and 1975 model year MGBs. All rubber-bumpered MGBs benefit also from lowering, which can be achieved by fitting blocks under the axle at the back and revised spring-mounting points at the front or by fitting re-shaped springs.

Worthwhile improvements to handling can also be made on the MGA, B and C by lowering the rear only, and, or, fitting stiffer rear springs to the MGB or MGC, at the expense of an odd appearance with the lowered rear end, and slightly more tail-happy handling with the stiffer springs. To this end, a variety of rear springs are available for the MGA, B and C from British Leyland, with the stiffest being the springs made for the police versions of the MGB and MGC GT. MG specialists Brown & Gammons and John Chatham Cars have devoted much research to such suspension modifications; Brown & Gammons cover MGAs, Bs and Cs, with a special line in lowering rubber-bumpered cars, whereas Chatham concentrates heavily on the MGB, C and V8. After a certain amount of trial and error, the best wheel, tyre and suspension set-up for my road-going MGC V8—which is of similar overall weight and weight distribution to that of a standard MGB—has turned out to be: Seven-inch by fourteen-inch Minilite bolt-on wheels all round; Goodyear G800 Grand Prix tyres; Koni shock absorbers all round adjusted to their first setting at the front and second setting at the back; and MGC GT rear springs lowered two inches. Under extremely violent acceleration, particularly on bumpy surfaces, it is possible to 'wind up' the rear springs, in which case radius arms under the front of the springs would take care of that; it is also possible, with equally violent cornering, on a smooth surface, to make the rear axle move sideways, which would call for a Watt linkage or an A-bracket to be made up. Although these linkages are worthwhile for competition, they are expensive and difficult to make and maintain, and present a grave obstacle to ground clearance; in any case such spirited driving is hardly necessary on the road!

Although wire wheels score heavily in terms of appearance and originality, they are definitely inferior to good alloy wheels when it comes to handling, particularly on the standard MGC. Not only do they have the handicap of higher unsprung

Above: University Motors' customised MGC GT.

Left: Interior of the MGC V8 using Porsche Recaro seats, Motolita steering wheel, Panther Westwinds trimming, late-style MGB steering column flasher, and Daimler gearlever overdrive switch.

A John Aley roll cage as fitted to the MGC V8.

weight, but they are less rigid than alloy wheels. It would be sacrilege, however, to abandon the peg-drive wheels fitted to the MGA Twin Cam and De Luxe models as these wheels, although heavier than modern alloy wheels, are rigid and really historic, having been fitted only to sports racing cars of the 1950s and a few exotic machines.

Additional advantages with fitting good alloy wheels and light tyres to an MGA, B or C include lightening the steering. With reduced unsprung weight, the steering is lighter and a smaller steering wheel can be fitted without making parking difficult. Minor problems encountered when fitting Koni shock absorber conversions to MGB V8s centre around the exhaust system, which is wider than that on the four-cylinder car. Sometimes it is necessary to rehang the pipe slightly further into the centre of the car, to avoid contact with the damper bodies, which are mounted further inboard than with the lever arm shock absorbers. At least this means that there is no danger of the damper arm fouling a rear brake pipe, which is a common problem on the standard car!

There is little that can be done to the braking to improve it other than fitting a Special Tuning dual circuit system to non-export MGBs and MGCs or competition linings. These linings are advantageous in that they are far less prone to fading under heavy use although they need a much greater effort at the pedal and are not recommended for tyres in traffic. When fitting these linings, most drivers consider it wise to replace the rear brake cylinders with those from a Mini (0.75 in diameter) to maintain the balance of the front and back brakes. With the MGC V8 it has also been found desirable to fit an MGB brake servo in place of the standard

MGC servo which has proved to be too powerful for the lightened car, with the result that it is very easy to lock the brakes.

Competition clutch units and lightened flywheels come into similar categories as the use of competition brake linings; fitting a lightened flywheel or a competition clutch means that more careful use of the pedal must be made. Advantages are a much more responsive engine with a lightened flywheel and longer clutch life with a competition unit. Generally, however, clutch life on the MGA, B or C is extremely good providing the appropriate unit is used with an engine (for instance, it is essential to use the MGB V8 clutch with a Rover conversion, and so on).

One of the most niggling problems over the years with the MGA, B and C has been the location of the twin six-volt batteries on pre-1974 model year cars. Fitting a single twelve-volt battery to a roadster to replace the awkwardly-located six-volt batteries involves only the use of extended battery leads, a battery clamp and a piece of wood for a spacer between the battery and the rear bulkhead when the new battery is located in the boot above the rear axle. It is a good idea to fit a battery cut-off switch at the same time; all parts (other than the piece of wood!) can be obtained from Lucas depots. A similar conversion is possible in the GT, although it intrudes into the interior and needs a special cover making up for the battery; in this case it is better to use post-1974 model year parts.

In the same way the fuel pump—which is also exposed to road dirt and damp and is difficult to reach under the floor near the rear axle—is well re-located in the roadster's boot. With powerful engine conversions, such as those on the MGC and V8, it is often necessary to use the twin SU pump from a Rover saloon to combat fuel starvation at high revs under full load.

Sealed cooling systems combined with electric fans are well worth while fitting to MGAs, Bs and Cs without this feature. They save valuable brake horse power and are much quieter in use. A useful ready-made overflow tank is that concealed in the front valence of the Austin and Morris 1100s which abound in British scrapyards.

A neat and convenient touch in the cockpit can be the fitting of the gearlever overdrive switch from a Triumph Dolomite, or post-1969 Daimler or Jaguar (as used from the 1977 model year on the MGB), in place of the dashboard overdrive switch, and electric windscreen washers in place of the normal antique push-button plumbing. Electric washers can be obtained in kits or readily adapted from the installation in saloons such as Jaguars and Daimlers.

Seats are a matter of personal preference with a wide variety on the market, but one ingenious modification that can do much to improve comfort in the MGA is achieved by sawing through the weld where the runner framing meets the perimeter and inserting a 1.5-inch vertical piece of metal and re-welding. The results give better lumbar and thigh support and are ideal according to people who consider its driving position too upright. One of the chief advantages of such a modification is that the appearance is still virtually as standard. In an age when much importance is placed on originality, non-standard appearance can be the chief disadvantage of many modifications that would be attractive otherwise.

XIII

Concours and Competition Preparation

THERE ARE more similarities than many people realise between preparing a car for concours and the more violent forms of competition, such as circuit racing, hill climbing and rallying. To achieve high placings, let alone victories, equally high standards of preparation are necessary, although a great deal of fun and satisfaction can be had with an MGA, B or C with little more than elbow grease and application. That's because they are real sports cars, designed for competition as well as more mundane transportation. To take concours first, you stand a good chance of winning an award (such as a highly-commended certificate), if you can present a good, original, undamaged car that is really clean. First, degrease the engine, gearbox rear axle and underside; then everything (including the engine bay and underside) should be scrubbed and hosed down; next polish all the metal work you can reach in the engine compartment, clean the hoses, paint the radiator and everything else that ought to be painted but which is frequently peeling; then paint the underside and exhaust system where necessary, clean the suspension thoroughly and the inside of the wings and battery bays, not forgetting the shock absorbers. Only then should underseal be applied, if desired. It's no good just slapping underseal around under the car to cover up the muck; it will show through and it is bad for the car, because it traps moisture between the underseal and the metal, which leads to corrosion.

On the outside of the body, touch up the stone chips, scratches and so on, then cut and polish it all and clean the chrome and the glass, inside and out. Scrub rubber bumpers, windscreen surrounds and tyres (including the spare). Pay special attention to the wheels, cleaning them thoroughly inside and out and touching up any damaged paintwork before treating them in the same way as the body. Blacken the tyres, if necessary, but not overmuch. Remove and scrub interior parts and thoroughly cleanse any leather before treating it. Don't forget the hood and tonneau cover on a roadster. Slightly faded upholstery is acceptable providing it has been well looked after. Once this basic preparation has been completed it is attention to detail that counts for a highly-commended certificate: little things like cleaning the back of the driver's interior mirror where grubby fingermarks can be seen from the outside that the driver might forget!

More advanced concours preparation involves starting with a new car or

restoring your car to as-new condition. When restoring a car, for concours, competition or personal satisfaction (even for sale), it is essential to approach the job meticulously. First of all, carry out a detailed examination of the car, noting everything that needs attention or replacement. Then find out how long it will take to get the job done or how much it will cost, and, providing you can afford the time and money involved, then work out a work plan.

To restore the majority of ageing MGAs, MGBs and MGCs, it is necessary to dismantle them as far as possible, which will involve removing the body on the MGA and the front wings on the MGB and MGC. When dismantling the car it is essential that the owner, or the same trusted friend or operative, is present throughout the whole procedure to make notes on any potential problems. As parts are removed they should be labelled, especially if there is likely to be any difficulty in recognising them months, or maybe years, later when they are returned to the car. All parts should be filed in boxes providing the parts are not very big. It should be self-evident where the big parts belong on the car! Use a logical sequence with the boxes: keep the speedometer with its cable, for instance, rather than just dropping the cable into the nearest box and having to hunt for it much later. Keep the car on its wheels for as long as possible, unless you have a big workshop, so that it can be moved around.

As parts, such as rechromed numbers, are returned, wrap them up in the blankets and store them somewhere safe, such as under a bed . . .

Abingdon competition cars were always prepared to concours standards. This is the rear view of one of the Le Mans MGA prototypes.

Right: Underbonnet view of the Le Mans MGA when fitted with a push-rod engine.

Below: Fitters hard at work in the competitions department at Abingdon preparing a new MGB roadster, GRX 307D, for the Monte Carlo Rally in 1966.

When everything is reduced to a manageable state and major components have been sent away for attention (such as the chromework) start cleaning everything carefully. But only dismantle one component at a time until you have gone through all the boxes. Then wrap the stuff up so that it doesn't suffer from damp and dirt. Keep note of the specialists to whom you have dispatched parts for renovation so that you can chase them at appropriate times, and make notes on the work plan about possible delays, Mother's Day and the big club meetings so that you don't lose touch with reality.

When the mechanical cleaning is done and the specialists are well under way, you can start on the bodywork and chassis. Sandblasting on steel parts is ideal as it shows up imperfections such as rust holes, while dramatically cutting the cleaning time. But don't try it on precious alloy panels except in the most skilled hands as it can blast them to pieces or quickly dent them. It is best to remove paint on alloy by hand. Interior panels, no matter how battered, should be saved as they can be invaluable for patterns for new panels. These can be easily copied on an MG using materials supplied by firms such as Roy Creech in South London. The labour content on a proper restoration can be enormous, but it is the only way to win a concours with a second-hand MGA, MGB or MGC, unless it is one of those exceptionally rare cars that have been kept in mothballs from new.

Mind you, mothballing can have its problems. Cars under storage should be kept in dry, well-ventilated buildings with particular attention paid to the condition of rubber components (including brake cylinder seals) when the car is returned to active service. The best way to keep the car fit and well during storage is to turn the engine and gearbox, and if possible, the rear axle over a few times each week on the starter motor with the coil disconnected to save wear from cold starting. Also pump the brakes and clutch a few times to keep their seals well lubricated. Keep the battery well charged and the tyres pumped up even if the car is on chocks. Make sure also that the brake and clutch fluid has not absorbed water during storage or you could soon be in trouble when the car is returned to the road.

Preparation for racing and rallying involves the same sort of work without the fanatical attention to the paintwork. Almost invariably, fairly extensive modifications are made, particularly to the engine, depending on the type of competition visualised. Until recently, the works-recommended degrees of engine tuning were followed by most competitors until these theories—developed the best part of twenty years ago—were blown sky-high in a notable series for *Cars and Car Conversions* by David Vizard. He frowned upon the established ideas of bolting on 1.75-inch SU carburetters or a 45 DCOE at an early stage of tuning as being a waste of money. Vizard pointed out that the 1800 cc B series engines rarely produced more than 140 bhp in their most advanced states of race tuning, which was far from impressive. Even the least successful modern pushrod engines were producing 25 per cent more power in relation to capacity. The chief problem with the B series engine, as Vizard saw it, lay in the head. This was a poor breather chiefly because its valves were on the small side. Small valves are inherent with a small bore and long stroke, but despite this, not all the available space had been used in the head, probably because the factory liked to play ultra-safe for fear of valve seat cracking. The intake port was found to be of low efficiency in its shape, so that a standard 1.5-inch SU carburetter accounted for only 6.5 per cent of the flow restriction. Changing to 1.75-inch SUs, or even a 45 mm Weber—at substantial cost—improved breathing by only 2.5 per cent. Far bigger relative gains were to be obtained by simply fitting better air filters (Vizard recommended American K and N filters) or open ram pipes. Obviously a poor, or choked air filter, would be a considerable handicap to B series engine power and a simple and cheap modification could be affected in this area.

Aldon Automotive, of Birmingham, tested Vizard's theories on a dynamometer and found that fitting 1.75-inch SU carburetters with the standard-shaped head was worth only an extra 1.5 bhp. Dynamometer tuning, however, proved to be the best way of extracting more power from a B series engine when on a limited budget.

When gas-flowing the B series head, Vizard discovered that the inlet valves worked most efficiently with orthodox seating when everything else was standard. He also found that bigger ports needed a very high lift cam (more than 0.39 inches) but that it was possible to improve efficiency with standard valves by 10 per cent as a result of careful gas-flowing. Larger valves, such as the 1.65-inch Pinto 2000 proved to be of little use in the standard B series chamber as they tended to shroud the intake area. Good flow was only possible with bigger ports and a high-lift cam. A rounded edge to the split between the two siamesed valves also proved better than the existing sharp edge. With a group two Pinto valve (1.74 inches) reduced to 1.714 inches for reliability, a Weber 45DCOE picked up 6.8 per cent in gas flow over open SUs. Therefore it was apparent that it was better to spend money on head work and a new camshaft rather than simply polishing the head and bolting on bigger carburetters.

Similar work was needed on the exhaust side, with the boss under the valve coming in for immediate attention; to fit larger exhaust valves it was necessary to cut away part of the cylinder block, with similar improvements resulting to those experienced with the intake. Higher compression ratios were found to be advantageous with 10.5 : 1 or 11 : 1 for the road and up to 14 : 1 for racing.

One of the best period modifications for the B series engine is the HRG-Derrington alloy cylinder head introduced in 1958. This head, designed by MG's erstwhile rivals, HRG, and marketed by ace Brooklands tuner Vic Derrington at Kingston upon Thames, weighed only 16 lb—half the weight of a standard MGA head. It had four separate inlet ports and the sparking plugs were inclined towards the highest concentration of petrol/air mixture on the compression stroke. Providing you had a special plug spanner, all standard parts, such as valves, could be used in this head, which was generally fitted in conjunction with Derrington manifolds. In this form, with twin 1.5-inch SUs, lightened valvegear and a 9.3 : 1 compression ratio, it was worth an extra 12 per cent on power (translated into 5 seconds less from 0–70 mph), and proved both smooth and flexible with slightly better fuel consumption and no running on. In more advanced states of tune it was worth up to 25 per cent more power.

One of the most successful Twin Cam engine tuners was Bob Olthoff, who copied Jaguar's well-known pre-E type XK head when modifying his car. He curved the normally-straight inlets so that the gas was already turning when it reached the valves. It was another instance of an independent mind reaching different conclusions to those of the factory and being proved right! When Olthoff began working at Abingdon, a works big-valve head was fitted to his car, with a subsequent drop in power and performance. In company with works engines, Olthoff's was bored out to 1762 cc and his chassis modifications were among the most successful of the day, and ultimately suitable for road and track.

Initially, his car was fitted with a South African Teleflow telescopic shock absorber conversion: like Konis and Spax, these dampers improved handling, providing particularly stable cornering. However, they contravened regulations in force in England when Olthoff brought his car over and he had to fit the original Armstrong lever arm dampers. He modified the valves to stiffen their operation and the results were so successful that these changes were adopted for the competition shock absorbers.

The Appendix J international regulations in force in the early 1960s for Olthoff's type of car specified that weight could not be reduced below 95 per cent of the standard machine's quoted weight. Therefore he confined his weight reduction programme to fitting fibreglass wings front and rear with aluminium inner wings and propeller shaft tunnel. He also lowered the rear suspension by 1.5 inches using spacers and softer springs, which, in conjunction with the competition shock absorbers, improved roadholding. Further bodywork modifications were confined to fitting a works hard top and fairing in part of the radiator air intake and substituting special valances for the bumpers. Olthoff worked out the nose section by attaching pieces of cotton to various points on the front of the car, then subjecting it to a blast from a ventilation system. Such experiments led to the removal of the grille, the fitting of a hand-made plate over part of the radiator intake, cleaning up the front valance and raising it for better airflow. Twin 42 DCOE Weber carburetters were fed from an air intake on the right-hand side of the grille opening with a matching intake on the other side to cool the driver. Louvres relieved under-bonnet pressure and reduced engine temperature in conjunction with an oil cooler in the radiator intake.

For racing, a short exhaust system exiting in front of the nearside rear wheel was used with a special distributor. A 4.55 : 1 limited slip rear axle was fitted with a close ratio gearbox—a popular modification to road-going MGAs. The advantages of such gearing, which used a much higher overall first gear, were frequently demonstrated on the track where standard cars would leave the line quicker only to be overtaken by close ratio cars (which had one less change to make) within a few hundred yards. Once rolling, the close ratio gearbox meant that in effect the car had one extra ratio within its power band.

The works specification MGAs, such as Ian Prior's Sebring car, featured numerous interesting modifications. These cars used a Twin Cam chassis with the Dunlop disc brakes and knock-on disc wheels all round, front anti-roll bar, front suspension drilled to save unsprung weight, extra fluid reservoirs in the engine compartment to feed the front shock absorbers, adjustable rear shock absorbers and an extra chassis member behind the twenty-two gallon fuel tank. Their 1588 cc pushrod engines used twin 1.75-inch SU carburetters, an extractor exhaust, and the water passages between the head and the block were closed off, with an extra water pipe at the back to compensate. The valve gear was lightened and a special distributor and camshaft fitted. A close ratio gearbox and competition clutch were fitted with a limited slip rear axle using ratios to suit individual events.

Further details included a larger capacity water radiator, an oil cooler, twin SU fuel pumps in the boot, a single twelve-volt battery in the front bulkhead, extra air intakes for the engine and driver, two-speed wipers, push-button ignition, wood-rim steering wheel, racing seats, alloy body, gearbox cover, transmission tunnel and floor behind the seats, drilled pedals, Plexiglass in place of side and rear glass, works body valances and headlight covers, apart from numerous external lights.

These sort of modifications are the most extreme normally carried out on a racing MGA, but there have been one or two extraordinary machines competing in modified sports car racing. Rob Haigh's was one of the best examples, developed over four seasons in the mid-1970s. The car started life as a 1956 roadster and quickly acquired an MGB engine and close ratio gearbox. Haigh eventually tuned the engine to give around 140 bhp when bored out 0.080 inches to 1892 cc (for the 1500 cc–2000 cc class) using an 11.5 : 1 compression ratio, big valve head, British Leyland super sprint camshaft, 48 DHLA Dellorto carburetter and Janspeed exhaust. He used a 3.9 : 1 rear axle ratio with locked differential, BBS 15-inch × 10-inch alloy wheels and Dunlop slicks. Girling alloy calipers were used with 11-inch discs at the front and 10.5-inch discs at the back. The rose-jointed front suspension used double wishbones and Armstrong coil spring/damper units. The same suspension medium was used at the back with the MGA rear axle located by twin radius arms and Panhard rod. The steering was by Ford Escort high ratio (1.75 turns lock-to-lock) rack with the wheels' inset arranged so that the kingpins were in the centre of the tyre area. The chassis was substantially as standard with a massive roll cage featuring hoop and rear braces, lateral side members and a cross member running beneath the scuttle. Weight was kept to a minimum by the extensive use of glassfibre and aluminium in the body, which had a frontal dam and rear spoiler with fully streamlined undertray. In this form, Haigh's MGA was successful in this highly-competitive British formula against cars such as Lotus Elans and Dave Bettinson's outrageously fast Lotus Seven.

Works specification MGBs were prepared in a similar manner to the Sebring MGAs except that a substantial proportion of the body had to be steel because of the car's monocoque construction. Bill Nicholson's track car, 286 FAC, has been prepared very closely to works specification using a stage six 1800 cc engine with a nitrided crankshaft special connecting rods, pistons, camshaft, timing wheels, oversize sump and so on. A competition clutch and overdrive close ratio gearbox are used with a limited slip rear axle and wire wheels. The suspension is lowered at the back by re-cambering the springs and at the front by mounting the wishbones higher in the cross member and modifying the springs to suit. Armstrong competition dampers are used all round with a 0.75-inch front anti-roll bar. Front wings, bootlid, doors and bonnet are in aluminium.

MGBs prepared for full-scale rallying are rare birds, but their preparation is

Oil coolers are essential wear for competition engines.

interesting. The 1964 roadster driven by Derek Skinner in the late 1960s and early 1970s used similar engine modifications to those on a circuit car with a close ratio overdrive gearbox and 4.5 : 1 rear axle ratio. The ride height was raised an inch with spacers, GT springs and 0.75-inch anti-roll bar at the front and police GT springs at the back. Armstrong competition shock absorbers were fitted all round. The engine and gearbox were protected by a Supersport shield, the battery carriers with steel skids and the petrol tank with an alloy shield. The exhaust system was beefed up with a second pipe over the original and a skid for the front silencer. The middle muffler was omitted and a Triumph 2000 silencer run across the back behind the petrol tank. An alternator was needed to keep its battery of lights working but the rest of the car was surprisingly standard except for glassfibre front wings to cut the cost of replacements for frequently-damaged steel items. Michael Pearson's V8 rally car is in similar trim except that he uses the stronger GT shell and the V8 gives about 225 bhp against 140 or so!

Numerous tuning kits have been marketed for the MGB for road use with Downton modifications among the most successful. These conversions generally

featured a gas-flowed cylinder head with 9.8 : 1 compression ratio and stronger valve springs; 1.75-inch SU carburetters with pancake air filters and extractor exhaust. Full balancing and a lightened flywheel were popular extras. Similar kits were made for the MGC with the choice of two or three SUs, and the results in both cases were greatly improved performance and fuel consumption.

One of the fastest MGCs ever was built for road use by John Chatham although in reality it was more like a works racing car and is prone to turn up in competition from time to time. This is the Red Rooster (JHU 21L) that still has an occasional outing in the author's hands. It uses a cast iron MGC engine which gives around 175 bhp in stage six tune but is mounted several inches further back than normal, resulting in better weight distribution. The main bulkhead is extensively modified for this bit of shoe-horning and the transmission tunnel moved back with a shorter propeller shaft and revised gear lever mounting. There's no room for a heater but Chatham is of the opinion that the car is hot enough anyway! An ex-works Austin-Healey style six-branch into two rally exhaust system exits under the passenger's seat and supports this theory. The C series engine is fitted with a gas-flowed 11 : 1 head according to the Abingdon gospel, triple 45 DCOE Webers and an oil cooler complete the extras on this fearsome engine. An equally-remote water radiator is cooled by a Kenlowe electric fan.

The Red Rooster uses a four-speed competition overdrive gearbox, limited slip differential and fourteen-inch by seven-inch knock-on Minilites. Triple SU pumps supply fuel at a prodigious rate (around 12 mpg) from the rear bulkhead next to the twelve-volt battery conversion. Ex-works MGB alloy bootlid and doors, fibreglass hard top and valances are used with Sebring-style fibreglass flared wings. The results are astounding: the Red Rooster handles like an MGB and is good for 150 mph on a high axle ratio.

Chatham also races a modsports MGC GT (when he has time from Austin-Healey commitments) built from one of the ex-works GTS shells. This car uses an all-alloy MGC engine giving more than 200 bhp for its all-up weight of around 15 cwt. Thirteen-inch by eight-inch Minilites, limited slip differential, discs all round, radius rods, Watt linkage, Konis and straight-cut competition overdrive gearbox take care of this power in the wet; ten-inch rims and slicks are run in the dry.

It is incredible the lengths to which enthusiasts will go to make their MGs faster!

Facing page, top: One of the smartest concours-winning MGC roadsters.

Facing page, bottom: An equally-smart MGC GT belonging to Pearly and Derek McGlen. This car is fitted with a Downton stage two conversion.

XIV

The Secret Dream Cars

It might seem that Syd Enever and his design team had a pretty easy time with only two cars, the MGA and MGB, produced in twenty-odd years, plus a couple of conversions. In reality they were kept busy, drawing and building a variety of cars, many of which never saw the light of day. The reasons so many of these projects, some of them brilliant, were killed is as varied as the designs: chiefly it was lack of capital and latterly a political situation dominated by former Triumph men. But you cannot help thinking that the over-riding reason why so many good ideas never reached fruition was that the MGA and MGB have always sold so well.

Most of these secret MGs had no names, only project numbers. Readers will remember the record car, EX181, and the 1955 Le Mans cars, EX182. Well, EX183 and EX186 (not all EX numbers were cars, some were engines and so on) were intended for Le Mans in 1956. EX183 looked like a normal MGA but it had a tubular chassis like the popular sports cars of the day. Listers, Coopers and Tojeiros had managed to build particularly light cars with such chassis which went very well with MG power. EX186 was completely different: it had a near-standard MGA chassis modified only to accept de Dion rear suspension and support a body bearing a close resemblance to a Mercedes Benz 300SLR. It was smaller, but the lines were similar.

Both projects, which used Twin Cam engines, were killed by BMC because of their change of policy over sports car racing, but Thornley and Enever learned a lot from them. Thornley was to comment later that the tubular chassis idea would have cost too much and Enever decided that he was not too keen on de Dion rear suspension. At that time, he considered it only a half-way house—'in total weight it's heavier than independent rear suspension and it's still liable to tramp.' He would have preferred independent rear suspension to eliminate tramp, but recognised that it would have added to the car's cost and that the average customer might not have noticed a big improvement.

One of the next projects (although no EX number has been revealed for it because it was not officially an Abingdon car) was Ted Lund's Le Mans MGA, followed by further wind tunnel experiments in which a nose similar to that on EX181 was grafted on to an MGA. This nose was carried over to EX205/1 and EX205/2, fixed-head and open versions of a project in 1958 that was to become the

MGB four years later. The number priorities are interesting in that they would seem to indicate that Thornley and Enever were already tending to favour the GT style. As Thornley was to say years later in *Motor*: 'The average age of our customers has gone up and up, partly forced up by the insurance companies' strictness on the young, partly by the better acceptance of the modern sports car with its more sophisticated design and gentler suspension, instead of the kidney-shaking type of thing we had years ago.'

They were realists, however, and Enever said: 'We've got to back it both ways until things find their own level. We should find out whether the GT style sells better—we should like it that way.' Also, they were perpetually amazed at the customers' insistence on hard-to-clean wire wheels. But they were not so dogmatic that they wouldn't give the customer what he or she wanted: thus all their prototypes had easy-clean disc wheels (which were cheaper to produce in any case, and more rigid from the design point of view) whereas the majority of production cars had wire wheels fitted as optional extras. In the same way, open cars were introduced first, followed by the fixed heads.

The MGB took four years to produce because it was a complete departure from previous practice and the EX205 cars were a good deal different in concept from the final product, in any case. The EX205 designs were bigger and more bulbous (as Thornley and Enever considered moving upmarket), with a longer wheelbase than the MGA and took a long time to pare down to the definitive MGB shape as it became evident where MG's true market lay.

Meanwhile, further experiments were being made at updating the MGA. Coil spring and radius arm suspension, like that on Haigh's modsports car nearly twenty years later, came under consideration as well as fully independent rear suspension. As a result of Leonard Lord's interest—he was a compulsive designer as well as chief executive of BMC—a new body was commissioned from the Italian stylists, Frua. This project, EX214, started as a series of sketches at Abingdon and was turned into a special-bodied MGA in Italy. It is interesting to note that Frua were used at this juncture although Pininfarina had by then been contracted to BMC for such work and the Austin A40 of 1958 was the first sign of their subsequent influence. Much speculation has arisen over the use of Frua, but the most likely explanations appear to be that Pininfarina had only just taken over the BMC contract and were busy with other projects at the time, and that Lord was always keen to keep minions on their toes by promoting what amounted to inter-house rivalries. At any rate, EX214 turned out to be rather ostentatious and distinctly Maserati-like, and Pininfarina got the upper hand at BMC after that.

It also seemed a good idea at that time to try the MGA with more power, to promote it into the Triumph and Big Healey performance fields, a theory which MG enthusiasts have found appealing for years. Austin were busy designing a new family of engines in the vee formation, with a two-litre four-cylinder version proposed for the MGA as EX216. This wide engine fitted in without much difficulty because MGA bodies were dropped on to the chassis during assembly at Abingdon, but one of the factors that went against such an installation was that the entire front end of the body, even if it retained the same outward shape, would have had to have been redesigned to allow the engine to be taken out again without removing the body! It is also one of the principle reasons V8 installations are impractical in the MGA.

This V4 engine was also featured in early MGB prototypes and accounted for the wide bonnet that went into production and eventually made the V8 practical. The V4 (and its natural V6 three-litre extension) were heavy, difficult to balance, and eventually too expensive to produce so they did not materialise in anything other than prototype form. Seven years later Ford eventually came to terms with these problems and produced the V4 and V6 Capris which were their idea (and incidentally, closely akin to Thornley's and Enever's) of a sports car. Even as the MGB was being developed—with coil spring rear suspension at one point—a V6 version was being considered that was eventually to become the in-line six-cylinder MGC. It is ironic that Ford's V6 Capri introduced after the MGC was dropped was to prove such a success.

MG's version of the Ford Capri was EX227, the MGB GT prototype of 1964. It amounted to an Austin A40 hatchback grafted on to the MGB shell and Abingdon did remarkably well, in conjunction with Pininfarina, to produce such a good-looking car from such a conflict of ideals: the soft, rounded shape of the MGB roadster with the angular rear end of the A40. In some respects, it was just what Thornley and Enever wanted, a cheap alternative model to extend their range. But it was not their ideal. They would have liked to have designed their fixed-head car from the start, not just as an adaptation of existing components. Designing with a stressed top would have enabled them to take a lot of weight off the bottom half of the structure with the result that it could have been bigger to meet their original ideas with EX205. This is the exact concept that Ford were to follow with their Capri, resulting in similar performance and a much larger rear seat.

As soon as the GT was in production, Abingdon began thinking about what should follow the MGB, with late 1969 as the production target. Changing the

This was the EX234, a brilliant and outstandingly-pretty car that could have been the MGD.

MGB's rear suspension drastically would have cost so much in bodyshell tooling that they decided to design a completely new car. To justify the cost, this had to be applicable also to the smaller Midget/Sprite range. They were also due for a redesign in any case, having been in production in their contemporary shape for the same length of time as the MGB. The idea of larger and smaller engined versions of the same car in this form (the Midget/Sprite were using a 1275 cc engine by then) mirrored Ford's thinking with the Capri, although Abingdon's exercise EX234, was designed as an open car from the start. BMC, soon to become British Leyland, still could not afford to sanction two completely new designs, a fixed-head and a roadster.

The tragically-beautiful ADO21 that might have become the MGE and been on top of the world today.

EX234 was a brilliant car and outstandingly pretty. It was around the same size as the MGB, except that it had an 87-inch wheelbase rather than 91 inches, two plus two configuration and all independent suspension. Wishbones were used at the front with trailing arms and a chassis-mounted differential at the back. Front and rear systems were interconnected by BMC's Hydroelastic system. Fitting a B series 1798 cc engine or an A series 1275 cc unit would have made the car an MGD or a Midget, but the project was still-born because of the myriad problems that arose with the formation of British Leyland in 1968 and the enormous amount of work needed to keep the existing MG models on the market in America now that they were subject to severe Federal regulations. The decision not to go ahead with EX234 for the 1970 model year was as heart-breaking for Abingdon as the shelving of EX175 has been in 1952. And sadly, EX234 never came down off the shelf.

The next, and last, car designed under Enever's aegis was even more outstanding, despite its Austin designation, ADO 21. It was a mid-engined wedge-shaped car that would have taken the Austin Maxi 1750 cc engine and gearbox (which were expected to replace the B series from 1969) or the similar Australian BMC E6 six-cylinder engines which could be had in 2.2-litre or 2.6-litre forms. At the same time, Triumph were asked to design a front-engined sports car to replace their ageing TR series, which had fallen well behind the MGB in sales. As brilliant as the MG design turned out to be, it was cancelled because Triumph's need was more pressing, and the ill-fated TR7 took precedence.

Both bodies were the product of Harris Mann at Longbridge, but although they used the same basic shape, they were as different as chalk from cheese with the MG bearing a resemblance to Fiat's recent best-seller, the mid-engined X1/9. The MG was far better looking than Fiat's subsequent product, and oddly enough its predecessor, EX234, had also resembled the X1/9's ancestor. This was hardly surprising, however, as EX234 was designed by Pininfarina.

The cancellation of ADO 21 was tragic in that its configuration, using de Dion rear suspension and fuel tank between the engine and the passenger compartment (reflecting Enever's apprehension at impending front-end impact legislation in America), and MacPherson strut front suspension (one of the best features of Lotus and Ford design) had subsequently been proved ideal.

XV

Comparisons with Contemporary Rivals

ONE OF THE reasons for the extraordinary sales success of the MGA and MGB is that there have been few competitors since 1955. The stiffest competition has always come from the Triumph TR range and the market has usually been big enough to absorb the entire output of both factories—at least until the advent of the less successful TR7. The MGC suffered badly from comparison with the MGB in what was already an ailing market for cheap three-litre sports cars, and the MGB GT V8 suffered equally at the hands of British Leyland's pricing policies of the day in comparison with the Ford Capri three litre, and the difficulties in getting enough engines.

The reason for the lack of competition for the MGA and MGB in Britain and the vast American market is that no other manufacturer, with the exception of Triumph, has been able to consistently produce a competitive car in the same quantities for the same price. Morgans have always been competitive in terms of performance and, until they became a cult car in the late 1960s, price. But they have never been a threat to MGs because they have never been produced in anything other than minute quantities. They are also darned uncomfortable! The Sunbeam Alpines made from 1959 were undoubtedly more comfortable than the MGs, but lacked the rugged appeal and were considered something of a 'softies' car. The Big Healeys outperformed both the MGs and contemporary Triumph TRs in a straight line but always cost more, and more important, cost a great deal more to run and insure. Lotus, with the Mark 6 and Seven kit cars, were competitive on price and performance but even more spartan and eccentric than Morgans. The nearest any Continental manufacturers could get to the British pair of MG and Triumph were the Italian Alfas and Fiats, which initially cost around half as much again, and the Japanese Datsun 240Z, which was more directly in the class vacated by the Big Healey and the MGC. American domestic products such as the Chevrolet Corvette and Ford Mustang sold in great numbers in their homeland, but lacked the appeal (and roadholding) of the lithe little European sports cars. Outside America they were matched against an entirely different, and much more expensive brand of car.

In many ways it had to be admitted that the Triumph TR was a superior car to the MG, particularly the MGA. The TR2 made until October 1955 was

The Allard Palm Beach fell by the
wayside before it ever got into serious
production.

quicker (103 mph, 0–60 mph in 11.9 seconds, standing quarter mile 18.7 seconds)
and more economical (32 mpg) but it was not so good looking as the MGA. It was
also a lot noisier and the handling was not so forgiving as that of the MG. It sold
as well at the same price, but there was room for both, the rugged TR and the
altogether more civilised MG, backed by a nostalgic charm dating back to Kimber's
days. The TR's brakes were not quite so good as those of the MGA until the
advent of the disc-front-braked TR3 in September 1956 (a drum-braked TR3 had
succeeded the TR2 in October 1955). Fuel consumption also fell to MGA standards
when the more powerful (and heavier) TR3 was introduced. Although a detachable
steel hard top was available for the TR (putting it in the GT competition class),
Triumphs never made anything like the MGA fixed-head coupé.

Most of the cars made by Morgan in this period used Triumph TR engines
(and the earlier Standard Vanguard version), and generally cost almost the same as
the MGA and TR, sometimes £10–£15 cheaper. The top speed was no higher than
the MGA, usually slightly lower, because of the Morgan's ancient outline. But thanks
to its light weight, acceleration was in the TR class, although the chassis with its
front suspension dating back to 1910, was rather prone to bump steer. Production
never exceeded a handful of cars, however. Triumph had wanted to buy Morgan at
one time, then produced the TR2 when they were rebuffed, so in many ways the
TR could be seen as the modern, mass-produced Morgan.

The Big Healey was a real get-up-and-go sports car with around 103 mph,
0–60 mph in 10.3 seconds, and 22.5 mpg, whether in four cylinder '100' form or

six-cylinder 100-Six. It sold well, especially in America, but because it cost about twenty-five per cent more than the MGA or TR did little to affect their sales. The Healeys aside, the nearest competition in the imported sports car field in the all-important American market were the Alfa Romeos, such as the lovely little Giulietta Spyder, in 1956. This, which was also available as a two-plus-two fixed-head coupé, cost at least fifty per cent more than an MGA or TR, but it was capable of 100 mph with only 1300 cc a 14.8-second 0–60 mph time, and 27 mpg. The roadholding was superb and the ride better than the MGA and the TR. 'It was the most fascinating small sports car we have ever driven,' said *Road & Track*. It was all the more appealing to the Americans because it had wind-up windows even on the open version, whereas the British cars stuck to sidescreens. Its price limited sales, however.

The Sunbeam Alpine of 1959 also distinguished itself with having a higher level of comfort than the MGA or TR. Besides being equipped with wind-up windows, it was plusher inside. However, this Rootes version of the MGA and TR lacked competition development. Its Hillman Husky estate car-based chassis and finned body proved less stable at high speeds although its vital statistics were up to MGA standards (99.5 mph, 13.6-second 0–60 mph, 27 mpg). Lower production runs were inevitable against such competition, and a combination of this and the higher standard of trim set the price around ten per cent higher than that of the big two sports car makers. The Sunbeam Alpine really became something of an alternative car for those seeking a softer tourer, although it did force MG, Triumph and Austin-Healey to follow suit with winding windows on their open sports cars a couple of years later.

Soon after the Sunbeam Alpine came out, Fiat introduced an attractive car in the same class, although it cost more than half as much again. This was because it used the limited-production Farina convertible body of their 1200 car with a production version of the OSCA 1.5-litre racing engine. As it was, the Fiat 1200 convertible was rather underpowered for 1960 and it was not possible to stretch that engine any further; the next size up in Fiat's range was a six-cylinder 1800 cc engine which was too long to fit in the 1200 chassis. Therefore the OSCA engine was slotted in. It was unusual for a racing engine in that it had a cast iron block, which was ideal for larger-scale production. This engine also provided excellent torque and good performance figures: 105 mph, and 0–60 mph in 10.6 seconds. The result was an excellent boulevard tourer, but little threat to MGA sales.

The MGA Twin Cam suffered heavily from the competition provided by the Austin-Healey 100-Six and later the 3000; at £843 basic (with £904 basic for the fixed-head coupé version), the MGA Twin Cam cost more than the 100-Six, priced at £817, and was not quite so quick. It had better brakes, roadholding and cockpit ventilation, but the brakes and roadholding were not too bad on the Big Healey. When it got a three-litre engine and disc front brakes with the 3000 designation in July 1959 the Healey was a much better buy.

The TR3A, which shared the Big Healey's skittish handling, fell into much the same category. It was cheaper than the MGA Twin Cam and faster, at least up to 80 mph. And then there was the question of reliability. The MGA's reputation definitely suffered because of its initially high thirst for oil and trouble caused by its high compression. Although it outperformed the small Alfa Romeos, their twin cam engine was much more reliable.

Alfa Romeo kept their basic design in production for the best part of ten years, although not many of their cars lasted that long; they were good mechanically, but suffered from a dreadful rust problem in damper climes. MG, along with Triumph, were quite good in this respect.

Triumph managed to get their new sports car, the TR4, on the market a year earlier than the MGB. It had more popular styling and wind-up windows like the Sunbeam Alpine, but it lost a little of its edge over the MGB in terms of performance: 102 mph maximum and a 10.9-second 0–60 mph. Its handling didn't improve either until independent rear suspension was introduced in January 1965. Even more important from the sales point of view, a gap had opened up in price: the cheapest MGB retailed at £690 against the TR's £750, further extended by high rates of purchase tax on the home market in the early 1960s. The Sunbeam Alpine came down to almost exactly the same price as the MGB, and although it was updated repeatedly its performance remained inferior with a 97 mph maximum speed and 14.4-second 0–60 mph time. In addition it was not so flexible as the MGB and TR4, an important point on the American market.

The Big Healey, which received wind-up windows in April 1962, remained the next step up in price and performance with 123 mph top speed and a 9.8-second 0–60 mph time, with even more flexibility.

Alfa Romeo pepped up the Giulietta with a 1600 cc engine in 1963 and called it the Giulia. It had more finesse than the MGB but its performance was no better and it never sold in the same quantity.

Car and Driver summed up the mood everywhere with some well-written words in 1964:

'There is a clique of automotive enthusiasts which still subscribes to the legend that a genuine sports car must be uncomfortable. Loyalty to such folklore involves a certain amount of frustration, because most contemporary vehicles have become too civilised to buffet passengers with wind, cramp and broil their legs, and flagellate their kidneys.

'Only the Morgan remains from a bygone era to reassure the believers that stiffness equals stability and discomfort equals desire fulfilled. There was a time when the MGs and Triumph TRs provided similar refuges from advanced automotive design, but both marques have given way to a growing demand for cars that handle properly and go fast with style and grace. The MGB 1800, for example, has roll-up windows and better weather protection than any of its predecessors. It goes faster thanks to more displacement, and it generally radiates a chicness that was absent in the A-series. But it is still an MG and the traditionalists need not despair completely.'

Soon after the competition increased: Triumph improved the TR with the long-overdue independent rear suspension (which made their ride much better than that of the MGB) although the option of the cheaper live axle remained for America, and a Japanese manufacturer, Datsun, started to look menacing on the American market with their Fairlady 1500 roadster. It was a sort of angular MGB with lots of extras (such as whitewall tyres, radio, clock and tonneau cover) included in the basic price. When these sort of options were added to the MGB (which had wire wheels as standard in the United States), it worked out at $150 more, and that's why the Datsun caught on. It started to sell really well when it was improved and turned into the Sport 1600 in 1965. Its performance was not far short of the MGB at 101 mph with a 13.3-second 0–60 mph time although its handling was nowhere near so good. A majority of readers in a *Road & Track* survey said that was why they preferred their MGBs to rivals such as the Datsun. At that time, too, the Japanese factory's quality control was not so good as that at Abingdon, and not many of these 'Japanese MGBs' have survived. However, Datsun continued to improve their cars, notably when they fitted an overhead camshaft two-litre engine and five-speed gearbox in 1967 to make the Sports 2000. This was a good deal faster than the 1600, with a 114 mph maximum speed, 0–60 mph in 10.2 seconds and a price not much more than an MGB—about the same as a Triumph TR4A. In appearance, it looked something like a cross between the two, and suffered a little as a result; a lot of Americans bought their MGBs because they considered the styling to be the best in its class. Few of these Datsuns were sold anywhere else other than in Japan for at that time the factory was fully extended with the American market alone.

Meanwhile Fiat produced a good-looking 1500 Spider based on their earlier OSCA-engined machine. With engineering by Lampredi from Ferrari and styling by Farina, it would have been a great success had it been faster. As it was, its 1500 cc saloon car engine endowed it only with a top speed of 94 mph and a 0–60 mph time of 17 seconds. However, it was superior to the MGB in that it had a superbly designed and easy-to-operate hood and a much bigger luggage boot. For some reason it retained the non-synchromesh first gear of the OSCA-engined car rather than adopting the all-synchromesh gearbox being fitted to Fiat saloons at the time. This cost it some popularity; even the die-hards in Britain were tooling up for the all-synchromesh gearboxes then!

Alfa Romeo at last abandoned their Giulietta/Giulia spider design for the adventurous new Duetto in 1966, marketing it at first with their 1600 engine and at a price far higher than that of the MGB. The 'flying saucer' styling was controversial but there was universal acclaim for its handling and performance: 113 mph, with a 0–60 mph time of 11.3 seconds. As ever, it remained the next step up, particularly as the Big Healey was in its final year.

Car and Driver picked their time well to run a pioneer comparison test between six sports cars in the under $4000 range in September 1966. It was the end of a period in which there was little to compete with very basic sports cars such as the MGB and ideally about the time that MG should have been intending to introduce something new, rather than just update the MGB to Mark II specification. Nevertheless, the MGB did well in *Car and Driver*'s test in September 1966, finishing second behind the new Alfa Duetto (priced at $4025 against the MGB's $2950) with the Fiat 1500 third, the Sunbeam Alpine fourth, the Datsun 1600 fifth and the Triumph TR4A sixth.

The Elva Courier was a special frequently using MG running gear. It
was much lighter than the MGA or
MGB and did well in competition.
Chris Meek's Courier is seen here at
Mallory Park at Easter in 1959 contesting third place in an *Autosport*
championship race with Ted Lund's
MGA.

Their evaluations were mostly based on those of racing driver Ken Miles, who
extracted best acceleration, top speed and lap times from the Alfa Duetto at New
York's National Speedway. 'When I get into it I immediately feel the car is part of me,
not some strange machine,' said Miles.

None of the testers 'really loved' the MG, but its overall performance was
so good that it couldn't be ignored. 'It's captured the look of a modern sports car
while retaining the blood-and-guts feeling of the traditional sports car,' said *Car and
Driver*. Miles added: 'The MG will give its owner a great deal of pleasure and long
life. The engine, transmission and brakes are very rugged, very well built but—
personally—it isn't my cup of tea because I don't like to put that much effort into
driving a car like this.'

Unlike the MG, everybody liked the Fiat, but it had the worst braking distance,
the worst lap time and the next-to-worst acceleration. 'It's a pleasant little car,'
said Miles, 'the sort of thing you'd buy your wife to pedal to and from the
market.'

The Sunbeam Alpine was the most innocuous car of the group; it had no
outstanding faults, and no noteworthy attributes. The Alpine's acceleration was
middling as were its lap times. 'The car actually handles fairly well, considering
that it has quite a high centre of gravity and a rather short wheelbase,' said
Miles. 'It has one severe handling fault. It won't stop.'

The Datsun gave the impression of being incredibly well put together, although
the suspension was far too jolting and proved to be no advantage to the roadholding.
'When the design people catch up with today's market they will have a very good
car indeed,' said Miles.

The Triumph which finished last came in for criticism on every score and seems to have been an exceptionally poor model. *Car and Driver* couldn't believe that all Triumphs were so bad and borrowed a rather well-worn demonstrator soon afterwards and pronounced it much better—but too late for their side-by-side test.

The new generation of cars that the MGB Mark II faced were a good deal more competitive. The Triumph TR went up to six cylinders and 2.5 litres in 1967 and became more of a competitor for the MGC although it still influenced decisions in the MGB-buying field. The fuel-injection TR5 was the fastest TR ever with 120 mph and an 8.8-second 0–60 mph time, although its price remained within a couple of hundred pounds of the MGB; the TR250 American version, with its Stromberg emission carburetters, had only a similar performance to the MGB.

The TR remained in open form only and Triumph introduced an intriguing new fixed-head coupé the GT6 as competition for the MGB GT in 1966. This cost very little more and was essentially an amalgam of the small open Triumph Spitfire with the more powerful six-cylinder two-litre engine that was to be used in the Triumph Vitesse saloon and drop head. The result was extraordinary, a miniature two-seater rather like a small E type Jaguar, with 105 mph top speed and a scorching 10.5-second 0–60 mph acceleration. It was cheap to run with 26 mpg and a good ride from its soft suspension—aimed at the American market—but the handling was a disaster. Triumph's retained the Spitfire's swing axle rear suspension lay-out until 1968, which made the car very hairy to handle at speed with so much extra power. It suffered in comparison with the MGB GT in that

To many people the Austin-Healey 100 was the next step up from an MGA. Like the TR2, the Austin-Healey offered superior performance, but inferior roadholding and it cost more than an MGA.

it was very small inside with no attempt at rear seats, but it was faster in a straight line. Sales figures were not very high, due in great part to the fact that Triumph's production lines had a great number of models to cope with at the time, and money was short for expansion.

Fiat updated their 1.5-litre sports range late in 1966 with the 124S series, a two-plus-two spider and a full four-seater sports coupé. These cars featured a twin overhead camshaft engine and the option of a five-speed gearbox at a price only £200 above that of the MGB GT in Britain and not much more than $100 in America. Performance was slightly inferior to that of the MGB GT with 100 mph top speed and a 13-second 0–60 mph time, achieved with a lack of flexibility typical of small Italian cars. But the first 124s were good looking and the coupé was much roomier than the MGB GT, with proper rear seats. When sales really got going in America in 1969, the 124 coupé became a serious competitor for the MGB GT among those who wanted something slightly softer and more sophisticated. A relatively low proportion of these outstandingly well designed cars have survived however, as they proved to be afflicted with a worse-than-average rust problem.

Meanwhile Alfa sales in America fluctuated badly as emission regulations kept them out in 1968 and 1970 until fuel injection replaced their Weber carburetters. The MGB kept selling throughout this difficult period with no apparent loss of performance, and in its home market the Italian cars had difficulty in establishing a firm foothold owing to high import duty.

Triumph revised the rear suspension of the GT6 to make it a much better, and safer, car in 1968, giving it more power at the same time. They also managed to keep the price down so that it was an altogether better bargain than the MGB GT

A Rolls-Healey prototype that might have been produced instead of the MGC.

if you didn't mind a mini-car. The GT6 Mark II's performance figures were: 110 mph top speed with a 9.4-second 0–60 mph time. Its size limited potential sales, however. In 1969, the TR5/TR250 was restyled as the TR6 with independent rear suspension as standard, available with the fuel-injection engine everywhere except America. Performance of the Federal-specification TR6 on carburetters remained much the same as the TR250 and MGB.

Also, for the first time, a Porsche became available in the same price bracket as the MG. This was the 914, a joint effort by Porsche and Volkswagen, introduced in 1969. It was made only in left-hand-drive form and was a significant competitor for the MGB only in foreign markets. In theory it could have been a great sports car with mid-engined configuration, removeable Targa-style top and Volkswagen reliability with the legendary name of Porsche. In practice it didn't live up to expectations, suffering from a lack of development, uncharacteristically poor quality control and dumpy styling. Top speed, with a 1700 cc four-cylinder engine, was 109 mph with a 0–60 mph time of 13.9 seconds. The price was about ten to fifteen per cent more than an MGB roadster, depending on options.

A far more formidable competitor was the Datsun 240Z introduced in Japan in 1969. Supplies started trickling through to the United States in 1970 at the same price as the Porsche 914, and only fractionally dearer than the TR6 and Fiat 124. The demand for this sleek six-cylinder fixed-head coupé which took its inspiration from the Big Healey and Jaguar E type was tremendous for a variety of reasons: its performance was in the Healey class, 122 mph, 0–60 mph in 8.7 seconds with improved fuel economy (21 mpg), four-wheel independent suspension, far more attractive styling than anything before from Japan, and it was well made despite its low price. Against such opposition the MGB could score only in terms of price, the fact that a roadster model was available, and that the market was big enough for both.

The waiting list for Datsun 240Zs was enormous when *Road & Track* tested sports cars in the $3000–$4000 range in June 1970, so they were able only to try the Fiat 124 Spider, the Porsche 914, Triumph TR6 and an MGB roadster. In their estimation, the Fiat was the best of the bunch with the Porsche and Triumph well behind but close together; the MGB trailed. Performance figures were remarkably similar, however, with the Porsche and Triumph managing 109 mph, the Fiat 106 mph and the MG 104 mph; the Triumph's 0–60 mph time was 10.7 seconds, the Fiat's 11.9, the MG's 12.1 and the Porsche's 13.9. Fuel consumption worked out at 31.5 mpg for the Porsche (well ahead of the others), 24.3 for the Fiat, 24 for the Triumph and 23.5 for the MG, so on paper there was not much between them.

Of the Fiat, *Road & Track* said: 'The overwhelming margin of preference for the Fiat (on our marking system) surprised everyone, including those who voted most strongly for it. The Fiat won by virtue of its overall balance. On the road, its steering, roadholding and ride made an unbeatable combination; in pampering the occupants its seating, interior fittings and weather protection were most effective, approached only by the Porsche. Every car in the group has a serious flaw; the Fiat's is its small, low-torque engine.'

Of the Porsche, they said: 'The 914's very unconventionality is responsible for both the high and low marks it received. Every feature was either praised or strongly disliked. Its awkward styling, noisy VW engine and cantankerous [gear] shift pattern put most drivers off at the start, but its excellent roadability, comfort and long-legged cruising qualities found favour . . . in two words, the Porsche 914 is futuristic but unresolved.'

Of the Triumph, they said: 'The strong, beautiful-sounding engine of the TR6 makes it one of the easiest and most enjoyable cars to drive—on good roads . . . then the car's extremely dated chassis and suspension make themselves known all too harshly. The dated character of the car also shows up in the styling and narrow cockpit, but in each case Triumph has done a better than fair job of improving a design that goes back to the TR4 of late 1961 . . . the top is nowhere near so convenient to put up or down as on the Fiat or Porsche, requiring a lot of careful folding, but is still vastly better than the disassemble-reassemble affair of the MG. The two words we'd choose for the Triumph are strong but dated.' Of the MGB, they said:

'It has had a long, successful life—even more than for the Triumph—but the end is in sight. Basically the MGB Mark II is a very good car. It has few serious faults but was consistently unimpressive compared to the outstanding qualities of one or more of the other cars in each category on our score sheets. The updating of the car—except for the much-needed all-synchro gearbox—has been so stingy that it simply looks and feels old. Its price—lowest of the four cars—is therefore an important factor.

'The MGB has enough power and torque to perform well in a straight line and it does much better than the Triumph in overall handling and ride though steering is notchy rather than progressive . . .

'If the MG functions decently, it falls down on aesthetics and convenience. The styling has suffered rather than benefitted from the recent modifications, while the interior is decidedly unattractive. In most cases, needed improvements have been made as cheaply as possible . . . capable but undistinguished would characterise the MG. Its low price may keep it on the market for some time but it is badly in need of replacement.'

As America for the first time experienced the horrors of a waiting list amounting to six months or more for a sports car, the Datsun 240Z, black market prices made a mockery of its $3600 list price. This interested General Motors, so they uprated the Opel 1100 GT coupé to 1.9 litres and produced a sort of mini-Corvette. This pretty little car was about the same size as the GT6 and performed nearly as well with a 113 mph maximum speed and 0–60 mph time of 10.8 seconds—enough to make an impact on the MGB GT's foreign market. Like the Porsche 914 it was available only in left-hand-drive form.

Therefore in July 1971 *Road & Track* chose a Datsun 240Z (supplies were filtering through even to England by then), a Fiat 124 1600 cc coupé, an Opel GT, and MGB GT and a Triumph GT6 for their next sporty comparison test in the

The Datsun 240Z, the car that took over where the MGC left off and hit MGB sales in the process.

$3000–$4000 bracket. Needless to say, the Datsun won hands down. The Fiat was second with similar comments to those in the earlier group test, the Opel third, the MG fourth and the Triumph fifth. Of the Opel, they said: 'It is a crisp little package but not impressive value for the money,' and they were afflicted with an unpleasant drumming in the tiny GT6. To sum up *Road & Track* said:

'One of our five drivers commented after the trip that the Datsun should be rated separately, as it is simply a class above the rest. But when all is said and tallied, the Fiat came surprisingly close and the Opel was far from unpleasant. As for the two Britishers, we do not wish to kick dead horses and sincerely hope that England will be able to get off her duff, produce some competitive cars again and challenge the other countries. We have reason to believe that British Leyland does intend to keep building sports cars and to come up not only with new designs but to redesign the product "mix" of MG, Triumph and Jaguar. One of these new products, we would predict, will be a medium-price GT replacing both the B and the GT6—one that we hope will render the choice of a good $3500 GT a bit more difficult to make.'

Datsun and Opel also marketed an automatic version with not quite such a good installation is that on the MG, but—like MG—withdrew the model through lack of demand. Potential buyers still wanted a car they could drive all by themselves, apparently.

However, automatic versions of the Ford Capri—introduced in 1969—sold well; this was because buyers thought of it more as a sporting saloon than as an outright sports car. Cars such as the Capri, Ford Escort Mexico, Vauxhall Firenza and Opel Manta sold well and made life more difficult for the MGB GT, offering

The sort of car that MG might have made had their design department been given their head in the 1970s: the mid-engined Lotus Europa.

more accommodation and similar performance. However, because the MGB was available in roadster form and at a competitive price it still sold well.

It must have seemed like a godsend when the Datsun 240Z went upmarket in 1974 to sell at $5200 in 260Z two-plus-two form against the MGB GT's $3950. The Datsun kept its place as the best-selling sports car in the world with the MGB GT selling steadily on its low price and traditional concept. Not even the advent of cars such as the Lancia Beta coupé and Toyota Celica GT in 1975 could kill the good old MG although the GT version was withdrawn from the American market after the launch of the Triumph TR7.

The TR7 was disappointing because it was too much like a saloon car. Its performance was about ten per cent slower than the TR6 and about ten per cent quicker than the MGB (it is better to quote percentages in this case as there was a considerable difference in performance between cars destined for California, the other American states, and Europe in this period). This difference in performance at only a small premium in price should have been enough to kill off the MGB— but it didn't happen because of the styling of the TR7, the hard top, and a bad reputation for reliability. The TR7 also suffered by comparison with the brilliant mid-engined Fiat X1/9 introduced at the same time. This baby Ferrari bore a remarkable resemblance to the ill-fated ADO 21 MG project and was dubbed 'the most significant sports car since the Datsun 240Z,' by *Road & Track* in a comparative test of sports cars costing less than $6000 (the equivalent of the old $4000 limit) in 1976.

The only seven cars to fall into this category were the Fiat 124 Spider, the Fiat X1/9, the MGB roadster, the MG Midget, the Triumph Spitfire, the TR6 and the TR7. The TR6 was not tested as its day was nearly past and it could not be bought then in the largest market, California. The MGB managed to beat its equally antique stablemates, the Spitfire and the Midget (which had acquired 1.5-litre engines to combat performance-sapping emission regulations since the halcyon days of the 1960s), but was placed only fourth behind, number one, the Fiat X1/9, two the TR7 and three the Fiat 124.

However, some clue to the MGB's continuing popularity was given by *Road & Track*'s summing up: 'Perhaps British Leyland will have the last laugh. The MGB could be the first replicar that never went out of production.' An all-time classic, in fact, like the Morgan.

The specialist magazines had been saying things like that for fifteen years and were well into their stride when the MGC was introduced in 1967. The MGC's most obvious rival was the Triumph TR5 against which it suffered by comparison. Triumph used a long-stroke six-cylinder engine with fuel injection, set further back than in the MGC, with the result that the car responded and handled much better, at the expense of legroom in the cockpit. Nevertheless, the cockpit in the Triumph was more comfortable because it had better seats. With a retail price only five per cent higher than the MGC and similar performance, the TR5 was a much better bargain in manual roadster form. There was nothing quite like the MGC in automatic roadster form and great hopes were pinned on this in the American market. But like Datsun later, MG found the demand of automatic sports cars like their's to be depressingly small. This was despite the success of home-brewed big sports cars such as the Ford Mustang and Chevrolet Corvette. In GT form, the MGC's closest competitor was the Reliant Scimitar three-litre which, again, shared a similar performance with much better accommodation and handling, for only £100 more. *CAR* magazine went as far as to lament that the Scimitar's Ford Zodiac V6 engine could not be fitted to the MGC! Perhaps it was not such wishful thinking, as Sunbeam (then owned by Rootes) fitted a Ford engine to their Tiger before being taken over by Chrysler, who could not countenance a rival's engine powering one of their cars. In practice, however, the MGC proved to be a much more durable car than the Reliant (or the Sunbeam Tiger which went out almost as the MGC came in). This is one of the reasons for it becoming a much sought-after car in the late 1970s.

MG's next attempt at a big sports car, the V8, should have been far more successful. It was practically as fast as the Datsun 240Z (same top speed, fractionally slower acceleration) and more economical (23 mpg against 21 mpg) and cheaper (£2294 against £2535). It could have been priced lower, and if the engine had been 'Federalised' it would undoubtedly have sold well despite its dated running gear. This was because it still handled well and had the great advantage, for the massive American market, of having a popular American-based power unit. Had the price been more realistic it would have been able to compete better with the Reliant Scimitar GTE (slightly slower, much bigger, only £200 dearer) and the Ford Capri three-litre which offered only marginally inferior performance and superior accommodation for £450 less.

It seems that *Road & Track* has almost been proved right: the MGB has been in production for so long now it is assuming the Morgan-like mantle of a brand-new vintage sports car. Its a pity that the MGB GT V8 did not survive long enough, as the Morgan Plus 8 with the same engine has been proved to be the ultimate vintage sports car today.

XVI

The MG Clubs

MG CLUB life has never been healthier. Just as the MGA, MGB and MGC have become established as classic sports cars, clubs for their owners have blossomed. For years, since 1930 when John Thornley helped start the MG Car Club, it was the only organisation in its field and became the biggest marque club in the world, thanks to his constant encouragement and the equally dedicated efforts of many other members. The MG Car Club was rarely challenged until business consultant Roche Bentley started the MG Owners' Club with his wife, Tricia, in 1973. Within six years membership has risen to more than 8000, composed mainly of owners of the MGA, MGB and MGC. In addition, two American offshoots of the MG CC, the North American MGA Register and the American MGB Association, have mushroomed as national organisations to cater for these sports cars.

How is it that such apparently individual organisations have been able to flourish when the field had been dominated for so long by the old-established MG Car Club with a membership of around 5000 in the United Kingdom and many more overseas? It is because the clubs are effectively complementary and in the case of the entirely-separate MG Car Club, there is a substantial proportion of dual membership. The naturally more conservative MG Car Club—a high proportion of whose members are of many years' standing—has an immaculate record of competition organisation in staging race meetings, hill climbs, rallies, driving tests and trials besides well-attended club meetings, affectionately known as Noggins and Natters, at hostelries throughout the world. A variety of social events, such as dinners, dances and film shows, are organised and the quality of their show days, with concours competitions, are second to none. Their summer Silverstone weekend is the highlight of their year with all aspects of interest catered for. But, because in recent years their administration has been essentially part-time, they have maintained a low profile in the marketing of spare parts and other commercial items.

The MG Owners' Club came into being—along with another, smaller, co-operative called the Octagon Car Club dealing with pre-1955 MGs—as an organisation aimed at helping, primarily, the owners of MGBs and MGCs to keep their vehicles on the road at a reasonable cost.

This side of club life was well catered for while Thornley was still at Abingdon and the MG Car Club received substantial support from the factory. However, when

Left: The MG Owners' Club staff hard at work with Roche Bentley in the centre.

Below: A typical MG Owners' Club get-together for a weekend outing.

BMC became British Leyland in 1968, drastic economies were needed and individual car clubs were no longer subsidised. One of the first, and most tangible, effects was the loss of the MG Car Club's superb factory-produced magazine, *Safety Fast*. It was replaced by a British Leyland publication called *High Road*, which embraced other marque clubs within the new organisation. This magazine could not concentrate so heavily on the products of Abingdon.

Within five weeks the MG Car Club had re-organised itself to bring out its own version of *Safety Fast*, with a new format more suited to their financial scope. This is the publication that today still binds the MG Car Club together as its prime means of international communication. But, although quality of production and content are high, it is essentially amateur in concept and is run, like the club, in a delightfully non-commercial manner. As a result, the needs of MGB and MGC owners receive no more than equal attention to those of the enthusiasts who run earlier models of MG, despite the great contrast in numbers.

It was into this breach that Roche Bentley stepped with a borrowed portable typewriter and a rubber stamp. He advertised in that exceedingly English institution, *Exchange & Mart*, and attracted many letters from owners anxious to trace second-hand parts for their cars. A card index system was established and members were asked to list, on their subscription forms, parts that were surplus to their requirements. This enterprise coincided with the rapid escalation in the cost of new spares and within weeks all manner of parts were changing hands through the emergent MG Owners' Club. A magazine full of for sale and wanted advertisements like those of *Exchange & Mart* followed in January 1974.

From these small beginnings, the MG Owners' Club has expanded to include the MGA (and some earlier models such as the T series in close co-operation with the Octagon Car Club) and provide members with a mine of information including recommended retailers, discounts negotiated in all areas of car running costs (such as insurance, tyres and labour bills), special offers of new spares as a result of bulk buying, regalia, literature, newsletters full of practical tips, and eventually a magnificent *Year Book*. The MG Car Club had been providing many of these services, but on a far less intensively organised scale.

Throughout this gestation period the MG Owners' Club maintained close checks on the quality of supplies through personal contact and questionnaires to all members. A club caravan started attending national car meetings and soon the MG Owners' Club started organising its own events. Membership multiplied to such an extent that it became a full-time job for the Roche Bentley, and his brother Martin. By 1977 a further four full-time staff had been taken on and a network of spares secretaries and area meetings organised. Today the MG Owners' Club has moved into motor sport in a very low key manner and still has the same ideals, to provide an organisation that enables MGs, particularly the A, B and C, to be maintained in good condition and run at a reasonable cost. In the face of such competition, the MG Car Club has adopted a more aggressive attitude to recruitment to the ultimate benefit of MGA, MGB and MGC owners, many of whom had been forming the opinion that the elder club was more interested in the earlier cars because of its natural support for them.

In the United States, the North American MGA Register was started in 1975 by Mac Spears, John Wright and Len and Ruth Renkenberger, along the lines of the highly-successful New England T Register, a group of MG Car Club members which had grown into a national organisation. By the middle of 1978, its membership had registered more than 1000 MGAs, plus many variants of the MGA and signed on numerous associate members. The objectives and activities are similar to those of the New England T Register, to expand the appreciation of MG cars made in their period, with national meetings and local chapters in most states and Canada.

The American MGB Association was organised on similar lines after being founded at Inwood, New York, in 1976. Its membership has grown rapidly to around the same size as the North American MGA Register at a rate in keeping with that of the MG Owners' Club in Britain. There are strong similarities in the way these organisations operate except that the American MGB Association does not concentrate heavily on second-hand spares. In other parts of the world, MG club events are run on strongly-traditional MG Car Club lines. But no matter which club, they are all receiving stronger British Leyland moral support now that the group has become more interested in the fortunes of its individual marques. National secretaries and local organisers are:

United Kingdom, MG Car Club, General Secretary, Gordon Cobban, PO Box 126, Brentwood, Essex CM15 8RP, membership Mrs Sheila Laurence, 67 Wide Bargate, Boston, Lincs PE21 6LE. *MGA Register*, Stuart Holley, 12 Sweet Briar Close, Shaw Clough, Rochdale, Lancs OL21 6NX; *MGA Twin Cam Group*, P Richer,

Above left: The MG Car Club Johannesburg Centre concours in 1973.

Above right: Later model MGs line up for an MG Car Club concours at Silverstone in 1978.

9 Grenville Way, Whitley Bay, Tyne and Wear NE26 3JJ; *MGC Register*, Peter Sullivan, 54 Woodland Way, Theydon Bois, Essex CM16 7DZ; *V8 Register*, Victor Smith, 4 Albany Close, East Sheen, London SW14 7DX.

MG Owners' Club: General Secretary, Roche Bentley, 13 Church End, Over, Cambridgeshire.

North America, MG CC: The North American MGA Register, General Secretary, Ruth Renkenberger, 5 Miller Fall Court, Derwood, Maryland, 20855 USA; *The MGA Twin Cam Registry*, Lyle F York, PO Box 1068, 5105 Kingswood Lane, Anderson, Indiana, 46011 USA; *American MGB Association national headquarters*, General Secretary, Marian Farrell, 111 Roger Avenue, Inwood, New York, 11696 USA.

Canada, MG CC: Canadian Classic, Harold Lunner, PO Box 48452, P S Bentall Centre, Vancouver, British Columbia V7X 1A2 Canada.

Europe, MG CC: Norwegian Centre, John Erik Skjefstad, Kastanjevien 19, Oslo 4, Norway; Sweden, Lennarth Gustafson, Vardshusvagen 6, 141 43 Huddinge, Sweden; *Danish Centre*, Svend Carstensen, Genuavej 45, 2300 Kbhvn S, Denmark; *Danish Centre West*, Poul H Jensen, PO Box 6, 6330 Padborg, DK Denmark; *Holland*, W van der Veer, J F Kennedyplantsoen 54, Voorschoten, Holland; *MGA Type Owners*, Holland, Bram Hoogendijk, Gerberalaan 28, Naaldwijk 2250, Holland; *Luxembourg Centre*, Tom Maathuis, 1 Rue Tomm, Fouhren, Luxembourg; *Belgium*, Pierard Franz, 37 Rue Delvaux, 6040 Jumet, Belgium; *Deutschland*, Postfach 94, Breitlacher Strasse 40–44 6000, Frankfurt 90, West Germany; *Switzerland*, Arnold Flammer, Burggraben 24, CH-9000, St Gallen, Switzerland; *Italian Centre*, F. Filippello, Via Vetulonia 38/A, 00183 Roma, Italy; *Dalmatia Centre*, Slobodan Jelich, 58000 Split, Hektorvicca 34, Yugoslavia.

Japan, MG CC: Japanese Centre, Y Kuboyama, 5–8–605, Kitamachi 3-Chome, Kichijoji, Musachino-shi, Tokyo 180, Japan.

Australia and New Zealand, MG CC: Gold Coast Centre, Valda Thompson, PO Box 103, Surfers' Paradise, Queensland 4217, Australia; *New South Wales Centre*, Frank Bett, PO Box 5165 GPO, Sydney 2001; *Newcastle Centre*, The Secretary, PO Box 62A, Newcastle 2300 NSW, Australia; *Western Australia*, Vic Longden, PO Box U1924, GPO Perth, Western Australia 6001; *South Australia*, Roy Kingham, 93 Chief Street, Brompton, South Australia 5007; *Auckland Centre*, C M Grant, PO Box 6483, Auckland 1, New Zealand.

South Africa, MG CC: Johannesburg Centre, Mrs M Nunn, PO Box 52336, Saxonwold 2132, Transvaal, South Africa; *Cape Town Centre*, Hon Sec, PO Box 2808, Cape Town, South Africa; *Natal Centre*, Hedley M Adams, PO Box 10260, Marine Parade 4056, South Africa; *Port Elizabeth Centre*, 39 York Road, North End, Port Elizabeth, South Africa; *Northern Transvaal Centre*, PO Box 17006, Groenkloof, 0027, Pretoria, South Africa.

XVII

Log Book Specifications

Part One: Colour Combinations

ONE of the most perplexing problems when restoring an MG—or almost any other car for that matter—is discovering the original colour combinations. For instance, what sort of upholstery was available with Old English White? Also, how do you tell the original colour of your MG should it have been subjected to repeated, multi-coloured resprays? Taking a good look inside the top of the scuttle is often the best answer. It's a pretty long-lasting part of the body and people don't often spray in there.

Index of colour combinations

MGA 1500 Roadster

Body	Hood	Interior
Black	Ice Blue	Red
	Black	Green
Orient Red	Black	Red or Black
Glacier Blue	Ice Blue	Grey or Black
Old English White	Black	Red or Black
Tyrolite Green	Ice Blue	Grey or Black

MGA 1500 Fixed-Head Coupé

Body	Interior
Black	Red or Green
Orient Red	Red or Black
Old English White	Red or Black
Island Green	Grey or Black
Mineral Blue	Grey or Black

NB: All roadsters had black carpets; all coupés had grey.

Early Twin Cams
Colour schemes as per equivalent 1500 MGA

What better registration number to remember the MGB by?

Late Twin Cams
Colour schemes as per equivalent 1600 MGA

MGA 1600 Roadster

Body	Hood	Interior
Chariot Red	Beige	Red or Beige
	Grey	Black
Iris Blue	Blue	Black
Alamo Beige	Beige	Red
Dove Grey	Grey	Red
Old English White	Grey	Red or Black
Black	Grey	Red or Beige

MGA 1600 Fixed-Head Coupé
Colour schemes as per roadster

MGA 1600 Mark II
Colour schemes as per 1600

MGB Roadster (early)

Body	Hood	Interior
Tartan Red	Red	Red or Black
Iris Blue	Blue	Black or Blue
Chelsea Grey	Grey	Red
Old English White	Grey	Red or Black
Black	Grey	Red or Black

MGB Roadster 1964 model year

Body	Hood	Interior
British Racing Green	Grey or Black	Black
Tartan Red	Black or Red	Black or Red
Old English White	Grey or Black	Black or Red
Iris Blue	Blue or Black	Blue or Black
Black	Grey or Black	Red or Blue

MGB Roadster 1966 model year

Body	Hood	Interior
British Racing Green	Black	Black
Tartan Red	Black	Black
Old English White	Black	Black or Red
Mineral Blue	Black	Black
Black	Black	Red or Black
Pale Primrose	Black	Black

MGB GT

Body	Interior
Tartan Red	Black
Mineral Blue	Black
Sandy Beige	Black or Red
British Racing Green	Black
Grampian	Black or Red
Old English White	Black or Red
Black	Black or Red
Pale Primrose	Black

MGB Roadster, MGB GT, MGC Roadster and MGC GT, 1968 model year

Body	Hood	Interior
Glacier White	All hoods Black	Black
British Racing Green		Autumn Leaf
Teal Blue		Autumn Leaf
Midnight Blue		Black
Flame Red		Black
Blaze		Black
Bronze Yellow		Black
Bedouin		Autumn Leaf
British Racing Green		Black
Blue Royale		Black
Pale Primrose		Black

MGB GT and MGC GT only 1968 model year

Body	Interior
Bermuda Blue	Black
Antelope	Black

MGB Roadster and MGB GT 1970 model year

Body	Hood	Interior
Glacier	All hoods Black	Navy
Teal Blue		Autumn Leaf
Flame Red		Navy
Blaze		Navy
Bronze Yellow		Navy
Green Mallard		Autumn Leaf
Aqua		Navy
Harvest Gold		Navy

MGB roadster and MGB GT 1971 model year

Body	Hood	Interior
Glacier White	All hoods Black	Navy
Teal Blue		Ochre or Autumn Leaf
Flame Red		Navy
Blaze		Navy
Bronze Yellow		Navy
Green Mallard		Ochre or Autumn Leaf
Aqua		Navy
Harvest Gold		Navy
Lime Flower		Navy
Damask Red		Navy
Black Tulip		Ochre

MGB roadster and MGB GT 1972 model year

Body	Hood	Interior
Glacier White	All hoods Black	Navy
Teal Blue		Autumn Leaf
Blaze		Navy
Bronze Yellow		Navy
Green Mallard		Autumn Leaf
Harvest Gold		Navy
Lime Flower		Navy
Damask Red		Navy
Black Tulip		Autumn Leaf

MGB roadster, MGB GT and MGB GT V8 1973 model year

Body	Hood	Interior
Glacier White	All hoods Black	Black or Autumn Leaf
Tahiti Blue		Black or Autumn Leaf
Flamenco Red		Black
Harvest Gold		Black
Damask Red		Black
Tundra Green		Autumn Leaf

Bracken	Black or Autumn Leaf
Citron	Black
Glacier White	Black
Chartoise	Black
Brooklands Green	Autumn Leaf
Tahiti Blue	Autumn Leaf
Damask Red	Black
Flamenco Red	Black
Sand Glow	Autumn Leaf

Part Two: Mechanical Specifications, Dimensions and Production Figures

MGA 1500 roadster

58,750 (including coupés) built between August 1955 and May 1959, chassis numbers from HD 10101–68850

Engine
Four-cylinder, CUBIC CAPACITY 1489 cc; BORE AND STROKE 73.025 mm × 88.9 mm; MAX. POWER 68 bhp at 5500 rpm (soon increased to 72 bhp at 5500 rpm); MAX. TORQUE 77 lb/ft at 3500 rpm; COMPRESSION RATIO 8.3 : 1; CARBURETTERS two 1.5-inch SU.

Chassis
WEIGHT (dry) 1988 lb; WHEELBASE 7 ft 10 ins; FRONT TRACK 3 ft 11.5 ins; REAR TRACK 4 ft 0.75 ins; LENGTH 13 ft; WIDTH 4 ft 9.25 ins: HEIGHT (with hood erect) 4 ft 2 ins; TURNING CIRCLE 30.75 ft; FRONT SUSPENSION independent wishbone and coil; REAR SUSPENSION live axle, semi-elliptical leaf springs; BRAKES Lockheed hydraulic drums all round; GEARBOX four-speed (overall ratios with 4.3 : 1 rear axle) 4.3, 5.908, 9.52, 15.652, reverse 20.468; STEERING rack and pinion; SHOCK ABSORBERS Armstrong lever arm; WHEELS AND TYRES Dunlop 5.60–15 steel disc or wire.

MGA 1500 coupé

As MGA 1500 roadster except produced from October 1956 to May 1959, chassis numbers from HM 20671–68850. Weight 2105 lb.

MGA Twin Cam roadster

2111 (including coupés) built between spring 1958 and spring 1960, chassis numbers from YD1 501–2611, and YD2 501.

Engine
Four-cylinder, CUBIC CAPACITY 1588 cc; BORE AND STROKE 75.39 mm × 88.9 mm;

MAX. POWER 108 bhp at 6700 rpm; MAX. TORQUE 104 lb/ft at 4500 rpm; COMPRESSION
RATIO 9.9 : 1 (8.3 : 1 from chassis no 2251); CARBURETTERS two 1.75-inch SU.

Chassis
As MGA 1500 except weight (dry) 2185 lb; FRONT TRACK 4 ft; REAR TRACK 4 ft 1 in;
TURNING CIRCLE 35 ft; BRAKES Dunlop discs all round; WHEELS AND TYRES Dunlop
5.90–15 centre-lock disc.

MGA Twin Cam coupé

As MGA Twin Cam roadster except chassis numbers from YD3 501. Weight 2245 lb.

MGA 1600 roadster

31501 (including coupés) built between May 1959 and Spring 1961, chassis numbers
G/HN 68851–100351

Engine
Four-cylinder, CUBIC CAPACITY 1588 cc; BORE AND STROKE 75.39 mm × 88.9 mm;
MAX. POWER 79.5 bhp at 5600 rpm; MAX. TORQUE 87 lb/ft at 3800 rpm; COMPRESSION
RATIO 8.3 : 1; CARBURETTERS two 1.5-inch SU.

Chassis
As MGA 1500 except WEIGHT 2015 lb; BRAKES Girling discs front, drums rear.

MGA 1600 coupé

As MGA 1600 roadster except chassis numbers G/HD2 68851–100351. WEIGHT
2075 lb.

MGA 1600 Mark II roadster

8719 (including coupés) built between Spring 1961 and July 1962, chassis numbers
G/HN2 100352–109070

Engine
Four-cylinder, CUBIC CAPACITY 1622 cc; BORE AND STROKE 76.2 mm × 88.9 mm;
MAX. POWER 86 bhp at 5500 rpm; MAX. TORQUE 97 lb/ft at 4000 rpm; COMPRESSION
RATIO 8.9 : 1; CARBURETTERS two 1.5-inch SU.

Chassis
As MGA 1600 except GEARBOX four-speed (overall ratios with 4.1 : 1 rear axle) 4.1,
5.633, 9.077, 14.924, reverse 19.516.

MGA 1600 Mark II coupé

As MGA 1600 Mark II roadster except chassis numbers G/HD2 100352–109070.
WEIGHT 2075 lb.

MGA 1600 De Luxe

Engine as MGA 1600 Mark I or Mark II, chassis as MGA Twin Cam.

MGB roadster

Approximately 500,000 made (including coupés and V8s) from July 1962, chassis numbers G/HN3 101–48765 (three-bearing engine to October 1964); G/HN3 48766–138799 (five-bearing engine, to October 1967); G/HN4 138800–187210 (Mark II, to October 1969); G/HN5 187211–218651 (Mark III from October 1969).

Engine

Four-cylinder, CUBIC CAPACITY 1798 cc; BORE AND STROKE 80.26 mm × 88.9 mm; MAX. POWER 95 bhp at 5400 rpm; MAX. TORQUE 110 lb/ft at 3000 rpm; COMPRESSION RATIO 8.8 : 1; CARBURETTERS two 1.5-inch SU. From 1975 model year recalibrated to 84 bhp (DIN) at 5250 rpm for British models, max. torque 104 lb/ft at 2500 rpm; North American models, 65 bhp (DIN) at 4600 rpm, max. torque 92 lb/ft at 2500 rpm, compression ratio 8 : 1, carburetter 1 Zenith-Stromberg.

Chassis

WEIGHT (dry) 2030 lb; from Mark II 2140 lb; WHEELBASE 7 ft 7 ins; FRONT TRACK 4 ft 1 in; REAR TRACK 4 ft 1.25 ins; LENGTH 12 ft 9.3 ins; 13 ft 2.25 ins from 1975 model year; WIDTH 4 ft 11.7 ins; HEIGHT (with hood erect) 4 ft 1.4 ins; from 1975 model year 4 ft 3 ins; FRONT SUSPENSION wishbone and coil; REAR SUSPENSION live axle, semi-elliptical leaf springs; BRAKES Girling discs front, drums rear; GEARBOX four-speed (overall ratios with 3.9 : 1 rear axle, optional overdrive 3.14, from January 1963) 3.91, 5.37, 8.66, 14.21, reverse 18.59; from Mark II, 3.91, 5.40, 8.47, 13.45, reverse 12.10, optional overdrive 3.14; optional automatic transmission 3.91, 5.67, 9.34, reverse 8.17, automatic option deleted 1973; STEERING rack and pinion; SHOCK ABSORBERS Armstrong lever arm; WHEELS AND TYRES 5.60–14 on 4-inch rims (steel disc), 4.5-inch rims (wire); all rims 4.5 inch from 1970-model year.

MGB GT

As MGB, built from October 1965, chassis numbers G/HD3 71933–139823; G/HD4 139284–187210 (Mark II, to October 1969); G/HD5 21900– (Mark III from October 1969).

Engine
As MGB

Chassis
As MGB except WEIGHT (dry) 2190 lb; from Mark II 2260 lb; HEIGHT 4 ft 1.75 ins; from 1975 model year 4 ft 3.25 ins.

MGC roadster

4542 made between July 1967 and August 1969, chassis numbers G/CN 101–9099.

Engine

Six-cylinder, CUBIC CAPACITY 2912 cc; BORE AND STROKE 83.34 mm × 88.9 mm; MAX. POWER 145 bhp at 5250 rpm; MAX. TORQUE 170 lb/ft at 3400 rpm; COMPRESSION RATIO 9 : 1; CARBURETTERS two 1.75-inch SU.

Chassis

WEIGHT (dry) 2460 lb; WHEELBASE 7 ft 7 ins; FRONT TRACK 4 ft 2 ins; REAR TRACK 4 ft 1.25 ins; LENGTH 12 ft 9.3 ins; WIDTH 4 ft 11.7 ins; HEIGHT (with hood erect) 4 ft 2 ins; FRONT SUSPENSION wishbone and torsion bars; REAR SUSPENSION live axle, semi-elliptical leaf springs; BRAKES Girling discs front, drums rear; GEARBOX four-speed (overall ratios with 3.07 axle) 3.07, 4.24, 6.65, 10.56, reverse 9.5; with optional overdrive (axle ratio 3.31) 2.71, 3.31, 4.33, 6.32, 9.86, reverse 8.87; with optional automatic transmission (axle ratio 3.31) 3.31, 4.79, 7.91, reverse 6.92; from chassis number 4236 (overall ratios with 3.31 axle ratio) 3.31, 4.33, 6.32, 9.86, reverse 8.87; with optional overdrive (axle ratio 3.7) 3.03, 3.7, 4.84, 7.61, 11.03, reverse 9.91; automatic unchanged; STEERING rack and pinion; SHOCK ABSORBERS Armstrong telescopic front, lever arm rear; WHEELS AND TYRES Dunlop 165–15 on 5-inch rims (steel disc or wire).

MGC GT

4457 made between July 1967 and August 1969, chassis numbers G/CD 110–9102.

Engine

As MGC roadster

Chassis

As MGC roadster except WEIGHT (dry) 2610 lb, HEIGHT 4 ft 2.25 ins.

MGB GT V8

2591 made between April 1973 and September 1976, chassis numbers G/D2D1 101–2903

Engine

Eight-cylinder, CUBIC CAPACITY 3528 cc; BORE AND STROKE 88.9 mm × 71.1 mm; MAX. POWER 137 bhp (DIN) at 5000 rpm; MAX. TORQUE 193 lb/ft (DIN) at 2900 rpm; COMPRESSION RATIO 8.25 : 1; CARBURETTERS two 1.5-inch SU.

Chassis

WEIGHT (dry) 2387 lb; WHEELBASE 7 ft 7 ins; FRONT TRACK 4 ft 2 ins; REAR TRACK 4 ft 1.25 ins; LENGTH 12 ft 9.3 ins; 13 ft 2.25 ins from 1975-model year; WIDTH 4 ft 11.7 ins; HEIGHT 4 ft 2.25 ins; 4 ft 3.5 ins 1974; 4 ft 4 ins from 1975-model year; FRONT SUSPENSION wishbone and coil; REAR SUSPENSION live axle, semi-elliptical leaf springs; BRAKES Girling discs front, drums rear; GEARBOX four-speed (overall ratios with 3.07 axle ratio and standard overdrive) 2.52, 3.07, 3.87, 6.06, 9.63, reverse 8.65; STEERING rack and pinion; SHOCK ABSORBERS Armstrong lever arm; WHEELS AND TYRES Dunlop 175–14 on 5-inch rims (steel disc).

Index